According to Dr. Michael E. Salla and many other experts in the field of ET research, for almost 70 years the US government has engaged in an extensive "official effort" of disinformation, intimidation and tampering with evidence in order to maintain a non-disclosure policy about extraterrestrial presence.

Writes Dr. Salla: "Ever since I began to publish the early versions of the chapters in this book in January 2003 as 'Study Papers' on my website, http://www.exopolitics.org, I have received a consistent stream of supportive letters encouraging my research, and unsolicited information from former government, military, intelligence employees confirming many of my hypotheses. This has given me hope that eventually full disclosure of the extraterrestrial presence on the planet will occur, since interest is high and so much information is now in the public arena."

Michael Salla presents an astounding and eye-brow raising alterative history of the past 100 years. He postulates that since at least the 1930s every major war and policy decision has been in response to an undisclosed extraterrestrial presence on Earth. He traces actual events, ranging from the Nazi development of flying saucers to the recent US invasion of Iraq, to this unworldly element within government and societal issues.

Salla's case could be easily dismissed as fringe conspiracy theory except that it is well supported by the data, answers many of recent history's most perplexing mysteries and, with each passing year, is gaining credence with thinkers all around the globe. Read and contemplate this thesis today. Tomorrow, it may be the news headlines.

—Jim Marrs
Author of *Rule by Secrecy* and *Alien Agenda*

Historians will eventually learn a host of academics in America well knew there was an extraterrestrial presence engaging the planet Earth and the human race, but did not have the courage to speak out against the government imposed truth embargo or risk the criticisms from uninformed colleagues. Dr. Michael Salla is not one of them. Lacking neither the courage nor the intellectual honesty to take on the most important issue in history, he is helping to found an extraordinary field of study and policy—Exopolitics. This new way of thinking about the world is the logical and inevitable extension of the citizen/science process underway in earnest since 1947 to confirm and understand the extraterrestrial presence.

For six decades the great universities of a free nation have, as regards this issue, completely abrogated their responsibility to seek and to teach the truth, however inconvenient that truth might be to the State. This is unacceptable and will be changed. In due course there will be various departments of extraterrestrial studies in every university and college in America. And that powerful and appropriate circumstance will owe much to Michael Salla.

—Stephen Bassett
Executive Director of the Extraterrestrial Phenomena
Political Action Committee

EXOPOLITICS

Political Implications of
The Extraterrestrial Presence

EXOPOLITICS

Political Implications of
The Extraterrestrial Presence

Michael E. Salla, PhD

A Dandelion Books Publication
www.dandelionbooks.net
Tempe, Arizona

A Dandelion Books Publication
Dandelion Books, LLC
Tempe, Arizona

Library of Congress Cataloging-in-Publication Data

Salla, Michael E.
    Exopolitics: political implications of the extraterrestrial presence

Library of Congress Catalog Card Number 2003112497
ISBN 1-893302-56-3

Cover and book design by Amnet Systems Private, Ltd.,
www.amnet-systems.com

Dandelion Books, LLC
www.dandelionbooks.net

Acknowledgements

This book marks a personal transition where I traveled from being a respected university academic with a regular salary, professional status and network of scholarly peers in the field of peace studies, to a place firmly on the outside of the hallowed halls of academia. In this strange territory, my new research interest in extraterrestrials and their political implications were dismissed, my peer network vanished, and my hope for remuneration for my research was non-existent.

This book would not have been possible were it not for the encouragement and support of a number of individuals who believed in the importance of this project, and my abilities to break new ground in a field which inspired little scholarly interest. These individuals stood by me as I fiercely continued my efforts to research and write in this new field while my personal finances dried up, and I found myself struggling to complete the final research and writing.

First I must thank Carol Adler, President of Dandelion Books, who at a very early stage when just a few online articles had been published on my website, www.exopolitics.org, gave her enthusiastic support for a book to be eventually published from these first efforts, that would deal with the political implications of extraterrestrial presence not disclosed by national governments. She gave me the confidence that my work was suitable for a far wider audience than I was reaching from my website, and inspired me to continue my efforts to continue the research and writing. Thank you very much, Carol!

A number of individuals stand out for their unwavering support for me while doing the necessary research and writing for this book, and in their personal encouragement despite the setbacks I was experiencing. First, I'd like to thank my good friend, Dr. John King, who has been untiring in his support and encouragement, and generously provided me with his holiday home while I completed chapter three of this book. Great thanks to Janice Smith, who was a steadfast friend in her unwavering support in those transitional periods when I needed it most.

Many thanks also to Susan Burton, who provided the warm hospitality and research environment for writing chapters two and four. Great thanks also to Art Miller, who also opened his home and provided the research environment so I could complete the final chapter to this book and edit the entire manuscript for submission to Dandelion Books, and to Navin Kulshreshtha for being the catalyst to make it happen. Finally, I am grateful to Hugh Matlock who also opened his home and provided the research environment so that I could safely get this book through the various stages of the production process.

I also wish to thank the following individuals for their generous financial support that allowed me to complete the research, writing and editing for this book: Janice Smith, Frank Scott, Warren Bellis, and Vonda and Fred Janson. I also thank Jim Grapek for his financial support just when I needed it.

Finally, I wish to thank my children, Sebastian and Kalinda, for the sacrifices they had to endure as I pursued a field of study that may have sparked the fire of scholarly passion, but drained the financial resources so vital to fulfilling a child's expectations of a "normal" lifestyle in an affluent Western society. I dedicate this book to them and the world we bequeath them.

Preface

The key actors, processes, and institutions that drive politics at the domestic and international levels are directly related to an extraterrestrial presence on our planet that has not been disclosed to the general public nor to most elected public officials since the 1930s.

Evidence presented in this book suggests that the extraterrestrial presence goes to the very core of how key actors, processes and institutions operate in international politics. An international political system based on disinformation, intimidation and manipulation has been constructed to hide the truth about the extraterrestrial presence and to maintain a nondisclosure policy that has existed for nearly 70 years.

Key ideas and evidence in this book will be disturbing for those who believe that the main actors, processes and institutions that influence the study of international politics have been thoroughly identified and understood by scholars, diplomats and policy makers. Any graduate student entering an elite American university to study international relations is given a thorough grounding in identifying and analyzing the respective actors, processes and institutions in international politics in order to emerge as a competent practitioner of this social science.

It is these graduate students from elite Master's level international politics programs at US universities that go on to fill the various state department, think tank, media, congressional and non-profit organizations in the US that require employees to have a firm understanding of international politics.

As a former Assistant Professor in one of the elite graduate programs listed in the Association of Professional Schools of International Affairs, it was my professional duty to assist graduate students in identifying the main actors, institutions and processes responsible for international conflict. My job in particular was to identify and develop appropriate conflict resolution strategies so that scholars, diplomats and other interested parties could resolve these conflicts to achieve regional and global peace.

In May, 2001, at the end of five years of employment in the School of International Service, American University, Washington DC, I left thoroughly discouraged with the conceptual tools, theories and models I had researched, taught and applied in my academic appointment. I began to explore alternative theories and concepts that would help me identify the core factors that drive and perpetuate international conflict.

This book contains the result of my research, conducted without official approval by supervisors in my new academic appointment as an untenured researcher of "Transformational Peace" in the Center for Global Peace, American University. It reveals the core actors, institutions and processes that drive international conflict and are directly related to an undisclosed extraterrestrial presence. Understanding this ET presence is essential for the study and practice of international politics, and establishment of peace on our planet.

If I am correct in my analysis of the evidence supporting such an extraterrestrial presence, then it is clear that the study of the main actors, institutions and processes that make up the discipline of international politics, are wholly inadequate. Most scholars, diplomats and policy makers committed to the study of international politics and to the resolution of international conflict are operating under premises that are severely deficient.

This has made a bad situation worse, since it means that not only are the general public and elected officials denied knowledge about an extraterrestrial presence, but also, scholars become complicit in this non-disclosure effort. Development of complex theories on international politics that are based on deficient assumptions about the true nature of what drives international politics, are a distraction from what is really occurring.

Anyone in the construction industry knows how important it is to get the foundations right for a structure to be durable and withstand unpredictable environmental forces. Yet in the arena of international politics, deficient foundations underlie the very fabric of how the scholarly community and informed general public discuss, understand and analyze international politics. Consequently, inadequate policies are developed that miss the point of what the extraterrestrial presence tells us about the nature of our societies, the technologies we use, and how

we go about resolving conflict among ourselves and with extraterrestrial races.

The extraterrestrial presence that has long been denied by
public officials "in the loop," has powerful political implications
at all levels of human society. More important, such a presence
lies at the core of international and domestic conflict. Yet the
actors primarily responsible for dealing with international politics and the resolution of international conflict are developing
policies that entirely overlook the political implications of the
extraterrestrial presence.

Conventional policy makers do not address the core roots
of international politics and conflict, since they ignore how the
extraterrestrial presence influences the actors, institutions and
processes that drive international politics.

The research conducted for this book is an effort to analyze
what I believe are the core actors, institutions and processes
that help understand the political implications of the extraterrestrial presence on our planet. I have attempted to faithfully
use the strongest evidence available for determining the
extent, scope and intentions of this presence.

Undoubtedly, there will be flaws in my analysis since this is
an entirely new field of politics, with no obvious precedents to
follow, tremendous difficulties in gaining reliable information,
and few supporters in the academic community with whom to
discuss and compare this type of research.

If the central premise of this book is correct, which the evidence suggests is the case, then non-disclosure of the extraterrestrial presence would have as its corollary an extensive
"official effort" of disinformation, intimidation and tampering
with evidence, to maintain a non-disclosure policy that has
existed for almost 70 years.

Although I cannot vouch for the veracity of all sources used
in this book, they have been chosen because they represent
the best available evidence of an extraterrestrial presence on
the planet.

Also, even if I have been disappointed by the reaction thus
far from academic colleagues, academic administrators, scholarly

think tanks, the mainstream media and "political leaders"; but the general public has been very supportive.

Ever since I began to publish the early versions of the chapters in this book in January 2003 as "Study Papers" on my website, http://www.exopolitics.org, I have received a consistent stream of supportive letters encouraging my research, and unsolicited information from former government, military, intelligence employees confirming many of my hypotheses. This has given me hope that eventually full disclosure of the extraterrestrial presence on the planet will occur, since interest is high and so much information is now in the public arena.

Indeed, my own research would not have been possible were it not for the heroic efforts of former military and intelligence officials who came forward to give public testimony, thereby risking severe penalties for breaking their secrecy oaths; and the efforts of individuals such as Dr. Steven Greer, Dr. Richard Boylan and others to make these testimonies available to the general public.

Also significant in making my research possible has been the seminal work of Budd Hopkins, Dr. David Jacobs, and Dr. John Mack, in analyzing hundreds of individuals experiencing the "abduction" phenomenon. This work has provided valuable information on the intentions, activities and communications relevant to the ET presence.

It is my sincere hope that this book contributes to the effort to bring about full government disclosure, once individuals begin to realize the enormity of the consequences for inaction in responding to the extraterrestrial presence on this planet. Although I don't want to overplay the element of danger of the public not responding, my research confirms that the policy consequences of the general public not taking the extraterrestrial presence seriously are profound.

I certainly don't want to advocate either the position that "extraterrestrials mean us harm" or that "they are here solely to assist us." Evidence suggests that extraterrestrials are a multifaceted phenomenon with multiple agendas, activities and histories that interact with global humanity's own subjective experiences, aspirations and belief systems.

Overall, I believe the extraterrestrial presence represents an opportunity for global humanity to deal quickly and effectively with issues that have affected us for many millennia. It is how we perceive and respond to the extraterrestrial presence that ultimately determines their political significance for us. Their competing intentions, agendas and activities, although politically significant, are secondary to the frames of reference we choose in determining what the extraterrestrial presence politically means to us.

Ultimately, we are a sovereign race whose political future lies firmly in our own hands, not in visiting/resident extraterrestrial races—no matter how advanced their technology, superior their mental/psychic abilities, or benevolent their intentions. The political implications of the extraterrestrial presence on our planet is therefore entirely up to how you and I choose to perceive them.

We need to choose wisely with truth, honesty, vigilance and courage as our constant companions.

Michael E. Salla, PhD
Washington DC
September 1, 2003

Table of Contents

Chapter 1

The Need for Exopolitics: Implications of Extraterrestrial Conspiracy Theories for Policy Makers[1]

According to a September 2002 Roper poll, two-thirds of US citizens don't believe their government is disclosing the truth about an Extra-Terrestrial (ET) presence over the last fifty years in the USA, and 60% supported the Federal government releasing this information.[2]

In a May 2001 press conference at the National Press Club in Washington DC., twenty "whistleblowers" from a pool of more than one hundred former US military, government and aviation officials gave verbal testimony and provided physical evidence on their participation in clandestine government projects involving reverse engineering of ET technology, collaborative projects with ETs or suppression of information involving UFOs.[3]

The television mini-series produced by Steven Spielberg, *Taken*, was seen at least in part by 31 million US viewers in the sixteen day period from its first episode on December 2, 2002, and has stimulated speculation that the public is being prepared for official government disclosure on the ET presence in the near future.[4]

The history of the ET presence has generated numerous books, films, articles, web sites and conspiracy theories on the various activities and intentions of ETs, and clandestine efforts by different governments to respond to the ET presence. Many of the popular conspiracy theories that emerge out of the growing literature on the ET presence are often inconsistent in terms of the intentions, activities and impact of the ETs and of the clandestine government organizations created to respond to the ET presence.

These conspiracy theories span the spectrum from a belligerent desire by ETs to deprive humanity of its sovereign control of the planet, to a benevolent desire to help humanity solve its myriad of social, economic and environmental problems; and evolve as a species. As far as the involvement of clandestine government organizations are concerned, conspiracy theories range from non-elected government officials intent on arrogating political power through a "shadow government," to an enlightened effort to prepare the general public for the startling truth concerning the ET presence.

The intentions and activities of ETs and of clandestine government organizations created to interface with ETs, if both are found to be true, have important implications for the way elected government officials and the general public ought to respond to the whole ET phenomenon as a political challenge with a range of policy options.

This becomes especially important with the increasing likelihood that official government disclosure of an ET presence will instantly catapult the topic from the shadowy world of conspiracy theories, alternative science and New Age philosophy to mainstream public policy. Such disclosure will lead to the birth of a new field of public policy, 'exopolitics', which can be defined as the policy debate over the choices governments and populations need to make in formulating and implementing legislative and policy responses to the presence of ETs in human affairs.

Rather than leaving serious study of this new field of public policy to a hypothetical post-disclosure world, this book advocates that the majority of public opinion supporting disclosure of government information on ETs; the expanding literature on the ET presence; and the quality of evidence substantiating an ET presence, indicate that exopolitics is already a part of the political landscape.

There is a need to outline the main concepts, theories and information sources used in exopolitics as an emerging field of public policy. This will assist both the general public wishing to familiarize themselves with the various policy issues associated with the ET presence, and undisclosed "specialists" who have information on a particular aspect of the ET presence (typically on a "need to know basis"), but lack the breadth and holistic vision of what is occurring in the entire spectrum of activities.

In this chapter, I will review the primary sources supporting an ET presence, the main conspiracy theories or perspectives that are generated by these sources; the main advocates of the different perspectives, the supporting evidence for each perspective, and the moral orientation of the respective ET elements found in each perspective. I will then analyze the implications for policy makers and the general public for those perspectives most supported by the evidence.

I conclude the chapter with a number of policy recommendations that support the need for exopolitics as a field of study. This chapter lays the conceptual foundations for subsequent chapters and for developing suitable policy responses to the ET presence.

Sources of Information

The literature on the ET presence comes from a diverse number of sources that differ greatly in terms of their reliability, accuracy, and scholarly standards. Virtually all of these sources operate within the political context of an official government policy that denies any ET presence or a systematic cover up of such a presence by clandestine government organizations.

An extensive discussion of the history of the UFO/ET phenomenon has been conducted by authors such as Richard Dolan, who reports how the cover up has become part of the "national security foundations of the ET presence in the US and around the globe."[5]

The existence of such an official cover up adds to the difficulty of studying the claimed ET presence and accuracy of sources supporting the various perspectives on such a presence, since official non-disclosure suggests either wholesale misrepresentation or deception by those supporting such perspectives, or a covert government program designed to keep this information from elected public officials and from the general public.

If the latter is indeed the case, which the evidence to be presented in this chapter indicates, then it is clear that the study of exopolitics will be compounded by officially sponsored acts of disinformation, official denial, and even intimidation by clandestine government organizations.

Another of the key approaches by military/intelligence organizations is that of "disinformation," whereby investigators of the ET/UFO presence are thrown off track by public officials who release distorted or false information. Disinformation, in the sense of information that has a factual core, is presented or "spun" in a way that steers individuals away from sensitive issues and towards those areas that might distract or consume the energy and resources of others.

For example, the famous Eisenhower briefing document, based on what may have been a factual briefing on the ET presence, has been claimed by some to be clever disinformation designed to divide and distract researchers of the ET presence.[6]

There have been testimonies by former military/intelligence whistleblowers that parts of their official duties were to hide, tamper or destroy evidence associated with an ET presence.[7] Among these former officials is John Maynard, a military intelligence analyst for the Defense Intelligence Agency who served in the US military for 21 years. Maynard revealed the following in an exclusive interview in October 2001:

> I became involved [in UFOs] while overseas in Germany, Turkey and Korea. These areas were not noted for a lot of UFO activity. I was primarily afforded the opportunity to investigate peripherally a few incidents and implement disinformation or misinformation programs to divert attention away from the military and toward the paranormal and/or UFO [followers] in those areas. However, a point I never revealed to the military, was that my grandmother brought me up believing that UFOs existed.
>
> Regardless of that point, I was still a staunch conservative (politically) and placed my military duties ahead of my beliefs. I had a "country, duty, and honor"-type attitude.

I believed that because of my dedication, and what appeared to be naïveté on my part, my military superiors did not question my actions when it came to debunking UFO sightings. However, I became very intrigued as to why UFOs were not to become public knowledge and that they (the government) preferred that any UFO information for public consumption stay in the realm of the paranormal and/or the unreliable UFO resources.

It took me several years to figure out that this blatant disregard for public opinion was a plan designed to keep and maintain the pressure of proof on certain elements of our society. The plan was basically to place the burden of proof on the UFO researchers and to steer the public away from the military organizations that were directly involved in UFO research. In this plan I deduced that the military was using the media to keep these UFO researchers from making too much of the issue by having the media brand them as kooks, weird, paranoid and unbelievable; better yet, by having people who go around chasing after shadows in a belief that UFOs are real and the government is hiding something. To date, this plan has worked well above average, and the general public still has an opinion that follows whatever the media tells them.[8]

Another of the key approaches by military/intelligence organizations is that of intimidation which has existed since the beginning of the cover up of the ET presence and can be dated to the mysterious death of a former US Secretary of Defense. A possible high profile victim of intimidation designed to maintain secrecy around the ET presence has been argued to be James Forrestal, the Secretary of Defense under President Truman.[9]

Forrestal suffered a nervous breakdown in 1948 after complaining of being shadowed by "foreign looking men" whose description was similar to the now famous "Men in Black" later to play a prominent role in intimidating ET/UFO witnesses.[10]

Truman announced that he would dismiss Forrestal in January 1949. After formally leaving his position in March, events unfolded quickly and by May 22, Forrestal was found dead after allegedly jumping from his 16th floor VIP suite at the Bethesda Naval Hospital.

Events surrounding Forrestal's suicide included significant security lapses that have long fuelled speculation that Forrestal was murdered by a powerful organization that could easily penetrate the secure Bethesda Naval hospital. A number of prominent government and military officials insist that Forrestal was murdered because he desired to reveal the truth about the ET presence.[11]

If disinformation and intimidation are but two aspects of a series of "official" policies and practices to maintain secrecy of the ET presence, then this raises important questions about how to confirm the accuracy and verifiability of sources supporting the ET presence.

Highly credible witness testimonies may be undermined by key documents or records going missing that substantiate the credibility and/or claims of witnesses and/or government/military officials. On the other hand, it cannot be simply assumed that testimonies and documents concerning the ET presence are factual reports or accurate documents by independent witnesses/former government employees. Such reports may in cases be part of an officially sanctioned program of "disinformation" designed to distract public opinion in whole or in part from the truth about the ET presence.

I will now begin by describing the main sources supporting the ET presence, which provide the content of the different ET perspectives to be outlined later in this chapter. These sources will be grouped in terms of seven categories, presented in the order that would appear most persuasive for the critical reader in a pre-disclosure political environment. They will be assigned a ranking in terms of evidentiary strength somewhere in the range: **Strong-Moderate-Weak**.

In developing these rankings, I use as guide the same reasoning as would a jury in a court of law, in sifting through available evidence on a particular case.

Emphasis is on identifying the strongest evidence and reaching a verdict on its plausibility in determining guilt or innocence. The rankings are not used to dismiss the relevance of the evidence of an ET presence provided by different sources, but solely to determine what evidence provides the strongest support for an ET presence in the minds of the general public and interested public officials. These rankings will subsequently be used in analyzing the political significance of different issues relevant to the ET presence that will be examined in later chapters.

Category A—Whistle Blowers

These are reports and testimonies of former government or military officials, and/or civilian aviation personnel who have had first hand experience of UFOs and/or evidence of the ET presence.

The most famous UFO incident in the US is the reported crash of an ET occupied saucer shaped craft in Roswell, New Mexico, in 1947. Initial finding of Major Jesse Marcel, the Army Intelligence officer sent to the site, was that debris from the crash was from a "flying disk."

The information officer at the Roswell Army Airbase then authorized a press release on the morning of July 8.[12] This imme-diately caused worldwide headlines and after Major Marcel was ordered to Washington, DC, Brigadier-General Roger Ramey announced to the world press that Major Marcel was mistaken and the "flying disc" was an experimental weather balloon.

In a subsequent interview years after the incident that boosted claims of a government conspiracy to cover up what happened at Roswell, Major Marcel asserted that he was silenced by superiors, and said, "It was not anything from this Earth. That I'm quite sure of . . . Being in intelligence, I was familiar with all materials used in aircraft and in air travel. This was nothing like this. It could not have been."[13]

Over the last five decades since the Roswell crash, a slow but steady stream of former government or military officials have come forth to reveal information about the ET presence. It should be pointed out that these former officials have usually taken secrecy oaths not to reveal information about their former duties and run the risk of considerable financial or criminal penalties for violating their oaths, as well as risking reputations and friendships developed over the years of their official service.

In the case of the US military, the relevant oath is called the "Oath upon Inadvertent Exposure to Classified Security Data or Information," and James Goodell, a former Air Force officer, describes the consequences of taking this oath:

> . . . you sign away your constitutional rights. You sign a piece of paper saying that if you violate your security agreement . . . without a trial, without the right of appeal, you're going to go to the Leavenworth federal penitentiary for twenty years. That's a real big incentive to keep your mouth shut.[14]

A prominent whistle blower recently revealing his official activities involving the ET presence is a former senior Pentagon official, Colonel Philip Corso (ret), who served in the Eisenhower Administration and later headed the Foreign Technology Desk in the Army's Research and Development department. After more than thirty years of silence, Colonel Corso publicly revealed in his 1997 book, The Day After Roswell, that he led a top secret clandestine project to reverse engineer ET technology recovered from the Roswell crash.[15]

He wrote that his project successfully released a number of these reverse engineered ET technologies for both the military and civilian sectors. Companies that benefited from this clandestine project included IBM, Hughes Aircraft, Bell Labs, and Dow Corning. Corso claims that the rapid technological advances over the last 50 years, in fiber optics, integrated circuit chips, night-vision equipment, and super tenacity fibers such as Kevlar body armor, were a direct result of these clandestine projects.

Despite repeated denials of secret government programs to reverse engineer the ET technology recovered at Roswell and other crash scenes, sustained government efforts at suppression of the ET presence continue to be compromised by the disclosure of former military, government and aviation officials that they have participated in these clandestine projects and/or witnessed UFO's and/or even ETs.

Dr. Steven Greer, director of the Disclosure Project, a non-profit organization dedicated to ending the official secrecy of the ET presence, introduced a select number of these witnesses to the press and general public at a May 2001 Press Conference at the National Press Club in Washington DC. Dr. Greer has gathered the testimonies of more than 100 witnesses on tape and video format and made these available for the general public and for a congressional inquiry.[16] One of the more revealing testimonies is that of former Apollo Astronaut, Edgar Mitchell:

> . . . when I learned that aliens really do exist, I wasn't too surprised. But what did shock me when I started investigating extra-terrestrial reports a decade ago is the extent to which the proof has been hushed up. It isn't just the US government which has kept quiet about alien visits. It would be arrogant of an American like myself to assume that ETs would only choose to visit my country. Indeed, I've heard convincing stories about governments all over the world that know of alien visits— including the British government.[17]

As a source of information on an ET presence, former government, military and aviation officials have high credibility due to the activities they performed as a part of their official positions. The financial and legal penalties these former officials risk in violating their secrecy oaths, and the possible damage to their reputations and friendships, suggest that individuals with high integrity are disturbed about continued non-disclosure of the ET presence and a hidden government conspiracy to cover this up through a campaign of intimidation, disinformation and secrecy.

In a court of law, whistleblower testimonies are powerful and can alone succeed in determining guilt or innocence even when no physical evidence can be produced. In conclusion, this category of information can be ranked as **"strong"** due to the verifiable credentials of those claiming to have first hand experience of an ET presence, the coherence of their testimonies, and their overall number.

Category B—Abductions/Contacts

Much of the information derived from individuals claiming to have been abducted/contacted by ET craft has come through the pioneering work of Budd Hopkins, Dr. David Jacobs and Dr. John Mack, in treating individuals apparently suffering the effects of such visitations.[18] These reports have grown in number and typically focus on an experience which has surprising uniformity whereby individuals claim to have been abducted and undergone a series of medical procedures by one or more ET races.

Using a variety of therapeutic tools, including hypnosis, Dr. Mack found surprising consistency in the disparate and unrelated cases he examined which he outlined in his first book:

> Each of the thirteen people whose cases are described in this book—indeed, each of the seventy-six abductees with whom I have worked—tells a unique story. The individual differences can probably be accounted for on the basis of the diverse personalities of the experiencers and the varieties of circumstances within the abductions themselves. But what I have found to be so extraordinary from the beginning of my study has been the readily identifiable patterns that emerge when the case narratives are examined carefully.[19]

Mack has published his findings in a number of books and scholarly journals, which subsequently became the topic of a popular film. In 1995, Mack co-hosted a conference at the Massachusetts Institute of Technology that featured a number of scholarly presentations of the "abduction phenomenon" and its significance for humanity.[20]

The growing number of abduction cases has led to this category rising in importance as a credible source of evidence for an ET presence. Estimates of the number of abductions in the US go as high as several million, signifying a huge database of potential information on the ET presence. This database is continuously being refined as researchers develop the analytical tools and therapeutic techniques for adequately dealing with abduction/contact cases.

Overall, the second category of information is distinguished by the coherence and consistency of the disparate abduction reports and evidence gathered of an ET presence. Researchers and collators of this information are highly credentialed in the use of psychological techniques, and have pioneered rigorous standards for assessing the evidence. In a court of law, such testimonies would be very persuasive due to their consistency and coherence. This source category will hence be ranked **strong**.

Category C—Witness/Sightings Reports

The third category of information sources on an ET presence are testimonies of those who have witnessed ETs/UFOs. These form the bulk of the available literature on the ET presence, and are often accompanied by physical evidence in terms of photographs, radar images, videos, or even ET artifacts.

Sightings of UFOs/ETs from shortly after the Second World War were so overwhelming in their frequency and scope that the US Air force launched three consecutive inquiries, designated Operation Sign (1947–48); Operation Grudge (1948–52); and Operation Blue Book (1952–69).[21]

Project Blue Book dismissed the overwhelming mass of the evidence given in 12,618 sightings as misidentified aircraft or explainable by natural causes, and left a relatively small proportion of cases, 701, as "unidentified." An independent assessment by the University of Colorado, the Condon Report, recommended terminating Project Blue Book.[22]

Rather than ending the matter of UFO visitation, this only generated more controversy over what many argued to be the Chairman's bias in ignoring important evidence and recommending termination of the Project.[23] For many, the Condon report was yet another instance of a cleverly orchestrated secret government conspiracy to hide the truth from the American public.

Despite the controversy over termination of the most well known official inquiry into the UFO phenomenon, new witness reports continued to stream in, adding to the already impressive amount of material supporting an ET presence. Prominent among those dissatisfied with the termination of Project Blue Book and desiring a more thorough and transparent inquiry was Dr. Allen Hynek.[24]

A prominent astronomer, Dr. Hynek served as the Astronomical consultant on projects Grudge and Blue Book between 1949–69; and began as a prominent debunker of what he disparaged as the "'psychological postwar craze' for flying saucers that seemed to be sweeping the country and at the naïveté and gullibility of our fellow human beings who were being taken in by such obvious 'nonsense'."[25] He subsequently became a powerful advocate of the credibility of the evidence supporting an ET presence; and gave interviews, wrote extensively, and organized scholarly research of the UFO phenomenon as Director of the Center for UFO studies.[26]

An initiative funded by Laurence Rockefeller in the early 1990s resulted in a report that was distributed to the US Congress and to policy makers around the world. It was subsequently published as the *UFO Briefing Document: Best Available Evidence*.[27] This was a compilation of the best sightings cases that could be used to compel governments to fully disclose all information on UFOs/ETs.

Steven Greer's Disclosure Project was also significant in compiling witness testimonies concerning UFOs/ETs.[28] Organizations such as the Mutual UFO Network continue to maintain a popular website, hold annual meetings with the most recent evidence on sightings, and sponsor discussion of developments in the field of UFO investigation.[29]

Overall, the third category of information is distinguished by the coherence and consistency of the disparate witness reports and evidence gathered of an ET/UFO presence. The researchers and collators of this information are highly credentialed and typically use rigorously developed scientific assessment standards.

Although this category provides strong evidence of the existence of UFOs as aircraft surpassing the capabilities of publicly known aircraft, there is debate whether these are genuine ET piloted craft or top secret military vehicles. In a court of law, such testimonies would be very persuasive of UFOs but would lead to some uncertainty over the extent of ET involvement. This source category will hence be ranked **strong-moderate.**

Category D—Documentary Evidence

In the 1980s a number of documents began to be "leaked" to UFO investigators that provided remarkable support for the existence of ETs and government efforts to respond to the ET presence. These leaked documents covered such topics as President Truman's executive order establishing a top secret committee to coordinate ET affairs, composition of the policy coordinating group established by Truman—Majestic 12; a briefing document to President Eisenhower; reports by a secret "Interplanetary Phenomenon Unit" embedded in Army Intelligence; and a report by Albert Einstein and Max Oppenheimer on relations with ET races.[30]

Ever since their appearance, the Majestic documents have aroused great controversy. Well known critic Phillip Klass declared: "Either [the documents] are the biggest news story of the past two millennia or one of the biggest cons ever attempted against the public."[31]

Another source of evidence on ET/UFO related issues concerns previously classified documents obtained through a variety of individuals gaining access to government/military departments through Freedom of Information Act (FOIA) requests. The most extensive collection of previously classified documents gained through FOIA requests is the Black Vault, an online website started by John Greenewald, Jr. in 1996.[32] The database has extensive information on a range of projects that are of interest to researchers of the ET presence.

However, the most sensitive information on the ET presence is not released through the FOIA process due to the exemption that exists for de-classification of documents that have national security implications. A federal judge can simply uphold the right of the relevant agency to not release the information that falls under one of the nine exemptions that relate to declassification of classified documents.

These exemptions include: national defense or foreign policy, privacy of individuals, proprietary interests of business, and functioning of the government.

In sum, evidence available for substantiating a range of issues, projects and events concerning ET presence is limited in scope and detail, and only relates to declassified documents that a Federal judge would deem insufficient in terms of national security implications to warrant exclusion from FOIA. Furthermore, it cannot be discounted that released documents may in some cases be part of a coordinated disinformation strategy designed to mislead researchers of the ET presence.

Leaked documents obtained outside of the FOIA process raise important questions about their legitimacy and accuracy, but nevertheless contain a wealth of information from classified documents that, if genuine, previously held the highest security classification of "top secret."

In sum, the role of public officials responsible for ET affairs in releasing documents either through FOIA or leaking, raises the possibility of disinformation in the timing and significance of different documents. Consequently, this category can be given an evidentiary ranking slightly below the first two categories. A **strong-moderate** ranking is therefore assigned to this category.

Category E—Remote Viewing

The fifth category of sources comes from participants in Remote Viewing projects. Remote Viewing is an intelligence gathering technique that was the subject of several government-funded projects organized at the Stanford Research Institute from the early 1970s to 1989.[33] These projects were initiated as a result of a study of psychic techniques used by the Soviet Union and its satellite states.

According to Shiela Ostrander and Lynn Schroeder, authors of a 1970 book, *Psychic Discoveries Behind the Iron Curtain*, The United States was lagging well behind the Soviets in the use of these psychic techniques for such activities as intelligence gathering. Indeed, it will be argued later, in Chapter Three, that the psychic techniques used by Nazi Germany in communicating with ET races was instrumental in giving it a technological edge on both the West and the Soviet Union.

Confirmation of a remote viewing program came in September 1997 with an official CIA response to an FOIA request from John Greenewald for information on the CIA's and US military's remote viewing program and use of psychics:

> As you may already know, Project Star Gate was one specific, rather short-lived, program that dealt with research into the parapsychological phenomenon known as "remote viewing." However, during recent years we have come to use "Star Gate" as a rubric for a series of CIA and US Military remote viewing research projects. All records related to your second item, "all documents related to remote viewing and the use of psychics in DoD Operations" are included in the Star Gate collection described below. The projects discussed herein are defunct; today CIA does not fund remote viewing research.[34]

In the US, Remote Viewing was pioneered by researchers Russell Targ and Harold Puthoff who trained remote viewers to spatially dislocate a part of their consciousness to designated locations, unknown to the remote viewers, in order to gain intelligence information.[35] Remote viewers were simply given a set of coordinates consisting of randomly generated numerical codes, and instructed to report on what they observed.

The apparent success of these projects as an intelligence gathering tool for an ET presence and other topics of interest to various intelligence agencies, led to numerous individuals being trained in the rigorous standards and protocols of this process. A number of these remote viewers subsequently wrote of their experiences in observing the ET presence, and began training others in this process.

Among the more prominent of these has been Dr. Courtney Brown, who has written two popular books on Remote Viewing that focus on the ET presence, and is attempting with many others to develop Remote Viewing as a scientifically credible intelligence-gathering tool.[36]

The information on ETs gathered by remote viewers is often startling in its implications. For instance, Brown describes remnants of a Martian civilization and the relationship with Earth: "There *are* Martians on Earth but one must think clearly about the implications of this before ringing the alarm bell. These Martians are desperate. Apparently they have very crude living quarters on Mars. They cannot live on the surface. Their children have no future on their home world. Their home is destroyed; it is a planet of dust."[37]

Perhaps more significantly, remote viewers described a federation of worlds responsible for controlling evolving planets such as Earth. In various sessions, remote viewers described the nature of headquarters of this Federation, and the ways these ET races influenced behavior.[38]

Given the novelty and relatively recent emergence of Remote Viewing as an intelligence gathering tool that has a plausible, though controversial, scientific foundation, in "psychic research" this category of information may be ranked below the first four in terms of reliability and objectivity. The relationship and history of remote viewing in terms of psychic research certainly places itself outside of mainstream expectations of reliable and credible information on the ET presence.

The quality and credentials of remote viewers might impress a jury in a court of law, but testimony provided by remote viewers would be insufficient on its own to determine guilt or innocence in a case. Although the information provided by remote viewers has been consistently shown to have high degrees of accuracy, the degree of subjectivity involved places this category of evidence slightly below "witness" or "whistleblower" testimonies. Remote Viewing can therefore be assigned an evidentiary ranking of **moderate.**

Category F—Independent Archeology

A sixth category of sources is the work of archeologists who specialize in translating or interpreting archeological evidence of a historic ET presence. Often led by independent archeologists who operate outside of mainstream archeology based in public institutions and universities, the theories and translations of the extensive public archives and monuments from the ancient world offered by these independent archeologists, continue to attract world wide audiences.

Among the more publicly prominent is Erich von Daniken, whose *Chariots of the Gods* became a phenomenal best seller when published in 1969.[39] Another best selling author is Graham Hancock, whose *Fingerprints of the Gods*, proved to be hugely popular with its speculative theories based on forgotten ancient civilizations and astronomical pointers to the homes of distant ET ancestors.[40]

Another perhaps less prominent but no less controversial example is the Sumerian scholar, Zechariah Sitchin who translated thousands of ancient Sumerian cuneiform texts that described an ancient ET presence on the planet.[41] Sitchin describes his controversial approach to translating Sumerian and other ancient biblical texts in the prologue to his first book published in 1976:

> The Old Testament has filled my life from childhood. When the seed for this book was planted, nearly fifty years ago, I was totally unaware of the then raging Evolution versus Bible debates. But as a young schoolboy studying *Genesis* in its original Hebrew, I created a confrontation of my own. We were reading one day in Chapter VI that when God resolved to destroy Mankind by the Great Flood, the "sons of the deities," who married the daughters of men, were upon the Earth. The Hebrew original named them, *Nefilim*; the teacher explained it meant "giants"; but I objected: didn't it mean literally "Those Who Were Cast Down," who had descended to Earth? I was reprimanded and told to accept the traditional interpretation.
>
> In the ensuing years, as I have learned the languages and history and archaeology of the ancient Near East, the Nefilim became an obsession. Archaeological finds and the deciphering of Sumerian, Babylonian, Assyrian, Hittite, Canaanite and other ancient texts and epic tales

increasingly confirmed the accuracy of the biblical references to the kingdoms, cities, rulers, places, temples, trade routes, artifacts, tools and customs of antiquity. Is it not now time, therefore, to accept the word of these same ancient records regarding the Nefilim as visitors to Earth from the heavens?[42]

Although formerly independent, Sitchin and other authors in this category typically produce high quality works that continue to generate controversy among mainstream archeologists. The controversy and subjectivity surrounding these debates of the archeological evidence of an ancient ET presence and accurate translations of ancient texts, require a low ranking to this category of information.

In a court of law, such evidence might be deemed helpful in uncovering the context or background to a phenomenon, but would hardly be conclusive. Therefore, evidence in this category will be assigned a ranking of **weak-moderate.**

Category G—Channeling

The seventh and most controversial sources of information on an ET presence are the works of those claiming to be in telepathic communication with different ET races. A majority of these "channels" have few academic or professional credentials, yet this has not impeded them from gaining international prominence as leaders or spokespersons in the Alternative/New Age movement. In something akin to a burgeoning social movement with global reach and accompanying religious devotion, many hundreds of thousands if not millions of supporters attest to the transformative effect of these messages from ETs, and liberating value of these messages for all humanity.

In the foreword to one of the highly popular books by the "channel" Barbara Marciniak, her sister writes:

For over ten years a group of multidimensional beings—who call themselves the Pleiadians—have blended and merged their energies with my sister Barbara, creating a unique and engaging relationship. The infusion of the

Pleiadian energy into Barbara's life, my life, and the lives
of countless others has been marked by change. In addition, with the success of the Pleiadians' first two books . . .
Barbara and I found ourselves overwhelmed at times by
the abundance of mail we received . . . The Pleiadians
say Family of Light [humans committed to transformational change] are **systems busters** [emphasis added]
who travel through time to systems in need of change,
helping to facilitate the collapse of these systems.[43]

Marciniak and most of these "channels" support the idea
that an ET presence has existed on the planet for millennia,
and that there exists an officially sanctioned government
conspiracy that is global in its reach to keep this presence
secret from the general public. The testimony of channels in a
court of law would obviously be controversial and not likely to
be conclusive in any way. Nevertheless, the overwhelming evidence suggesting that ET races do communicate with humans
through telepathic exchanges, indicates the importance of not
excluding this body of evidence.

In terms of the evidentiary standards for information
sources, due to the highly subjective nature of channeled material, this category can be assigned the low ranking of **weak**. This
ranking does not dismiss the relevance of this information, but
solely acknowledges the difficulty of verifying and analyzing
such a form of communication for the development of public
policy, and responding to the challenges presented by non-
disclosure of the ET presence by various government officials.

In sum, the sources of information on an ET presence differ
widely in terms of: academic and professional credentials of
those making such a case; physical evidence provided; subjectivity of those interpreting or providing the evidence; coherence
and consistency of testimonies concerning an ET presence;
intentions and activities of ETs, and their moral orientation
which typically falls somewhere along the range, benevolent-
neutral-malevolent.

What follows is an attempt to analyze these different
sources of information and the conspiracy theories they generate

in terms of four main perspectives on an ET presence. Each of these perspectives will be analyzed according to its main themes, principal supporters, evidentiary strength, and moral orientation ascribed to the ET presence.

Intruder Perspective

In the "Intruder perspective," ETs are depicted as off-world beings that have traveled great interstellar distances and, without announcing themselves or gaining permission, have repeatedly violated US air space and abducted citizens for genetic experiments for purposes yet to be fully determined. In a popular 1987 book titled *Intruders*, author Budd Hopkins supports the idea of ETs being intrusive in their manner of collecting and experimenting with genetic material taken from abductees.[44]

A rather bellicose presentation of the Intruder perspective is made by Col. Philip Corso, who describes the ETs as repeatedly violating US airspace, abducting US citizens for the extraction and manipulation of genetic material, and having purposes that pose a direct threat to US national interests.

Col. Corso advocates that the US needs to use the recovered ET technology for building a new generation of weapons capable of shooting down ETs anywhere around the planet. Indeed, he claims that over the years the US has been very successful in using this reverse engineered technology to shoot down some of these ET craft, but more effort and resources need to be committed for a comprehensive global defensive shield.

Testimony provided by witnesses in the Disclosure Project support Corso's view that such a clandestine operation targeting ET flights has been underway for some time; however, they depict the ETs as not retaliating to these hostile actions by US military forces.[45]

Another supporter of the intruder perspective and its negative implications is Dr. David Jacobs whose book, *The Threat*, depicts the ET presence in the following terms:

> I do not like what I see. For the first time in over thirty years
> of researching the UFO phenomenon, I am frightened of

it. Understanding has not led to a feeling of contribution or accomplishment. Rather, it has led to profound apprehension for the future. The abduction phenomenon is far more ominous than I had thought. Optimism is not the appropriate response to the evidence, all of which strongly suggests that the alien agenda is primarily beneficial for them and not for us.[46]

In contrast, Dr. John Mack, who also adopts the intruder perspective, describes the ET presence in more morally positive terms. He views these intruder ETs as often being catalysts for transformational personal changes experienced by abductees as a result of their profound interaction with ETs.[47]
Mack finds that abductees often become committed to a number of progressive global causes that give value and meaning to their lives. Protecting the global environment, reducing the use of nuclear weapons and other destructive technologies, and peaceful forms of conflict management appear as consistent themes in the ET-abductee interaction according to Mack. Elaborating on this "transformational" aspect of the human abductee/contactee, Dr. Richard Boylan writes on the basis of his "dialogue" with such individuals:

One of the more common effects, in those Experiencers who have had competent debriefing and counseling, is a sense of altered and heightened conscious. Along with that goes the felt need to begin "cleaning up one's act" in respect to practices which are at variance with higher consciousness. Some experiencers feel drawn towards a vegetarian lifestyle, while other experiencers have felt an imperative to get rid of habits which interfere with their full awareness and consciousness. These have included jettisoning tobacco, alcohol, marijuana and other drugs, caffeinated coffee, free sugar, and other consciousness-changing substances from their diets. I have humorously complained about being turned into a "Zen monk" by the ETs. But the truth is that I have voluntarily made these changes, because they feel better and the old habits repel me now.[48]

The ETs described by abductees and those allegedly recovered from downed UFOs are commonly described as being approximately four feet tall, with a gray complexion (hence the name 'Grays'), with a large head disproportionate to its small thin and wiry body, with large almond-shaped eyes, a very small mouth, and no organs for sexual reproduction.[49]

Confirmation of such reports comes from an interview with a former Army/CIA officer who described a live Gray ET seen at a secret military facility: "He had the large head and bigger eyes, kind of slanted bigger eyes. He looked like he was wearing sunglasses because the lenses were real dark. He had kind of a slim face down to a peaked chin with just a little nose area, a tiny slit of a mouth and just holes in the side of his head for ear openings."[50]

The 'Grays' home star system is commonly reported as Zeta Reticulum, near the constellation of Orion. Some former officials and/or employees involved in clandestine government military projects report to have seen live ETs at various military bases. Michael Wolf, a former member of a National Security Council committee that oversaw the ET presence, claimed that he "met with extraterrestrial individuals every day in my work, and shared living quarters with them."[51]

The reports of joint ET-human bases give credence to reports that a treaty was signed as early as 1954, during the Eisenhower administration, granting rights to ETs to establish joint bases for technological sharing on US soil, and placing strict limits on the biological experimentation the Grays were conducting with US citizens.

The existence of such a treaty between the Eisenhower administration and an ET race has been disclosed by a number of government/military whistleblowers.[52] William Cooper, part of a Naval Intelligence briefing team for the Commander of the US Pacific Fleet, narrates the events surrounding this Treaty from classified documents he claims to have read as part of his official duties:

> [I]n 1954 the race of large nosed Gray Aliens which had been orbiting the Earth landed at Holloman Air Force Base. A basic agreement was reached. This race

identified themselves as originating from a Planet around a red star in the Constellation of Orion which we called Betelgeuse. They stated that their planet was dying and that at some unknown future time they would no longer be able to survive there. This led to a second landing at Edwards Air Force Base. The historical event had been planned in advance and details of the treaty had been agreed upon. Eisenhower arranged to be in Palm Springs on vacation. On the appointed day the President was spirited away to the base and the excuse was given to the press that he was visiting a dentist. President Eisenhower met with the aliens and a formal treaty between the Alien Nation and the United States of America was signed.[53]

Alluding to a treaty signed by the Eisenhower administration, Col. Phillip Corso, a highly decorated officer who served in Eisenhower's National Security Council, wrote: "We had negotiated a kind of surrender with them as long as we couldn't fight them. They dictated the terms because they knew what we most feared was disclosure."[54]

Another whistleblower to elaborate on this treaty was Phil Schneider, a civil engineer who had worked on the construction of secret underground facilities, and who was found dead seven months after giving a lecture in May 1995 with the following information:

Back in 1954, under the Eisenhower administration, the federal government decided to circumvent the Constitution of the United States and form a treaty with alien entities. It was called the 1954 Greada Treaty, which basically made the agreement that the aliens involved could take a few cows and test their implanting techniques on a few human beings, but that they had to give details about the people involved. Slowly, the aliens altered the bargain until they decided they wouldn't abide by it at all.[55]

Former officials involved in clandestine projects run by different government agencies, claim that the Grays communicate through telepathic thought exchange, and use thought to activate the advanced technology and navigation instruments of their space craft.[56] Based on interviews with a range of ET witnesses, contactees and military/intelligence personnel, Dr. Richard Boylan explains the telepathic communication used by ET races and its relationship to the psychological trauma often associated with ET encounters:

> Because extraterrestrial encounters often involve the sudden appearance of one or more extraterrestrials without warning in an unexpected location, such as one's bedroom at night, their appearance can feel, at first, like an invasion. The extraterrestrials' use of mental telepathy, and their faculty for reading one's thoughts and the contents of one's mind, can feel, to the previously traumatized person, like an old, familiar, and unwelcome intrusion into what is in our culture one's private space.
>
> Here we have the clash of two cultures, polar opposite in their assumptions. In human culture (Western modern industrial culture, anyway), the assumption is that one's thoughts and living space are private, because individualism is prized. In extraterrestrial cultures researched thus far, it appears that living space and thoughts are inevitably shared, because of the automatic, two-way nature of the mutual telepathic ability of all members of their society. They live in a shared mind-field "commons."[57]

Dr. John Mack, in his evaluation of patients exhibiting symptoms of ET abduction, claims that many of these communicated through telepathy with the Grays.[58] In reports on the content of the telepathic communication with the Grays, abductees/contactees have reported that the Grays' survival as a species is threatened due to genetic degradation as a result of the repeated use of cloning for reproductive purposes.

The Grays say they need to create a hybrid race that integrates the human and Gray genes in order for the continuation of their species. It is claimed that with the creation of this hybrid race, the Grays will somehow be able to transfer their "essence" or "consciousness" as individuals into the hybrid, thereby perpetuating the continuation of their race.[59]

The idea that telepathy is the standard communication means of ETs gives plausibility to the claims of numerous civilian sources that they have been contacted by ETs and conducted telepathic communication with them. This is especially important with information given by "channelers" who claim to be in communication with different ET races.

In sum, the "Intruder perspective" describes the intentions, abduction activities, genetic experiments, violations of US and allied airspace, and advanced technology of ETs as intrusive. Moral categories used to describe the Gray intruders are unclear. Although their activities are clearly described as intrusive and authors such as Philip Corso and David Jacobs voice their suspicions about their ultimate agenda, there appear to be few, if any, hostile actions taken against military forces around the globe—or against the civilian population taken aboard and later released from Gray ETVs (Extraterrestrial Vehicles).

Indeed, accounts by John Mack and Richard Boylan suggest that the transformational changes brought about in individuals makes the "abduction/contact" phenomenon a positive one for many if not most individuals.

Main focus for conspiracy theorists in this perspective are clandestine government agencies desiring to withhold the truth of the ET presence from the general public. Sources of information are drawn from all seven evidentiary categories described earlier. Of these, the whistleblower category stand out as the most compelling due to the integrity, credibility and coherence of expert testimonies.

The growing number of abduction cases and their analysis also provide strong evidentiary support for this perspective. Witness and documentary sources also provide strong-moderate evidentiary support. Given the strong evidentiary rankings ascribed to these first two categories, conspiracy theories surrounding the intruder perspective can be judged to have **strong** evidentiary support.

Manipulator Perspective

This perspective covers conspiracy theories suggesting that an advanced race of ETs with enhanced psychic abilities and superior technology, has been either overtly controlling or covertly manipulating humanity ever since the first human presence on the planet. Elaborating on this theme of ET "manipulation," Bill Cooper writes: "Throughout our history the Aliens have manipulated and/or ruled the human race through various secret societies, religion, magic, witchcraft, and the occult."[60]

It is claimed that these ETs played a direct role in creating the human species as a source of slave labor, and therefore feel entitled and even responsible for guiding/controlling the human race either overtly by direct control or covertly through human proxies.

According to William Bramley:

> . . . the human race was once a source of labor for an extraterrestrial civilization and still remains a possession today. To keep control over its possession and to maintain Earth as something of a prison, that other civilization ("Custodians") has bred never-ending conflict between human beings, has promoted human spiritual decay, and has erected on Earth conditions of unremitting physical hardship. This situation has lasted for thousands of years and it continues today.[61]

One of the most widely cited scholarly sources for conspiracy theorists falling into this perspective is the Sumerian scholar, Zechariah Sitchin.[62] In his translations of thousands of Sumerian cuneiform texts, Sitchin tells how an ancient ET race, described by the Sumerians as the Anunnaki or as the Nephilim in the Old Testament, created humanity by genetic engineering. Mixing their own DNA with that of the primates then existing on Earth, the Anunnaki created humanity in order to exploit it as a slave race and a natural resource for the Anunnaki.

There were, however, violent disputes between different factions of the Anunnaki that resulted in much regional destruction and decimation of the captive human population. Sitchin claimed these are the same beings variously described in the Book of Genesis and the Book of Enoch; and that biblical stories of the Elohim, rebel angels and the Serpent, referred to the conflict between different factions of the Anunnaki concerning how to manage humanity.[63]

There were apparently two distinct races among the Anunnaki. One was a humanoid race of giants, and the second, a non-human race that was "serpent-like" in appearance. This has given rise to the more popular term, 'Reptilian' for this second race. The author, R.A. Boulay, has extensively analyzed a variety of historic sources and argued there is sufficient evidence to support the conclusion that an ancient ET race of Reptilians inhabited the Earth and played a role in the creation of humanity.[64]

Sitchin describes these ET races as having overt control of the human population for millennia, but then largely disappearing from the scene approximately 4000 years ago after an intense factional battle between them.

Presumably, the bulk of the Anunnaki left the scene, believing it was no longer necessary to exercise direct rule over a humanity that was ready for self-rule. However, a rebel cohort that disagreed remained behind, intent on secretly monitoring and influencing human affairs from deep underground ET bases to demonstrate the inadequacy of humanity to exercise stewardship over the planet Earth.

References to "serpents" in biblical books suggest that elements of the Reptilian race stayed behind. Such a scenario is consistent with the chronology used by the Egyptian historian Manetho who claimed that prior to the 30 dynasties of human kings that ruled Egypt, there was direct rule by the Gods and the demigods.[65]

The view that remnant Anunnaki ETs are hidden on Earth is supported by Dr. Courtney Brown and others who have conducted extensive remote viewing sessions on the presence of ET races on and off the planet.[66] Brown has concluded that a rebel faction of Anunnaki, who he and others describe as Reptilians, is concealed on Earth and it is estranged from the larger body of their race.

According to Stewart Swerdlow, who claims to have participated in clandestine government projects located at the
Montauk Air force/Naval facility;[67] the investigative journalist,
Jim Marrs;[68] and the controversial British author, David Icke;[69]
this remaining band of Anunnaki on Earth has influenced
humanity through human proxies derived from ET/human inter-
breeding that eventually became the aristocratic "blue bloods"
of Europe and other nations. According to Icke,

> . . . a race of interbreeding ['royal' reptile-human hybrid]
> bloodlines . . . were centered in the Middle East and
> Near East in the ancient world and, over the thousands
> of years since, have expanded their power across the
> globe . . . creating institutions like religions to mentally
> and emotionally imprison the masses and set them at
> war with each other.[70]

These human elites maintained certain esoteric traditions
by which they could maintain contact with those Anunnaki
rebels concealed in different locations on Earth. Brown, Marrs,
Bramley, Icke and others claim that this advanced race covertly
influences humanity in order to produce resources that sustain
these hidden ETs.[71]

The author/channel Alex Collier, claims that the small number
of Anunnaki beings at the moment concealed on Earth eagerly
await the return of the Anunnaki elite, who they hope will end
the secrecy of the Anunnaki history and presence, and reestablish overt Anunnaki control. This will end the need to rule
covertly through unreliable human proxies.[72] Brown describes
the Anunnaki remnants as often being in conflict with the ET
intruders, the Grays.[73]

In the *Stargate Conspiracy*, Lynne Pickett and Clive Prince
describe the process by which this advanced race of ETs established religion as a control instrument for humanity.[74] They
argue that clandestine government agencies are aware of the
Anunnaki remnants on Earth and are divided over how to
respond to the anticipated return of the Anunnaki elites in the
immediate future, that may attempt to reestablish overt control
over the planet.

Brown, Picknett and Prince claim that clandestine government programs are using "exotic" technologies such as psychotronic weapons activated by thought, enhanced psychic abilities, "star gates," and even time travel, to militarily prepare for the return of the Anunnaki who possess a technology supposed to be superior to anything reverse engineered from downed Gray space craft.[75]

A number of individuals who claim to have participated in clandestine military programs with ET races have also reported interacting with or witnessing a large Reptilian species that presumably is associated with the historic Anunnaki presence on the planet. Andy Pero, who claims to have been recruited as a super soldier by a clandestine government organization, gave testimony of such an encounter:

> On one occasion I was introduced to a Reptilian being while in an underground base sometime in 1989–90. At first I saw a 7-foot tall human Aryan looking man. He walks towards me and I notice that his image phases out as if something interfered with an energy field. He does something to a device on his belt and tells me, "OK, I'll show you." He then pushes some button and then I see his image change into a 7-foot tall lizard like creature who looked like he weighed over 400 lb.[76]

According to other participants including Michael Relfe, Al Bielak and Preston Nichols, Reptilian beings are involved with time/interdimensional travel technology, mind control, psychotronics and other exotic weapons.[77]

Conspiracy theories falling into this perspective suggest that humanity needs to counter subversive efforts of the concealed Anunnaki remnants, and prepare for the potential threat posed by the returning Anunnaki who may attempt to deprive humanity of their sovereignty by reestablishing overt control on the basis of global mismanagement by human elites.

This perspective suggests those Anunnaki remnants concealed on Earth continue to manipulate international events through human proxies, to create the right international environment to influence the decision of their superiors. War, poverty and environmental collapse are presumed to constitute a favorable climate for the return of the Anunnaki elites. They would present themselves as saviors of humanity who would solve these problems and "punish" human elites responsible for them.

Categories used to describe the Anunnaki presence, in contrast to the Gray ET presence, clearly fall into the malevolent end of the moral spectrum. There are few morally redemptive features of the ET presence concealed on Earth, and there is also suspicion concerning the intentions of the larger body of Anunnaki presumed to be returning. In contrast to the intruder perspective that focused on a clandestine government conspiracy not to reveal the ET presence, this perspective focuses on an ET conspiracy to subvert and control humanity through human proxies.

Primary information sources for conspiracy theories in this perspective are drawn, in order, from the last three categories of Remote Viewing, Independent Archeology, and Channeling. Although these sources have weak to moderate evidentiary strength, the small number of whistleblowers who have come forward to support the manipulator perspective suggests ranking this category at the upper end of **moderate** evidentiary support.

Helper Perspective

According to conspiracy theories that fall into this perspective, ETs are here to help humanity deal with a myriad of political, socioeconomic and environmental problems, but this is not disclosed to the general public by clandestine government agencies. The ETs in this category are described as humanoid in appearance, with a height of 7 feet or more, often having the physical characteristics of Northern Europeans and typically called Nordics or Semites.[78] Dr. Michael Wolf claims to have worked with these humanoid races in secret military facilities in the US, and claims that the "the Semitics and Nordics [ETs] come from Altair 4 and 5 and from the Pleiades [star systems]."[79]

A more controversial description of these helper ETs is Billy Meiers who claimed to have been visited by beings from the

Pleiades who allowed him to photograph their ships and to have extended communication with him.[80] Meier quickly attained celebrity status. People were coming from around the world to hear his story, the secret history of the ET-Earth connection, and the esoteric ET philosophy.

Some of the principal supporters of the helper perspective include Dr. Steven Greer, who has personally interviewed and analyzed hundreds of whistleblower testimonies on the ET presence; Dr. Richard Boylan who has interviewed a range of "contactees" and military/intelligence "insiders" with knowledge of the ET presence; and Alfred Webre, a former Science adviser to the Carter White House now based at the Stanford Research Institute. Webre is a pioneer in advanced communication techniques with ET races.[81] Numerous "channelers" of ET races also support the perspective of an advanced race of ETs quietly assisting humanity in its evolution.[82]

According to this perspective, the "helper ETs" are here to assist humanity in a number of interrelated ways. First, the helper ETs assist humanity in empowering itself by developing more advanced levels of consciousness whereby humans use a greater proportion of their inherent psychic capacity and spiritual potential.

The theme of self-empowerment through transformational activities such as prayer, meditation and connecting with the energy field of the planet is a recurring one in descriptions of what the Helper ETs are attempting to teach global humanity.[83] This was the theme promoted by Meiers in his account of the philosophy taught to him by ETs from the Pleiades who were apparently concerned that self-destruction had occurred when earlier human civilizations had integrated Pleiadian technology before self-destruction.

According to Meiers:

> Semjase and the Pleiadians who had chose to return again to Earth were descendants of a peaceful Lyrian [star system Lyra] faction that now felt responsible for guiding Earth in its spiritual evolution, so the Earth humans could avoid the setbacks long ago experienced by their Pleiadian ancestors.[84]

Courtney Brown argues that his remote viewing sessions consistently turn up evidence of a Galactic Federation of races that assists humanity in its evolution.[85]

A second way in which helper ETs assist humanity is to pass down knowledge of advanced technologies and alternative energy sources that are more harmonious with the biosphere which they regard as a living organism that needs to be protected. The early twentieth century inventor, Nikola Tesla, is often cited as having been assisted by ETs in developing and disseminating these environmentally friendly technologies.[86]

According to statements from witnesses in the Disclosure Project, a number of "free energy technologies" are possessed and used by the government, but are not disclosed to the general population.[87] Paul Czysz, who has worked for 38 years either with the US Air force or the exotic technologies department of the military contractor, McDonnell-Douglas, explains why these technologies are withheld as follows:

> The people that [sic] have access to [these advanced energy technologies] don't know how to let go of it, because they're afraid of who's going to get their hands on it. Even though there would be a tremendous benefit to mankind, they're also worried that somebody could take that same energy source and do the equivalent of what they did with the *USS Cole*—instead of blowing a hole in the side, they could just obliterate the whole ship.[88]

According to interviews of "government insiders," Richard Boylan claims that the B2 stealth bomber operates largely using anti-gravity technology for its propulsion system, but this is not disclosed to the general public who believe it relies on conventional fuel sources.[89]

A third way helper ETs assist humanity is to encourage humanity to achieve peaceful resolution of international conflict, and prevent nuclear proliferation and the use of other destructive weapons. A number of former government and military officials have provided testimonies that support this perspective of ETs as helpers. ETs have displayed significant concern about nuclear weapons and even, in some instances, have disarmed them. According to Captain Robert Salas in testimony given in December 2000 as part of the Disclosure Project, 16 nuclear-armed missiles were simultaneously disarmed in two separate launch facilities after guards reported UFOs hovering over two NORAD facilities in March 1967.[90]

Other sources report that during the early years of the Eisenhower administration, a group of ETs secretly met with US government officials appointed to deal with the ET question, and offered to assist with a number of environmental, technological, political and socioeconomic problems, with the sole condition that the US dismantle its nuclear arsenal.[91] When the government officials declined, this group of ETs subsequently withdrew and played no role in the government's clandestine program to reverse engineer ET technology for advanced weaponry.

It is claimed that these "helper ETs" would subsequently concentrate their efforts with consciousness raising of the general public; warning of the hazards of nuclear and "exotic" weapon systems reverse engineered from ET technology; limiting the environmental impact of clandestine projects; encouraging the development of alternatives to using fossil fuel as an energy source; and preparing the general populace for eventual disclosure of the ET presence.

Finally, the helper ETs describe the Milky Way galaxy, and indeed the universe, as being populated by numerous advanced civilizations.[92] By understanding more about ET races and interstellar politics, the helper ETs believe this will help the evolution of humanity. Alfred Webre, who briefly headed a 1977 Special Study on Communications with Extraterrestrials initiated by President Carter, has written a book based on the politics of ET races and their interaction with Earth:

Earth appears to be an isolated planet in the midst of a populated Universe. Universe society consists of highly organized and consciously evolving, advanced civilizations. Universe civilizations function within our own interstellar Universe, as well as within other dimensions in the Universe at large. Advanced Universe civilizations exist in other dimensions parallel to our own. They access our own planet, galaxy, and all of interstellar space. Life-bearing planets such as Earth are part of a collective Universe whole, operating under Universal law. Think of Earth as part of a Universe commons. Life is implanted and cultivated here under the tutelage of more advanced societies, in accordance with the over-all principles of Universe ecology.

Where necessary, Universal law applies restrictive measures to a planet that endangers the collective whole. Universe government can remove a planet from open circulation within Universe society. This fate appears to have happened to Earth in our distant past. Earth has suffered for eons as an exopolitical outcast among the community of Universe civilizations. Earth is isolated because it is under intentional quarantine by a structured, rational Universe society. There are signs around us of a Universe initiative to reintegrate Earth into interplanetary society. It is possible that Earth may be permitted to rejoin Universe society, under certain conditions, or at a future time certain.[93]

Rapidly growing information about these helper ETs comes from an extensive range of sources. Former military and government "whistle blowers" have revealed the activities of clandestine government agencies and interests opposed to incorporating ET technology into the public arena.[94] An extensive number of witnesses of these Helper ETs continue to make reports about being physically visited by helper ETs and communicating with them either by both verbal and/or telepathic means, that are collected and closely analyzed by many highly credentialed individuals and organizations.[95]

Further sources of information are participants in scientific remote viewing projects either conducted under government supervision or private organizations; and individuals who claim to be in telepathic communication with these helper ETs who often become popular "channels" of insights for the general public.

In sum, the Helper ET perspective depicts the ET presence as being clearly benevolent in their moral orientation. Their intentions and activities aimed to assist humanity deal with a range of global issues, including rogue ET elements intent on destabilizing global institutions and the biosphere, or abducting the human population for genetic experiments.

Conspiracy theories that stem from the helper perspective focus on the efforts of clandestine governmental organizations to suppress information about the presence of the ET helpers, and even contrive a military conflict with ETs in general in order to maintain the status quo. Primary information sources for conspiracy theories in this perspective are drawn from all the categories with the exception of the abduction category. The most persuasive is from the whistle blower category, suggesting **strong** evidentiary support for this perspective.

Watcher Perspective

The fourth perspective can be distinguished from the first three insofar as it relies exclusively on the last two categories of sources—individuals claiming to be in telepathic contact with ETs ("channels") and independent archeologists.[96] The main idea advocated by these authors is that many ETs are primarily here simply to observe how humanity resolves its numerous societal and global conflicts at a time when cosmic energy surges in the solar system and the galaxy adds to the intensity of these conflicts.

According to the Watcher perspective, humanity represents an elaborate galactic experiment designed by ETs who wish to observe how humanity responds to the galaxy wide energy surges.

The Watcher perspective views the entire universe as comprised of vibrating energy fields that wax and wane in long historical cycles that have their origin in cosmic and galactic energies. The energy fields emanate from the cores of galaxies, and elsewhere in the universe. At different points in these cycles, energy fields will be intensified by cosmic and galactic energies that have a cycle similar to that of our sun which every 11 years experiences an increase in the emission of Solar Flares, Coronal Mass Expulsions, and the various electromagnetic energies that make up the Solar Wind. These energy shifts prove to be profound in terms of their impact, and according to this perspective, the future of planetary civilizations is determined by how well they respond to these energy shifts.

Although it may appear strange at first to believe that reality is nothing but energy, quantum physics has indeed shown that sub-atomic particles are made up of rapidly vibrating energy fields rather than discrete particles that were earlier thought to be the ultimate substratum of reality. According to Robert Becker in his best selling book, *The Body Electric*, the human body is nothing but concentrated electrical and magnetic energy fields that respond constantly to the energy fields of the larger environment.[97]

Thus, the contemporary era, based on this perspective, corresponds to the end of a number of important celestial cycles revealed by the Mayan Calendar. One is the end of a Mayan cycle of 5,200 years and another is the end of a solar cycle of 25,920 years corresponding to the precession of the equinoxes.[98]

Some argue that cycles up to as long as 225,000,000 years also come to completion at this time.[99] According to John Major Jenkins, the solar cycle corresponds with the time it takes for the plane of our solar system (the ecliptic) to realign itself with the "galactic core" where cosmic and other energies from the center of the galaxy dramatically influence consciousness throughout the planet.[100]

These historic shifts in consciousness, according to Jenkins, are described in the Mayan, Vedic and Egyptian traditions and explain the dramatic rise and falls of different civilizations throughout the ages.

The profound consciousness shift occurs due to the cyclic transitions and realignment with the galactic core changing the intensity of all the "energies"—electromagnetic, solar, gravitational, cosmic, etc.—that influence life throughout the solar system. This means, for example, that all the thoughts, feelings and actions that combine to influence an individual's reality are either magnified or diminished.

In the case of a magnification, this has two polarized outcomes. One is that human civilization implodes due to the intensification of latent conflicts and dysfunctional energies that come to the surface of human collective life, in a kind of "planetary spring cleaning," and prove to be unmanageable. An analogy to help understand this is that of the psychological process of "projection" wherein unbalanced individuals project onto others their own unresolved psychological issues.

If this were to occur to an extreme degree with large numbers of individuals, such a society could implode in a violent cathartic release of repressed negative emotions.

The second outcome of a magnification of energies influencing human consciousness is that the energy surges make it possible for a jump in evolution from the "dimensional reality" in which a particular civilization finds itself, to a higher dimension where more refined powers of creation are possible. According to a number of authors, human civilization currently occupies a "third density level" and is preparing to make the transition to the "fifth density level" at the end of the current 5000-year cycle of the Mayan Calendar in December 2012.[101]

This philosophy of differing density levels that can also be described as making up a "multidimensional reality" can be understood by the metaphor of water molecules at different temperatures. At temperatures below 0°c, water freezes into ice crystals.

The degree of difficulty or energy used in manipulating these water molecules when in ice form in terms of movement, storage, shapes, etc., is a metaphor for the difficulties encountered by beings who live in a low density level such as the third density which human civilization reportedly occupies. At temperatures between 0 and 100°c, water is in liquid form wherein the molecules are much easier to move, store, and place in different shapes.

This is a metaphor for the ease with which civilizations are able to shape their external reality according to the energy used. Finally, water at temperatures above 100°c becomes a gas where it is easiest to manipulate the water molecules in terms of movement, storage and shape. Again, this is a metaphor for the ease with which civilizations are able to shape their external reality according to the energy used.

According to this perspective, the Watcher ETs are here to learn how humanity deals with the energy shifts that intensify the latent conflicts and dysfunctional energies from human history. They desire to observe whether human civilization implodes, or is successful in making the transition from a third density into fourth and then fifth density environments.

Although it may appear odd at first to be informed that advanced ET civilizations are here to observe and possibly learn from humanity, it may not be so strange if "galactic history" is explained from the perspective of a number of authors claiming to be in telepathic communication with ETs.[102] According to these authors, the Milky Way galaxy has witnessed intense armed conflict between large alliances of ET races divided by competing philosophies, histories and genetic heritages. In its most simple terms, these conflicts have been polarized around two competing visions about how the galaxy is best organized, and took place primarily in the constellation of Orion.[103]

One vision is that all ET races should have an equal role and voice in galactic decision making, while the other is that the oldest and most technologically advanced race, rightfully has a privileged position.

According to this perspective, the most powerful elites from the two sides many millennia ago, realized that the coming cyclic energetic changes, what can be termed the 'Great Shift', would in most likelihood lead to another galactic war due to the intensification of all the issues that were never completely resolved in previous conflicts and which lay dormant.[104]

This would be disastrous since this would mean great devastation and loss for those ET civilizations not able to make the transition to a higher density. Only a comprehensive galactic unity would guarantee that these latent conflicts would not result in a new Galactic War, and that most civilizations could successfully move up in density levels.

However, these elites from the respective ET races recognized that the intense divisions between them in terms of history, genetics and philosophy, would in most likelihood not be overcome in time for a comprehensive galactic union to be reached, thereby making another galactic war inevitable.

In order to overcome this problem and avert future disaster, the ET elites decided to sponsor a hybrid race that would comprise the diverse genetic pools found in the galaxy. As a result of genetics, and interventions by differing ET races at appointed times, this race of beings would experience a history that closely mirrored that of the galaxy. If this hybrid race could resolve its internal differences by the time of the Great Shift to achieve a comprehensive political unity, then this would provide an example for the rest of the Galaxy for how they could in turn deal with these energetic changes.

Thus the human race was born as a "Great Galactic Experiment" whose true purpose was known only among a few of the elite of the most powerful ET races.[105] Although these few elites from the oldest and most advanced ET civilizations presumably knew that only a galactic union would avert future disaster, this was not widely accepted among the bulk of the ET races that believed their favored viewpoint would prevail in a future galactic conflict. This is analogous to human conflict where hard line military leaders strongly believe they will militarily prevail in another confrontation, and thus, disagree with more prudent calls for dialogue and negotiation.

Those few ET elites that could prophesy such a future galactic calamity sponsored the evolution of humanity throughout the varied ET interventions in history, both benevolent and malignant, in order to demonstrate to the rest of the Galaxy how to handle the Great Shift. One of the principal advocates of the Watcher perspective is Barbara Marciniak, whose writings have become a seminal source in the channeling community. Marciniak, channeling a group of ETs from the Pleiades describes this "Great Galactic Experiment" as follows:

> Much of existence is focused on you at this time, although that is not to say everyone has their telescopes

pointed at Earth. However, there are legends in the cosmos, just as there are legends on Earth, and cosmic legends speak of this time of change and refer to you as a gem of a genetic library tucked away, an experiment made for a "just-in-case" time. And this experiment has been fought over and discounted, recognized and forgotten, valued and given away; you have experienced all these events in the collective of your consciousness, in the cells of who you are ... You are the Gods' secret tucked away in time, and they wait to see if you can change from one form of being into another in a nanosecond—in their terms; in yours, perhaps it takes a lifetime, a lifetime enriched and extraordinary, above and beyond ordinary existence.

You have an exquisite opportunity to create a completely unique kind of power and to bring purposefulness and meaning to Earth. Cosmic legends are full of this tale about you humans. Just as your legends on Earth are filled with tales of magicians, at this juncture in time you are looked upon in the Book of Earth as magicians yourselves, the whole lot of you, not simply a few. The heavens hold the rich imprint of electromagnetic aliveness, and as you move through space, your planet, solar system, and galaxy all traverse new territory. This territory has been planned for you to encounter, one that will recode your DNA in this lifetime to connect you to the multidimensional intelligence that exists beyond your biology, and is your inheritance.[106]

According to the Watcher perspective, recent human experience in terms of two World Wars in the first half of the twentieth century, and fears of a third World War either in the latter part of the twentieth or early twenty-first century, mirrored the history of earlier galactic conflicts. Insofar as humanity has been able to avert a third world war, the human experiment has thus far been a great success story.

Humanity has shown how a civilization can overcome a long history of racial and cultural differences, political and economic conflict, and environmental degradation at the same time the Great Shift intensifies all the aspects of these differences. This viewpoint is clearly outlined by the popular author, Jeleila Starr who claims to channel a higher dimensional ET race associated with the seeding of planet Earth:

> Earth is the third of 3 Grand Experiments in Polarity Integration. This means that she is a special planet set aside from all others and populated with every species in the known universe for the specific purpose of integration. In this melting pot of species, and with the aid of highly evolved incarnated souls and their angels/ guides, it is hoped that full integration of the Light and Dark can be achieved. If this occurs, peace will reign in the galaxy and universe. Why? Each species will have the blueprint, created in the Grand Experiment by their star-seeded children, to resolve any conflict no matter how ancient.
>
> It is these painful, ancient irresolvable conflicts between races and species that have resulted in numerous galactic wars that have brought about the necessity of this experiment. If Earth fails to achieve full integration, the galaxies will be destroyed because there won't be any way to resolve the conflicts. If Earth succeeds and peace is established, the Polarity Game will end and all souls who achieved integration will have the opportunity to move on to other realms and create new universes and games through which they can continue to learn and grow.[107]

The planet Earth, Humanity and the galaxy, it is claimed, have a deadline to prepare for this transition to a higher dimensional or "density" level at the end of the current 5200 year cycle of the Mayan Calendar in December 2012.[108]

In sum, the Watcher perspective suggests that a galactic/ cosmic conspiracy exists where humanity has been set up to create a solution to a galactic problem not of humanity's own making. The Watcher ETs are represented as merely observing how humanity integrates its diverse heritage and resolves the historic conflicts expected to emerge over the next decade. Rather than directly intervening in human affairs, the ET Watchers are portrayed primarily as observers who over the course of millennia are somehow able to influence or decide which other ET races are allowed to intervene in human affairs.

The ET Watchers are depicted as being able to calculate the effects of such interventions in a way that predisposes humanity to arriving at a uniquely human solution to a complex galactic problem.

The moral dimension of this perspective is primarily neutral due to the observational nature of the ETs described, and the long-term effort involved in promoting and learning from the "human experiment." The primary information sources for this perspective are drawn overwhelmingly from Category G, Channels. Additional evidence comes from independent archaeology and remote viewing but these lack the clarity and coherence of channeled information. The reliance on channeled information suggests **weak** evidentiary support for this perspective.

Despite its weak evidentiary support base, it integrates the earlier perspectives into what appears to be a coherent framework integrating all the other conspiracy theories concerning the ET presence.

Furthermore, those advocating this perspective write with clarity of purpose, coherence and persuasiveness that win many converts who desire to know the "big picture" about the ET presence and human history. One might view this perspective as the "mother of all conspiracies," whereby this grand galactic conspiracy by higher dimensional ET races, lays the foundations and rules for all other conspiracies involving ET races and human elites.

Summaries for all the perspectives examined, and the various conspiracy theories, moral orientations, primary sources and evidentiary support ascribed to each perspective can now be presented.

Table 1: Summary of ET Perspectives and Conspiracy Theories

Perspective	Source of Conspiracy	ET Moral Orientation	Primary Sources (Top 4)	Evidentiary Support
Intruder	Clandestine Government Organizations	Neutral	Whistleblowers Abductions Witnesses Documents	Strong
Manipulator	Remnant Anunnaki ETs	Malevolent	Remote Viewers Independent Archeology Channels Whistleblowers	Moderate
Helper	Clandestine Government Organizations	Benevolent	Whistleblowers Witnesses Remote Viewers Documents	Strong
Observer	Watcher ETs	Neutral	Channels Independent Archeology Remote Viewers	Weak

Implications of Exopolitics for Policy Makers

Much of what has been written so far will predictably have little impact in the policy making community, in the event of a continued government policy of non-disclosure of the ET presence and of clandestine government projects set up to deal with different aspects of this presence. Recent signals that the US and other governments are deliberately leaking information supporting the ET presence, suggest that some form of official disclosure might occur in the near future.

Interviews of a number of former/current government "insiders" affirm that key policy making bodies embedded in various levels of government, have been recently pursuing a policy of acclimation, preparing the general public for disclosure of the ET presence.[109]

The emergence of hundreds of former government, intelligence and military officials who have become or are willing to become, whistle blowers on their participation in clandestine projects and/or suppression of information involving ETs, supports claims that a gradual disclosure program is underway.[110]

Most prominent among the public disclosures of former military/intelligence officials are the revelations by Col. Phillip Corso in his book, *The Day After Roswell*. Corso's impeccable military credentials, former leadership positions in the Army's clandestine Research and Development Department, and association with prominent Republican leaders such as Senator Strom Thurmond, made him a key figure in the gradual disclosure program to prepare the general public.

Discussion of the political implications of an ET presence is clearly difficult in an official environment of non-disclosure of such a presence. This means making some effort to determine where evidentiary support is strongest in order for discussion of the political consequences of the ET presence to proceed with least reservations over accuracy and verifiability.

Of the four perspectives, two were found to have weak or moderate evidentiary support. The Manipulator perspective had a ranking of moderate evidentiary support. This suggests that any discussion of its policy implications, while possible, would need to be qualified by the need for stronger evidence to support any conclusions that stem from this perspective.[111] In Chapters Five and Six of this book, this perspective will figure prominently in analyzing motivations for US led military intervention in Iraq in 2003. The fourth perspective, the Watcher, had the weakest evidentiary support among all of the perspectives. Once again, this suggests that any discussion of its policy implications, while possible, would need to be qualified by the need for stronger evidence to support any conclusions that stem from this perspective.[112] For the remainder of this chapter, I will briefly review the two perspectives, Intruder and Helper, found to have the strongest evidentiary support, and their implications for policy makers.

The Intruder perspective has a high degree of evidentiary support and therefore deserves close attention in terms of its policy implications. This perspective portrays the ET presence as intrusive and a potential threat. As such, it lends itself to US and allied government policy responses that support the acquisition and use of reverse engineered ET weaponry in addition to other exotic weapons gained in clandestine projects.

This perspective suggests an ongoing military confrontation in which the US and allied governments militarily cooperate in ways designed to counter what is perceived as a potential ET threat. Although this may encourage greater global political cooperation, it does so on the basis of a clandestine and coordinated military build up that would at best translate into a form of non-belligerence, rather than global peace, which characterized much of the Cold War era.

A hidden war is therefore underway, in which physical evidence of this conflict with ETs is kept hidden from public awareness, but consumes national resources as those policy makers participating in clandestine government organizations try to upgrade defense industries to better contain or confront ETs anywhere on the planet where they may appear. In Chapter Four, this situation will be closely reviewed in terms of how various clandestine organizations embedded in military and intelligence branches of government have been infiltrated by ET races.

As analysis of this perspective pointed out earlier, intrusiveness can be distinguished from hostility or aggression. There is little evidence that the gray ETs have displayed hostility or aggression toward either military forces or the civilian population. It may therefore be concluded that it is premature to support a military confrontation with this ET race. This suggests that resources devoted to a secret military confrontation need to be restricted and placed under close scrutiny by elected public officials who would be more open to a responsible policy debate over how to interact with the Gray ET species.

The third perspective, the Helper, has strong evidentiary support that merits discussion of its implications for policy makers. This perspective poses a difficult challenge for those political leaders, since it is based on a policy of disarmament of a range of reverse engineered and exotic weaponry, nuclear weapons, and other destructive weaponry that presumably harm the biosphere. For example, weapons such as extremely long wave (ELF) sonic waves used for sonar tracking in the oceans, presumably to monitor ET activities, cause great harm to marine life.

Similarly, the High-frequency Active Auroral Research Project (HAARP) that uses microwaves deflected off the Ionosphere, also causes environmental damage and is argued to be an instrument of mind control.[113] These weapon systems were included in a comprehensive list of space-based weapon systems that Dennis Kucinich, a congressional representative from Ohio, introduced for consideration as a bill by the US Congress in October 2001.[114] In implementing such a wide-ranging disarmament program as outlined in Kucinich's bill, *The Space Preservation Act*, policy makers would be confronted with the dilemma of sacrificing what they perceive to be the chief means of a military defense in the case of future conflict with an ET race.

Helper ETs suggest that through a radical overhaul of human society to empower individuals, eradicate social and economic inequalities, adopt environmentally sustainable energy sources, and use new technologies for communication and transportation, humanity would ultimately develop a more viable form of global defense against ET interference.

Implications for global peace suggested by the ET helper perspective are that primary obstacles to peace are clandestine government projects that use reverse engineered technology and exotic weapons with little regard to the damage caused to the biosphere, the refusal to disclose the true nature and motivations of the ET helper's presence, and government secrecy over the discovery of alternative energy sources that can relieve pressure on the biosphere as a result of fossil fuel consumption.

Accordingly, efforts such as the Disclosure Project organized by Dr. Stephen Greer focus on the illegal secrecy of these clandestine projects and institutions, and the importance of alternative energy sources for preventing environmental catastrophe and international conflict.[115]

This perspective offers the most far reaching vision of global peace where humanity comes together to eradicate social, environment and economic problems by responsibly incorporating ET technology. Although the third perspective is morally desirable, it poses the greatest challenge to policy makers who have exercised clandestine control over the ET question and who have an ingrained disposition that military defense is the best insurance against intrusive ET activities and the technological superiority of such races.

It also suggests that the clandestine decision making processes originally designed as a safeguard against ET interference, need to be reassessed and placed under close scrutiny by elected public officials who would be more responsive to a genuine public debate over how to deal with the difficult question of disarmament and the ET presence.

Policy Recommendations: The Need for Exopolitics

It has been concluded that of the four perspectives comprising a range of conspiracy theories concerning an ET presence, two have sufficient evidentiary support to be immediately considered by policy makers, and to be closely studied in terms of their political implications. On the basis of evidence supporting these two perspectives, the following five policy recommendations can be made.

First, the quality of evidence substantiating an ET presence and clandestine government cover up has a significant degree of credibility and persuasiveness. This supports the creation of a new field of public policy, exopolitics, which would study these two perspectives in the current political climate of an officially sanctioned government policy of non-disclosure of the ET presence.

There is therefore a need to outline the main concepts, theories and information sources used in exopolitics as an emerging field of public policy. Furthermore, efforts need to be devoted to analyzing the policy implications of exopolitics in all areas where the ET presence has an impact.

Second, there is a need to promote official government disclosure of an ET presence, and to make more representative the policy making process that has evolved in government responses to such a presence. The magnitude of the issues raised by the ET presence requires vigorous public debate over the ET presence and how to interact with ET races.

This would lead to a more representative decision making process concerning the ET presence in contrast to what the evidence suggests is a restricted process run by a small number of government officials "appointed" in a manner which raises serious concerns over their accountability, constitutional status and lack of congressional oversight.

Third, there is a need to reveal the full nature of national security policies undertaken by clandestine government organizations in militarily responding to the ET presence. Evidence provided by a number of sources reveals a clandestine government policy that uses reverse engineered ET weaponry in addition to other exotic weapons gained in clandestine projects to target and bring down ETVs.

Evidence suggests that a covert military confrontation has been underway for more than fifty years whereby the US and other major governments have been secretly cooperating in ways designed to monitor, contain and engage in what is viewed as a potential ET threat. Such a coordinated military response around the globe to an ET presence consumes national resources as clandestine government organizations try to upgrade defense industries to better contain or confront ETs, while keeping the general public and elected officials ignorant of these military activities.

Fourth, there is a need to release into the public arena all knowledge about alternative energy sources that have a commercial application but are withheld on national security grounds. Substantial evidence suggests that reverse engineered ET technologies have been used in the development of energy sources for "black projects" such as the anti-gravity propulsion system that is claimed to fuel the B2 bomber. Given the environmental impact of the continued use of fossil fuel energy, there is a need to release into the public arena all available technologies that have commercial application.

Final policy recommendation is that there needs to be more effort in determining the extent to which congressional oversight is required for organizations created to deal with the ET presence. Evidence suggests that elected public officials including even sitting Presidents, have been denied access to information about the ET presence on the basis of national security considerations.[116]

Although the argument that national security considerations may at times require public secrecy and even non-disclosure to most elected public officials, more effort needs to be devoted to working out an effective and constitutional process establishing firm guidelines for such a process.

Even if the relevance of exopolitics as an emerging field of public policy may justifiably be questioned in a pre-disclosure political environment, the seriousness of the claims, evidence provided by those conducting exopolitical research, and policy implications drawn by exopolitical analysis, deserve close attention from academic researchers, policy makers and the general public. Exopolitics provides an opportunity for understanding how humanity can better share and manage the resources of this planet with other species, both terrestrial and extraterrestrial, thereby contributing to a more peaceful and harmonious planet for this and future generations.

Notes

1. This chapter is a revised and updated version of a Study Paper, "The Need for Exopolitics: Implications for Policy Makers and Global Peace," released on January 20, 2003 and published online at www.exopolitics.org. Many thanks to Dr. Peter Weinberger for his suggestions on the title of the original paper and for his thoughtful advice on organizing the material. Thanks also to Art Miller for helping correct typographical errors.

2. The Roper Poll, "UFOs & Extraterrestrial Life Americans' Beliefs and Personal Experiences," prepared for the SCI FI Channel, September 2002, Roper Number: C205-008232 (www.roper.com). The poll was conducted by a representative sample of 1,021 adults ages 18 and over. The telephone interviews were conducted from August 23rd through August 25th, 2002.

3. Stephen Greer, *Executive Summary of the Disclosure Project* (Crozet, VA.: Disclosure Project, April 2001). Website: www.disclosureproject.com. He claims an additional 300 witnesses are also available to give testimony.

4. CNN.Com, "'Taken' takes Sci Fi to new heights," Wednesday, December 18, 2002. http://www.cnn.com/2002/SHOWBIZ/TV/12/18/scifi.taken.ap/.

5. Richard Dolan, *UFO's and the National Security State: Chronology of a Cover-up 1941–1973* (Hampton Roads, 2002).

6. For discussion of the Briefing Document and similar official documents, see Jim Marrs, *Alien Agenda: Investigating the Extraterrestrial Presence Among us* (Harper Paperbacks, 1997), pages 160–80.

7. For witness testimonies about participation in destroying or tampering with ET/UFO evidence, see Steven Greer, *Disclosure: Military and Government Witnesses Reveal the Greatest Secrets in Modern History* (Crossing Point, Inc., 2001).

8. Theresa de Veto, "From Disinformation to Disclosure," *Surfing The Apocalypse* (October, 2001). Available online at: http://www.surfingtheapocalypse.com.

9. For discussion of events surrounding Forrestral's breakdown, dismissal and death, see Dolan, *UFO's and the National Security State,* pages 70–76.

10. For discussion of the mysterious 'Men in Black' see Albert K. Bender, *Flying Saucers and the Three Men* (Neville Spearman Limited, 1963). An extract is available online at: http://www.nexusmagazine.com/meninblack.html.

11. See, "Testimony of Master Sergeant, Dan Morris," *Disclosure,* ed., Steven Greer (Crossing Point, Inc. 2001), p. 359; and William Cooper, *Behold a Pale Horse* (Light Technology Co., 1991), pages 198–99.

12. For details of the Roswell incident, see Jim Marrs, *Alien Agenda: Investigating the Extraterrestrial Presence Among Us* (Harper Collins, 1997), pages 133–37.
13. Marrs, *Alien Agenda*, p.138.
14. Quoted in Dolan, *UFO's and the National Security State*, p. xx.
15. Corso, *The Day After Roswell* (Pocket Star, 1997).
16. Stephen Greer, *Executive Summary of the Disclosure Project.* Website: www.disclosure project.com.
17. Quoted in Greer, *Disclosure*, p. 55.
18. Budd Hopkins, *Missing Times* (Ballantine Books, 1990); David Jacobs, *Secret Life: Firsthand Accounts of UFO Abductions* (Touchstone Books, 1993); John Mack, *Abduction: Human Encounters with Aliens* (New York: Ballantine Books, 1994); Mack, *Passport to the Cosmos: Human Transformation and Alien Encounters* (Three Rivers Press, 2000).
19. John Mack, *Abduction*, p. 385.
20. For discussion of the conference and presentations, see C.D.B. Bryan, *Close Encounters of the Fourth Kind: Alien Abduction, UFOs, and the Conference at MIT* (Alfred Knopf, 1995).
21. The official Air force website on Project Blue Book is: www.af.mil/news/factsheets/Unidentified_Flying_Objects_a.html.
22. Condon, Edward U. and Daniel S. Gillmor (ed.). *Final Report of the Scientific Study of Unidentified Flying Objects* [Conducted by the University of Colorado Under Contract to the United States Air Force], (New York: Bantam Books, 1968).
23. For discussion of the debate surrounding the Condon report, see Dolan, *UFOs and the National Security State*, pages 312–70.
24. Allen Hynek, "The Condon report an UFOs," *Bulletin of the Atomic Scientists*, XXV(4), pages 39–42.
25. Hynek, J. Allen: *The UFO Experience* (Chicago: Henry Regnery Co., 1972), Part 1—The UFO Phenomenon. Introduction: An Innocent in UFO, Land, paragraph 4.
26. For more information on the Center for UFO studies, go to: www.cufos.org.
27. Don Berliner, Marie Galbraith, Antonio Huneeus, Whitley Streiber. UFO *Briefing Document, The Best Available Evidence* (Mass Market Paperbacks, 2000).
28. Greer, *Disclosure*.
29. MUFON has a website at http://www.mufon.com.
30. These "leaked" documents were published together by Robert and Ryan Woods, *The Majestic Documents Books*. The book and documents are available online at: http://www.majesticdocuments.com.
31. Quoted in Jim Marrs, *Alien Agenda: Investigating the Extraterrestrial Presence Among Us* (Harper Paperbacks, 1997), p. 165.

32. John Greenewald, *Beyond UFO Secrecy* (The Black Vault, 2002). Website URL is: http://www.blackvault.com. Another online source of UFO documents released by FOIA is available at: http://www.chez.com/lesovnis/htm/foia.htm.

33. In 1990, these intelligence agencies switched their financial support for remote viewing to Science Applications International Corporation. See Courtney Brown, *Cosmic Explorers: Scientific Remote Viewing, Extraterrestrials, and a Message for Mankind* (New York: Signet Publishing, 2000), p. 5. For an excellent overview of remote viewing, see Marrs, *Alien Agenda*, 441–519.

34. CIA letter (Reference: F-1997-02079) in response to John Greenwald, September 27, 1997. Available online at the Black Vault: http://www.bvalphaserver.com/secart72.html.

35. Russell Targ and Harold Puthoff, *Mind-Reach: Scientists Look at Psychic Ability* (London: Jonathan Cape, 1977).

36. Courtney Brown, *Cosmic Explorers*; and *Cosmic Voyage: A Scientific Discovery of Extraterrestrials Visiting Earth* (New York: Dutton, 1996). Extensive online information on remote viewing can be found at the homepage of the International Remote Viewing Association: http://www.irva.org/index.shtml.

37. Brown, *Cosmic Voyage*, pages 68–69.

38. Marrs, *Alien Agenda*, pages 493–96.

39. *Chariots of the Gods* (G.P. Putnam's Sons, 1969).

40. Graham Hancock, *Fingerprints of the Gods: The Evidence of Earth's Lost Civilization* (London: Three Rivers Press, 2000).

41. Zecharia Sitchin, *The Earth Chronicles*, Books 1–6 (New York: Avon Books).

42. Sitchin, *The 12th Planet: Book 1 of the Earth Chronicles* (Avon Books, 1976), p. vii.

43. Barbara Marciniak, *Family of Light: Pleiadians Tales and Lessons in Living* (Bear & Co., Santa Fe, New Mexico), p. xi–xii.

44. Budd Hopkins, *Intruders: The Incredible Visitations at Copley Woods* (Ballantine Books, 1987).

45. Executive Summary of the Disclosure Project Briefing Document 73–84. Website: http://www.disclosureproject.com.

46. David Jacobs, *The Threat: Revealing the Secret Alien Agenda* (Simon and Schuster, 1998), p. 20.

47. See John Mack, *Passport to the Cosmos: Human Transformation and Alien Encounters.*

48. Richard Boylan, "Close Encounters And Personal Transformation," cited online at: http://drboylan.com/ce4trnf2.html.

49. For descriptions of Grays by abductees, see C.D.B., Bryan, *Close Encounters of The Fourth Kind*; and Jacobs, *The Threat*. For a detailed online description which identifies different "Gray species,"

see Richard Boylan, "The Various Kinds of Star Visitors," available online at: http://www.drboylan.com/etraces.html.
50. Linda Moulton Howe, "UFOs and EBEs: More Insider Evidence," *Nexus* magazine (August-September, 1998): http://www. nexusmagazine.com/ufosebes.html.
51. Quoted by Richard Boylan, "Extraterrestrial Base On Earth, Sanctioned By Officials Since 1954": http://drboylan.com/ basespst2.html. Original Source, Michael Wolf, *Catchers of Heaven: A Trilogy* (Dorrance Publishing, 1996).
52. See Richard Boylan, "Official Within MJ-12 UFO-Secrecy Management Group Reveals Insider Secrets," in Boylan and Boylan, *Labored Journey To The Stars.* Available online at: http://www.drboylan.com/wolfdoc2.html. See also William Cooper, "Origin, Identity and Purpose of MJ-12": http://www. geocities.com/area51/shadowlands/6583/maji007.html; and Cooper, *Behold a Pale Horse* (Light Technology Publications, 1991), pages 201–05; Phil Schneider, MUFON Conference Presentation, 1995, available online at: http://www.ufocoverup-conspiracy.com/20.htm; See Dr. Neruda Interview #1: http://www.wingmakers.com; Boylan gives a more extensive coverage of events surrounding the Treaty signing in "Extraterrestrial Base On Earth, Sanctioned By Officials Since 1954," in Boylan and Boylan, *Labored Journey To The Stars.* Available online at: http://drboylan.com/ basespst2.html.
53. Cooper, "The Secret Government: Origin, Identity and Purpose of MJ-12," *Paper delivered at MUFON Conference 1989,* Available online at: http://www.geocities.com/Area51/Shadowlands/6583/ maji007.html.
54. Phillip Corso, *The Day After Roswell* (Pocket Books, 1997) p. 292.
55. Phil Schneider, "MUFON Conference Presentation, May 1995," available online at: http://www.geocities.com/Area51/Shadowlands/ 6583/coverup044.html.
56. Corso, *The Day After Roswell,* p. 79.
57. Richard Boylan, "The Differential Diagnosis of Close Extra-terrestrial Encounter Syndrome," online article published at: http://drboylan.com/diffdxce4a.html.
58. John E. Mack, *Abduction: Human Encounters with Aliens.*
59. For discussion of the hybrid race being created, see Jacobs, *The Threat,* pages 128–84.
60. Milton William Cooper, "The Secret Government: The Origin, Identity, and Purpose of MJ-12," available online at: http://www. abovetopsecret.com/pages/mj12.html.
61. William Bramley, *Gods of Eden* (Avon, 1989) 37. Also cited in Jim Marrs, *Rule By Secrecy, The Hidden History That Connects the*

Trilateral Commission, the Freemasons, and the Great Pyramids (Harper Collins, 2000) 406.

62. Zecharia Sitchin, *The Earth Chronicles*, Books 1–6.
63. The *Book of Enoch* describes in great detail this conflict. An online version can be found at: http://wesley.nnu.edu/noncanon/ot/pseudo/enoch.htm.
64. R.A. Boulay, *Flying Serpents and Dragons: The Story of Mankind's Reptillian Past* (Book Tree, 1999).
65. Manetho, *Manetho*, tr., W.G. Waddell (Harvard University Press, 1940).
66. Courtney Brown, *Cosmic Explorers*.
67. Stewart Swerdlow, *Blue Blood, True Blood: Conflict & Creation* (Expansions Publishing Co., 2002).
68. Jim Marrs, *Rule By Secrecy* (New York: Perennial, 2000).
69. David Icke, *The Biggest Secret*, 2nd Ed. (Bridge of Love Publications, 1999). For online information on Icke and his most recent work, go to: http://www.davidicke.com.
70. Cited by Jim Marrs, *Rule By Secrecy*, 406. Source: David Icke, *The Biggest Secret*, p. 1.
71. Rather than mining for material resources such as gold and other precious metals that Sitchin describes as being the initial reason the Anunnaki established humanity, Icke claims this race uses humans as a basic resource supplying hormones derived from emotions such as fear and anger, and using humans as a food source (*The Biggest Secret*).
72. Alex Collier, *Defending Sacred Ground: The Andromedan Compendium*, Edited by Val Valerian, January 1997, Revised July 1998. Website: www.lettersfromandromeda.com.
73. *Cosmic Explorers*, 159–221.
74. Lynn Picknett & Clive Prince, *The Stargate Conspiracy* (New York: Berkley Books, 1999).
75. The term 'exotic weapons systems' has been defined to include weapons designed to damage space or natural ecosystems (such as the ionosphere and upper atmosphere) or climate, weather, and tectonic systems with the purpose of inducing damage or destruction upon a target population or region on earth or in space. Space Preservation Act of 2001 (Introduced in the House), HR 2977 IH, 107th CONGRESS, 1st Session, H. R. 2977. Website: www.fas.org/sgp/congress/2001/hr2977.html.
76. See Interview with Andy Pero, "Project Superman," available at: http://www.hostileinvader.com/ProjectSuperman.html.
77. For two ebooks detailing Michael Relfe's memories of his encounters with Reptilians, see *The Mars Records*, published online at: http://www.themarsrecords.com. See also Preston Nichols & Peter Moon, *Pyramids of Montauk: Explorations in Consciousness* (Sky Books 1995) and "Interview with Al Bielek," *Connecting Link*

(Issue 19, Oct 1993) available online at: http://psychicspy.com/montauk1.html.

78. For a detailed description of the Nordic ETs, see Richard Boylan, "The Various Kinds of Star Visitors": http://www.drboylan.com/etraces.html.

79. Quoted by Richard Boylan, "Extraterrestrial Base On Earth, Sanctioned By Officials Since 1954, Now Revealed. Also Disclosed: Secret U.S.-USSR Manned Space Station, Positioned In Orbit For Past 30+ Years," in Boylan and Boylan, Labored Journey To The Stars. Available online at: http://drboylan.com/basespst2.html.

80. Kal K. Korff, Spaceships of the Pleiades: The Billy Meier Story (Prometheus Books, 1995).

81. Steven M. Greer, Extraterrestrial Contact: The Evidence and Implications (Crossing Point Publications, 1999). Richard Boylan, Labored Journey To The Stars: An anthology on human responses, governmental, civilian and Native, to extraterrestrial visitation, Rev., 2002. Alfred Lambremont Webre, Exopolitics: A Decade of Contact (Universe Books, 1999). His book is available online at: http://www.universebooks.com.

82. These include Barbara Marciniak, Family of Light (Bear and Co., 1999); Lyssa Royal & Keith Priest, "Preparing for Contact: A Metamorphosis of Consciousness" (Royal Priest Research, 1993); and Sheldan Nidle, First Contact (Vancouver: Blue Lodge Press, 2000).

83. See Marciniak, Family of Light, and Nidle, First Contact.

84. Cited in Marrs, Alien Agenda, p. 303. Original source: Gary Kinder, Light Years (Pocket Books, 1987) pages 98–99.

85. Brown, Cosmic Explorers.

86. For information of the connection between Tesla and ETs, see Tim Swartz, Timothy Beckley, The Lost Journals of Nikola Tesla: Haarp—Chemtrails and Secret of Alternative 4 (Global Communications, 2000).

87. See testimonies in section 5, Greer, ed., Disclosure, 489–559. Dr. Greer further claims these efforts have been stymied by vested interests opposed to alternative energy sources.

88. Testimony of Paul Czysz, Disclosure, ed., Greer, page 519.

89. Boylan, "B-2 Stealth bomber as antigravity craft," available online at: www.drboylan.com/waregrv2.html.

90. See "Testimony of Captain Robert Salas, US Air force," in Disclosure, Greer, pages 167–71. See also Executive Summary of the Disclosure Project Briefing Document, p. 49; available online at http://www.disclosureproject.com.

91. See Michael Wolf, Catchers of Heaven; and Bill Cooper, Beyond a Pale Horse. Website: http://www.abovetopsecret.com/pages/mj12.html.

92. See Nidle, *First Contact.*

93. Alfred Lambremont Webre, JD, Med, *Exopolitics: A Decade of Contact* (2000) an ebook published online at: http://www.universebooks.com/exoone.html.

94. See Greer, *Extraterrestrial Contact.* See for example, Richard Boylan and Lee K. Boylan, *Close Extraterrestrial Encounters: Positive Experiences With Mysterious Visitors* (Wildflower, 1994). Website: www.drboylan.com.

95. The most popular "channels" advocating this perspective include Barbara Marciniak, *Family of Light;* Robert Shapiro, *Shining the Light,* Vols. 1–6 (Light Technology Publications); Jelaila Starr, *We Are the Nibiruans: Return of the 12th Planet* (New Leaf Distributing Co., 1999), and Drunvalo Melchizedek, *The Ancient Secret of the Flower of Life,* Vol. 2 (Light Technology Publications, 2000).

96. Robert Becker and Gary Seldon, *The Body Electric: Electromagnetism and the Foundation of Life,* New York: Quill, 1985.

97. John Major Jenkins, *Maya Cosmogenesis 2012,* Santa Fe: Bear and Co., 1998.

98. Barbara Hand Clow, *The Pleiadian Agenda: A New Cosmology for the Age of Light* (Bear and Co., 1995) p. 49; John Major Jenkins, *Maya Cosmogenesis 2012* (Bear and Co., 1998).

99. John Major Jenkins, *Galactic Alignment: The Transformation of Consciousness According to Mayan, Egyptian, and Vedic Traditions* (Inner Traditions International, 2002).

100. The most well known author advocating this timeline is Jose Arguelles, *The Mayan Factor,* Santa Fe: Bear and Company, 1987. For discussion of different dimensions/densities, see Lyssa Royal & Keith Priest, *The Prism of Lyra: An Exploration of Human Galactic Heritage,* Rev. ed. (Royal Priest Research, 1993), pages 1–9.

101. Some of the popular sources for Galactic history include: Royal & Priest, *The Prism of Lyra;* Sheldan Nidle, *First Contact,* Barbara Marciniak., *Family of Light;* and Fred Stirling, *Kirael: The Great Shift,* Oughten House Publication, 1998. The most well-known author advocating this timeline is Jose Arguelles, *The Mayan Factor* (Bear and Co., 1987).

102. For the conflict in Orion, see Royal and Priest, *The Prism of Lyra,* 39–46.

103. The term 'Great Shift' is used by Fred Stirling, *Kirael: The Great Shift* (Oughten House Publication, 1998); Website: www.kirael.com.

104. The idea that humanity is a hybrid race comprising various ET genetic strands is promoted by Zecharia Sitchin, *Earth Chronicles* (Books 1–6). For discussion of the galactic politics surrounding the genetic make up of human races and the ET involvement, see Royal and Priest, *The Prism of Lyra,* pages 67–74.

105. Marciniak, *Family of Light*, pages 186–87. For a similar perspective, see Royal and Priest, *The Prism of Lyra*, 67–74.
106. Jelaila Star, January 3, 2003, website update.
107. The most well known author advocating this timeline is Jose Arguelles, *The Mayan Factor* (Santa Fe: Bear and Company, 1987). See also Jenkins, *Cosmogenesis*.
108. Richard Boylan, *Labored Journey To The Stars: An anthology on human responses, governmental, civilian and Native, to extraterrestrial visitation*, Rev., 2002: http://www.drboylan.com/aclmatn2.html; Arguelles, *The Mayan Factor* (Bear and Co, 1987).
109. See Greer, ed., *Disclosure*.
110. For discussion of this perspective in terms of its policy implications, see Marrs, *Rule by Secrecy*; and Courtney Brown, *Cosmic Explorers*.
111. For discussion of this perspective in terms of its policy implications, see Marciniak, *Family of Light*.
112. For discussion of this perspective in terms of its policy implications, see Marciniak, *Family of Light*.
113. Jerry Smith, *Haarp: The Ultimate Weapon of the Conspiracy: The Mind-Control Conspiracy Series* (Adventures Unlimited Press, 1998).
114. Space Preservation Act of 2001 (Introduced in the House), HR 2977 IH, 107th CONGRESS, 1st Session, H. R. 2977.
115. See Greer, ed., *Disclosure*. Online information available at: http://www.disclosureproject.com.
116. Chapter Five will discuss the evolution of US policy making concerning the ET presence and the erosion of executive oversight of clandestine organizations.

Chapter 2

Political Management of the Extraterrestrial Presence—The Challenge to Democracy and Liberty in America

Introduction[117]

Political management of the extraterrestrial (ET) presence on Earth has evolved during the course of the successive US Presidential administrations that had to deal with the policy issues that arose once irrefutable proof of such a presence was brought to the attention of policy makers.

This evolution of responses by Presidential administrations can be broken into five historic phases which demonstrate a gradual erosion of Presidential/executive oversight, and the growing autonomy/independence of clandestine organizations embedded in military-intelligence and national security branches of government. This erosion of Presidential/executive oversight in the form of ultimate control of the ET presence being gradually taken away from elected Presidents and/or their congressionally approved political appointments appears to have all the characteristics of a "political *coup.*"[118] Presidents, in the case of Republicans, have been reduced to rubber stamps for those controlling political management of ET issues; or, in the case of Democratic Presidents, to political irrelevance.

The first political management phase was crisis management during the Roosevelt administration when the ET presence became enmeshed within the foreign policy crisis of the Second World War, and was effectively controlled by a complex of scientific-military institutions set up under executive oversight to conduct the war effort.

The second phase was an effort by the Truman administration in the post-war era to establish a framework for politically managing the ET presence through a series of ad hoc committees responsible for setting policy and coordinating response by the scientific-military-intelligence communities.

The third phase was a comprehensive effort by the Eisenhower administration to manage the ET presence through improved policy coordination between different clandestine organizations embedded within military/intelligence and national security branches of government, and introducing more prominent roles for Corporate America and foreign policy elites in the political management of the ET presence.

The fourth phase was the effective loss of direct Presidential/Executive oversight during the latter part of the Eisenhower administration and the Kennedy administration, and the independence of clandestine organizations created to deal with the ET presence.

Evidence suggests that the recent military campaign in Iraq marks a disturbing fifth phase in the political management of the ET presence in which clandestine organizations effectively take control of a foreign government for the exclusive purpose of managing the ET presence.

For the purpose of this chapter, 'political management' will be defined as a coordinated series of policies for dealing with a set of issues that have important public policy implications. In the case of political management of the ET presence, this refers to the need for developing a coordinated and strategic approach to the ET presence that satisfactorily deals with all its public policy dimensions.

More important, political management of the ET presence involves coordinating the various agendas, reverse engineering programs, covert military operations, intelligence gathering operations, and policy studies undertaken by a variety of clandestine organizations embedded within the military, intelligence and national security branches of government.

Chief among the clandestine organizations to be identified as taking the lead in politically managing the ET presence in the US is "Majestic 12" (MJ-12—aka "PI-40" and "Special Studies Group"), embedded within the Covert Operations Committee of the National Security Council.[119] Prominence of Nelson Rockefeller and Dr. Henry Kissinger in influencing this clandestine organization, and supporting roles given to Corporate America and elite policy study groups such as the Council on Foreign Relations, give important insight into how the political management of the UFO presence has been historically conducted. This casts considerable light on motivations for the recent military intervention in Iraq, and the likelihood that it marks an important watershed in the political management of the ET presence.

In this chapter, I will identify the political management approach taken in the various phases of US administrative/clandestine organizational response to the ET presence. I will analyze the gradual erosion of executive oversight of these clandestine organizations, and the latter's increasing influence over the executive branch of government. I will also outline the increased role of Corporate America and the Council on Foreign Relations in politically managing the ET presence.

I further examine the most current political management style as evidenced by the US-led military intervention into Iraq and what this suggests concerning the way ET presence will be managed in the future. I conclude by identifying how political management of the ET presence has been conducted in a manner that represents a threat to the principles of democracy and liberty in the US.

Phase One-Crisis Management of the Extraterrestrial Presence

Evidence for the emergence of ET piloted craft over US skies has been claimed to exist from as early as the 19th century.[120] The emergence of the ET presence as a phenomenon that required political management can be dated to the first instance in which US policy makers had to grapple with irrefutable evidence of an ET presence and its tremendous policy implications.

Evidence from whistleblower testimonies from clandestine government organizations points to the crash of an ET craft off the coast of California in 1941. Its secret retrieval was what initially set off efforts by the Roosevelt administration to politically manage the ET presence.[121] Furthermore, in 1942 there was a naval bombardment in response to what at first was perceived to be a Japanese air raid, but upon closer evidence suggested was an intelligently piloted UFO.[122]

US participation in the Second World War from 1942 meant that these astonishing events involving ET piloted spacecraft had to be politically managed in the context of a global military conflict requiring coordinated policy responses for the sake of US survival.

The approach taken by the Roosevelt administration was based on maintaining tight secrecy, given the assumption that the "enemy"—Japan and Nazi Germany—would take any advantage of the ET presence it could discover through its intelligence assets, to bring about defeat of US forces on the battlefield. The Roosevelt administration delegated control of the ET presence to the US Department of War (renamed the Department of Defense) who were immediately aware of the military significance of such a development. Any technology and knowledge acquired from the ET presence would be used to develop weapons technology that could bring victory on the battlefield.

Witness testimonies provided considerable evidence that the US Navy led this clandestine military effort with a top secret project seeking to develop "stealth technologies" for Navy ships from as early as 1943.[123] Dubbed the "Philadelphia Experiment," this project established the primacy of the US Navy in reverse engineering ET technology, and subordination of the whole ET issue within military institutions.

An important characteristic of this phase of the political management of the ET presence was the leading role played by military funded scientific laboratories such as Los Alamos National Laboratory in New Mexico. These would play the critical role of reverse engineering ET technology. This "military-scientific complex" was critical to the war effort and for responding to the ET presence.

As Commander-in-Chief in a wartime situation, President Roosevelt's political management of the ET presence was synonymous with political management of the Manhattan Project that produced the first atomic bombs and other secret weapons technologies that were part of the war effort. Both secrecy and a clear chain of command were required, and no effort would be spared to fund Los Alamos and other scientific laboratories working directly under the military to utilize this ET "presence" for battlefield success.

There is no evidence that the Roosevelt administration developed any special organizational structures for dealing with the ET presence, other than simply subordinating the whole ET issue to the Department of War that was conducting the war effort. As Commander-in-Chief, Roosevelt and his most senior advisors would be extensively informed. They played a key role in exercising the necessary executive supervision of military projects using technology and intelligence gained from ET sources.

Most important, the Second World War meant there would be no congressional overseeing of the ET presence, since the latter's existence and military significance required utmost secrecy due to dire national security implications it had for the War effort. These ET related projects fell into the category of what is today called a "Special Access Program" (SAP).

SAPs are programs that have additional security measures attached to them over and above the normal classificatory system (confidential, secret, top-secret) attached to most classified information and programs. These SAPs are divided into two classes: "acknowledged" and "unacknowledged," and a further distinction is made for waived SAPs in which normal Congressional overseeing does not occur.

Essentially, a waived unacknowledged SAP (deep black) is so sensitive, only eight members of Congress (the chairs and ranking members of the four defense or intelligence committees divided between the House of Representatives and Senate) are notified of a waived SAP without being given any information about it. This would enable them to truthfully declare no knowledge of such a program if asked, thereby maintaining secrecy of this SAP.

If unacknowledged SAPs are "black programs," then "waived" unacknowledged SAPs are "deep black." ET related programs fall into the "deep black" secrecy category.

Phase Two-The Truman Administration and the Decision to Maintain Secrecy

When Harry Truman became President in 1945, a "successful" outcome of the Second World War was already clear. This meant that a more organized institutional structure could be developed for politically managing the ET presence.

The national security threat to the US was now over as far as the general public was concerned, which meant there would soon be pressure for Congressional supervision and public disclosure of the clandestine programs conducted by military and intelligence branches of government. Since the US military exercised complete operational and logistical control over all aspects of the ET presence during the emergency conditions of the war, there needed to be a process for deciding how to politically manage extensive policy implications of such a presence.

Undoubtedly, the first policy issue to be confronted was the extent to which the ET presence should be disclosed to Congress and the general public. More important, an institution needed to be created for ensuring policy coordination between the different military and intelligence units that were working on different operational aspects of the ET presence; and, critically, a means of ensuring that the President and his principal advisors would be sufficiently well informed to maintain executive oversight of the entire military-scientific-intelligence community that interfaced with the ET presence.

In 1947, Truman gave executive approval in the form of a memo to then Secretary of Defense, James Forrestal, for the creation of a clandestine committee to be formed that would play these three crucial roles of politically managing public disclosure of the ET presence; policy coordination of the various projects associated with the ET presence; and executive supervision of clandestine organizations dealing with the ET presence.[124]

Titled Majestic 12 (MJ-12), this group was claimed to initially include 12 senior individuals from the military, intelligence and civilian sectors who formed an ad hoc committee. MJ-12 was therefore a clandestine political entity created to politically manage all aspects of the ET presence in order to provide the best policy advice to the President. Significantly, MJ-12 was embedded within the National Security Council which was formed at the same time, for the purpose of coordinating policy recommendations from different government, military and intelligence departments into a coherent set of policy recommendations from which Presidents could choose.

The way in which policy advice would be gained was through a series of ad hoc committees that would be formed to investigate specific aspects of the ET presence. One of the more famous was an ad hoc committee including Albert Einstein and Robert Oppenheimer, who released a top secret report on "Relationships with Inhabitants of Celestial Bodies" in June 1947, that outlined a number of recommendations for responding to the ET presence in terms of their foreign policy implications.[125]

Thus, executive supervision of the ET presence occurred through the President, his advisors and appointed officials who would steer US policy on the critical policy issues concerning the ET presence on the basis of policy advice gained from top secret ad hoc committees.

A factor that increasingly impacted on the political management of the ET presence was the rise in public sightings of UFO craft in the post-war period, making it more difficult to maintain a public policy of secrecy. In 1947, there was an extraordinary increase in the number of public sightings of UFO craft that led to a groundswell of support of an official response, and public disclosure of the ET presence.[126]

The most famous of these was the 1947 Roswell incident that has spawned numerous books and testimonies from various individuals and officials.[127] This led to the decision of the Air force to launch an official public examination of the UFO presence. Project Blue Book began in 1952 and was the official public successor to earlier Air force investigations of UFOs from 1947–48 (Project Sign), and 1948–52 (Project Grudge).[128]

In the midst of the clamor generated by the public for news on the UFO presence, the Truman administration was evidently advised by the MJ-12 committee to maintain strict secrecy of the ET presence, while continuing to exercise executive supervision of clandestine projects concerning ET activity and their technology. Evidence of the nature of the executive control of the ET presence and the decision by MJ-12 to maintain public secrecy can be found in the circumstances surrounding the dismissal and death of James Forrestal as Truman's Secretary of Defense in 1949. Secretary Forrestal had, according to whistleblower testimonies, developed a clear difference of opinion on how the ET presence should be politically managed, and was said to have favored public disclosure.[129]

Forrestal, who was a member of the MJ-12 committee, was thwarted by President Truman, his principal advisors and others on the MJ-12 committee, who decided that the whole ET presence had to be politically managed in a way that maintained strict secrecy, thereby denying the general public and Congress the truth about the ET presence. Forrestal was dismissed due to what was officially claimed to be a "nervous breakdown" and later "committed suicide" from the 6th floor of the Bethesda Naval Hospital.[130] According to several military "whistleblowers," Forrestal was murdered.[131]

Testimonies by former officials support the view that a non-disclosure policy of the ET presence was in place and public officials that released classified information concerning ETs/UFOs were liable to severe penalties. According to John Maynard, a former military intelligence analyst with the Defense Intelligence Agency, officials were silenced by threats of severe penalties for disclosure:

> It was during that time [1970s] that I realized just how much the government was hiding under its classification and disclosure blanket. Even newspaper reports that had become part of the [UFO] file were being classified. It appeared to me that they literally did not want anyone to know what they knew. I guess curiosity got the best of me at that point. After that incident, I started to pay serious attention to what was going on, particularly

when it came to the classification of documents. I, more or less, became an official source to ask about classifying documents, which meant full research of the documents surrounding the one being classified.

They say that hindsight has 20/20 vision. I could have turned illegal at that point and made copies of the pages pertaining to UFO incidents. However, my security oath and duty to country stopped me from going that extra measure to the illegal. I have to tell you I seriously thought about it; however, I could not come to the point of making copies of any particular pages relating to UFO sightings and other encounters. I guess I was too much of a Boy Scout and I detested the thought of going to prison. Ah, yup, I am a big chicken when it comes to that.[132]

In conclusion, the political management of the ET presence by the Truman administration was one of firm executive supervision whereby he would be advised by his appointed committees such as MJ-12 in how to deal with the ET presence. Congressional leaders, at best, would only be verbally informed of the existence of ET related projects, but given no specific details as occurs in the procedure developed for waived Special Access Programs (deep black).

MJ-12 would provide policy recommendations for coordination and supervision of clandestine organizations embedded in military and intelligence departments, and the military funded scientific laboratories that pursued reverse-engineering programs and communication with ETs.

Phase Three-The Erosion of Executive Oversight of Clandestine Organizations

The election of Dwight Eisenhower in 1952, brought with it not only a Republican administration, but also a profound policy shift in how political management of the ET presence would be conducted—the formal involvement of Corporate America and the Council on Foreign Relations. The Rockefeller family had supported Eisenhower in his Presidential campaign and it was therefore no great surprise that he chose Nelson Rockefeller to be in charge of reorganizing the government. From 1953–59, Rockefeller was Chairman of the President's "Advisory Committee on Government Organization." In addition, he became the President's Special Assistant in Cold War Strategy (1954–55) and was critical in shaping Eisenhower's views and responses to the ET presence.

The Rockefeller family derived much of its wealth and influence from the Standard Oil Company founded by John Rockefeller. Standard Oil established a powerful monopoly in the US oil industry whose legacy continues today under the Exxon/Mobil/Chevron banners.[133]

Nelson Rockefeller, the grandson of John Rockefeller, was a "moderate Republican" who was a liberal in political issues and strongly supported the liberal internationalist idea of a global political institution, but conservative in the economic sphere.[134] In asking Nelson Rockefeller to advise him and reorganize the government in general and the policy making infrastructure concerning the ET presence in particular, Eisenhower was giving Corporate America a prominent role in the way in which the government attempted to address policy issues—a view consistent with the ideological underpinning of the US Republican party.

As far as the ET question was concerned, this meant Corporate America would play a prominent role in the clandestine efforts to reverse engineer ET technology.[135] The immediate consequence was that the scientific laboratories directly funded by the Department of Defense in the past were reorganized in terms of their location and funding base. These laboratories now received corporate funding through contracts awarded by military organizations, rather than being directly funded by the military, as was the case during the Second World War and the Truman administration.

Including Corporate America provided the important benefit of introducing a further layer of secrecy that could effectively keep prying Congressmen away from the truth about the ET presence. The Congressional supervision, in theory at least, possible for government/military funded scientific laboratories working on reverse engineering ET technology, would not also be possible for corporations nominally in charge of the scientific laboratories working on the same clandestine military projects, using the same personnel, resources and funding.

With Project Blue book underway and Congress attempting to discover what was really happening concerning the ET presence, a thorough re-organization involving a prominent role for Corporate America, in Rockefeller's view, was needed if secrecy was to be maintained. The "sleight of hand" involving Corporate America provided an important means for politically managing the ET presence—total secrecy could be maintained by simply invoking the mantra of private sector market forces, thereby ensuring immunity from congressional investigation.

The full extent of the budget and chief contracting companies of the "military-industrial complex," according to Phil Schneider, who was a Civil Engineer contracted to work on the construction of underground facilities was claimed to be the following:

> The black budget is roughly $1.3 trillion every two years. A trillion is a thousand billion. A trillion dollars weighs 11 tons. The U.S. Congress never sees the books involved with this clandestine pot of gold. Contractors of stealth programs: EG&G, Westinghouse, McDonnell Douglas, Morrison-Knudson, Wackenhut Security Systems, Boeing Aerospace, Lorimar Aerospace, Aerospacial in France, Mitsubishi Industries, Rider Trucks, Bechtel, *I.G. Farben*, plus a host of hundreds more.[136]

Confirmation of Schneider's alarming estimates comes from Catherine Fitts, a former Assistant Secretary in Housing and Urban Development who has provided extensive information on trillions of US dollars being siphoned through the Department of Defense and Department of Housing and Urban Development that find their way into the black budget operations of the military-industrial complex.[137] Fitts estimated that the black budget for the fiscal years 1998–2000 was 1.1 trillion dollars.

Another important policy shift by Rockefeller was the inclusion of the Council on Foreign Relations as the source for suitable recruits for a top secret policy committee whose exclusive task was to provide policy recommendations for the various political, economic, social, religious and legal issues concerning the ET presence. The Rockefeller Family became important benefactors in the establishment of the Council on Foreign Relations in 1921 by making significant yearly donations of $1,500; making a large donation of $50,000 for the Council's new headquarters in 1929; and donating the building that became the headquarters of the Council in 1945.[138]

A measure of the Rockefeller influence could be seen in their support for individuals who were appointed to powerful positions. In the early 1970s, for example, David Rockefeller, who eventually became Chairman of the Council, went against the wishes of a nominating committee to appoint William Bundy to the editorship of the influential journal, *Foreign Affairs*.[139] By bringing the Council on Foreign Relations to the center stage of how the Eisenhower administration would gain recruits for clandestine organizations designed to make policy recommendations concerning the ET presence, Nelson Rockefeller had maneuvered himself and his family into a key position for determining how the ET presence would be politically managed.

The most significant institutional reorganization as far as political management of the ET presence was concerned was the expanding and formalizing of MJ-12 as an autonomous institution fully authorized by executive order to deliberate upon and make policy decisions concerning the ET presence. MJ-12 became formally embedded in the Covert Operations Committee of the National Security Council—Committee 5412, named after National Security Council Edict 5412. MJ-12's earlier existence as an ad hoc committee appointed by executive authority, was now transformed into a permanent sub-committee institutionally embedded within the most secret of all the National Security Council's committees.

Evidence from whistleblower testimonies suggests that Truman's ad hoc committee, MJ-12, was reorganized to be comprised of two layers.[140] The outermost layer was a group of up to 40 individuals who would form a Study Group (hence the names PI-40 and Special Studies Group also attributed to MJ-12) whose function was to provide specialized studies and policy recommendations concerning ET issues for a smaller decision making group (MJ-12) that would actually make official policy recommendations for implementation after gaining executive approval by Eisenhower.

The Special Studies Group/PI-40 formed under Eisenhower held their first meetings at Quantico Marine Base in Virginia and its 35 members were drawn exclusively from the Council on Foreign Relations. The Study Group had two directors, Henry Kissinger and Zbigniew Brzezinski, and consisted of prominent individuals, including Dr. Edward Teller, Paul Nitze, David Rockefeller, and McGeorge Bundy (later Kennedy's Special Assistant for Foreign Affairs).[141] According to Cooper, the Rockefellers built a lavish retreat for the Study Group in an exclusive area in Maryland.[142]

MJ-12 now consisted of 19 individuals who reviewed the various studies, and deliberated on policy issues concerning the ET presence on the basis of a qualified majority system of 12 votes being necessary for an issue to be passed.[143] According to William Cooper, who served on the Naval Intelligence briefing team for the Commander of the Pacific Fleet, the President's Special Representative for Foreign Affairs headed this smaller group, and its composition was determined according to the following formula.

The President's Special Representative for Cold War Strategy (aka National Security Advisor—Nelson Rockefeller); the Director of Central Intelligence (Allen Welsh Dulles); Secretary of State (John Foster Dulles); Chairman of the Joint Chiefs of Staff (Admiral Arthur Radford); Director of the FBI (J. Edgar Hoover); six men from the executive of the Council on Foreign Relations ("Wise Men"); and six men from a secret scientific organization called the JASON group (led by Dr. Edward Teller) were all members of the Council on Foreign Relations.[144]

It is likely that among the main organizational rules governing membership of MJ-12/PI-40, all appointments had to be approved by MJ-12; individuals could not belong to both MJ-12 and PI-40; term limits applied to how long individuals

could stay on the policy making body, MJ-12; and no term limits applied in the case of PI-40.

As with the policy-coordinating role played by the National
Security Council in providing advice to the President, MJ-12
had a similar function in coordinating policy concerning the
different clandestine organizations involved in various aspects
of the ET presence. As the organization developed to study
specific policy issues concerning the ET presence, PI-40 had
a significant role in framing policy issues and determining
priorities that would influence the way MJ-12 made policy
recommendations.

As the architect of the institutional reorganization that led
to the expansion of MJ-12, and as the President's Special
Advisor, Rockefeller assumed the critical role of head of MJ-12.
Furthermore, Rockefeller through his family's connections also
could influence the selection of appointments from the Council
on Foreign Relations and the JASON Group for PI-40.
Accordingly, Rockefeller played a critical role in influencing the
strategic principles and imperatives that would subsequently
govern policy making on the ET presence. Rockefeller's influence gradually led to his estrangement with Eisenhower as a
result of the latter realizing that executive overseeing of the ET
presence was being eroded due to Rockefeller's reorganization.

Eisenhower's concern resulted from two main ways in which
executive overseeing was eroded: the role of Corporate
America, and the way information was provided by MJ-12/PI-40
in dealing with the ET presence.

The shift from the Roosevelt/Truman administration models
of government funded military-scientific laboratories that conducted clandestine military projects, to a model that made US
corporations nominally in charge of these clandestine projects,
led to a cooperation that Eisenhower believed became a threat
to executive government. This was immortalized for the general public by Eisenhower's famous warning in his January
1961, departure speech of the danger of the "military-industrial
complex":

> In the councils of Government, we must guard against
> the acquisition of unwarranted influence, whether

sought or unsought by the Military Industrial Complex. The potential for the disastrous rise of misplaced power exists, and will persist. We must never let the weight of this combination endanger our liberties or democratic processes. We should take nothing for granted. Only an alert and knowledgeable citizenry can compel the proper meshing of the huge industrial and military machinery of defense with our peaceful methods and goals so that security and liberty may prosper together.[145]

At the end of his administration, Eisenhower evidently felt the military-industrial complex had grown too powerful and had slipped out of his control and that of his principal advisors concerning the way the ET presence was to be politically managed. Essentially, clandestine military projects with Corporate America receiving funding through contracts awarded by the different military services and intelligence branches, meant that the President and his principal advisors had lost control of what was occurring in the clandestine projects and organizations that formed an elaborate "military-industrial complex" weaving through the various military and intelligence organizations that worked on different aspects of the ET presence. Loss of control of what was happening in military-corporate laboratories carried with it a loss of control of over the quality and accuracy of the intelligence information that found its way back to the President and his senior advisors.

The "military-industrial complex" evidently was able to frame issues and contingencies concerning the ET presence in ways that dictated government policy to the extent that Eisenhower and his advisors felt frustrated and alarmed. This suggested that the MJ-12 and/or PI-40 had been compromised by the military-industrial complex, and was framing policy issues and imperatives in ways that eroded executive overseeing of these clandestine organizations.

Nelson Rockefeller, the architect of the reorganization that included Corporate America of how the ET presence would be politically managed, resigned from his position as the President's Special Assistant for Government Reorganization in 1959 to successfully run for New York governor. Rockefeller's prominent role in both Corporate America and in MJ-12/PI-40, however, ensured that control of how the ET presence was to be politically managed increasingly lay with the MJ-12/PI-40 and the military-industrial complex responsible for reverse engineering ET technology, and the various intelligence agencies focused on the ET presence.

What Eisenhower was alluding to in his departure speech was that, at least as far political management of the ET presence was concerned, a political *coup* had occurred.[146] Eisenhower had been maneuvered into a role that merely gave constitutional validity to policy recommendations that were crafted on information that the President had no independent means of confirming. That Eisenhower felt this way is evidenced in reports by Brigadier-General Stephen Lovekin, one of the military officers who directly served under Eisenhower. Lovekin wrote:

> But what happened was that Eisenhower got sold out. Without him knowing it he lost control of what was going on with the entire UFO situation. In his last address to the nation I think he was telling us that the Military Industrial Complex would stick you in the back if you were not totally vigilant . . . And I think that he realized that all of a sudden this matter is going into the control of corporations that could very well act to the detriment of this country. This frustration, from what I can remember, went on for months. He realized that he was losing control of the UFO subject. He realized that the phenomenon or whatever it was we were faced with was not going to be in the best hands. As far as I can remember, that was the expression that was used, "It is not going to be in the best hands."[147]

The Kennedy administration marked an important milestone in the erosion of executive overseeing of the ET presence. Kennedy was made aware of the ET presence when, as a young Senator serving on the Foreign Relations Committee, he was informed of the ET presence. Like his Republican predecessor, the new Democratic President Kennedy found that the political management of the ET presence was dominated by the clandestine military and intelligence organizations in concert with MJ-12/PI-40. He discovered they released information on ETs in a way that was biased towards a particular outcome, the most obvious, the need for continued funding of their respective programs.

If an information "spin" was indeed occurring, and certainly that is what the Eisenhower experience suggests, then the ET presence would permanently remain in the category of a national security threat that required strict secrecy, with minimal government supervision and extravagant funding levels. Involvement of Corporate America in fulfilling military contracts meant that executive supervision would not succeed in discovering the true ramifications of the ET presence and what clandestine organizations were really up to.

This problem of having no way of checking and confirming the information supplied by clandestine organizations that was suspected of being "spun" in a way that supported particular outcomes was certainly what concerned Eisenhower, and was a problem that Kennedy also confronted.

Kennedy and his most trusted senior advisors evidently labored hard to reestablish executive supervision and control, but were similarly frustrated as was Eisenhower and his team of advisors. Kennedy's Special Assistant on International Affairs (aka National Security Advisor), McGeorge Bundy, and other cabinet members from the Departments of Defense and State, the Director of Central Intelligence and the Chairman of the Joint Chiefs of Staff were most likely members of MJ-12, but this did not apparently assist Kennedy in gaining the changes he required.

According to a former steward aboard Air Force One, Bill Holden, he and Kennedy had the following conversation when flying to Europe in the summer of 1963: "What do you think about UFOs, Mr. President?" Kennedy became serious for a moment, and replied, "I'd like to tell the public about the UFO situation . . . but my hands are tied."[148] Rockefeller's institutional reforms made it impossible for one individual, even a sitting President, to take control of the policy making process concerning the ET presence.

Kennedy's efforts to reestablish executive control and overturn the disturbing reality that the military-industrial complex was acting with minimal executive supervision in dealing with the ET presence and, more important, influencing how the ET presence was to be politically managed, certainly led to an escalating series of confrontations. For example, Kennedy's initiative to improve relations with the Soviet Union under Nikita Khrushchev and cooperate more in responding to the ET presence certainly disturbed those clandestine organizations that held real influence in how to politically manage the ET presence.

Documents have been found supporting the idea that Kennedy desired greater cooperation with the Soviet Union, and that this was opposed by the military-industrial complex.[149] Furthermore, it has been claimed that Kennedy issued an ultimatum to MJ-12, that "he intended to reveal the presence of aliens to the American people within the following year [1964], and ordered a plan developed to implement his decision."[150]

The institutional restructuring under Rockefeller that made it possible for Corporate America to participate in conducting highly classified programs with clandestine organizations embedded in military and intelligence departments, was not going to be overturned by an upstart Democratic President committed to a more transparent and cooperative national and international effort to politically manage the ET presence. It is likely that Kennedy's assassination was partly linked to his efforts to wrest back control over how to manage the ET presence.[151]

Those responsible could have come from any of the clandestine organizations that felt their operations threatened by Kennedy's policies. An outcome of the crisis involving the Kennedy administration would have been that the formal policy making group, MJ-12, would have begun making policy choices without necessarily gaining Presidential approval. This marked a departure from the Eisenhower administration where, at least, Eisenhower had to give formal approval for major MJ-12 policy recommendations to be implemented.

Kennedy's assassination marked the culmination of a process that in all constituted a "de facto political *coup*" where executive supervision of the ET presence came to an end in less than a decade. Eisenhower's Republican affiliation and choice of Rockefeller to reorganize government structures and play a leading role in reforming how the ET presence was to be politically managed, was what effectively led to the erosion of executive overseeing of the ET presence.

Eisenhower became aware later in his administration that he had lost control, and that a "silent political *coup*" was occurring. Kennedy's unsuccessful effort to reestablish control and his assassination marked a turning point in the erosion of executive supervision. The kind of executive supervision achieved under the Roosevelt and Truman administrations where the President and his senior advisors were fully informed and exercised firm control over the political management of the ET presence was now a distant memory.

Real control over how to politically manage the ET presence had slipped into the hands of the clandestine military and intelligence organizations that operated secretly, with no executive supervision and lavish budgets. It is therefore understandable why, at least from a bureaucratic perspective if not a national security standpoint, clandestine organizations had a strong interest in maintaining the status quo and opposing efforts to yield to greater transparency and executive supervision.

As the key policy coordinating body, MJ-12/PI-40, would certainly have been aware of the advantages of such a "de facto political *coup*" and most likely played a supporting, if not principal, role in the erosion of executive supervision of all aspects of the ET presence. MJ-12/PI-40 was institutionally positioned to benefit greatly from this loss of executive supervision, which meant that Presidential administrations knew less about what was really happening on ET issues, and would have to rely on MJ-12/PI-40 for accurate information on what was occurring within the military industrial complex.

MJ-12/PI-40 could play its policy coordinating role with little real interference or scrutiny from Presidents and their policy advisors who simply did not have the means for confirming or challenging the information provided to them by the various clandestine organizations involved in dealing with the ET presence, and/or the policy advice provided by MJ-12/PI-40.

The inability of Presidential administrations to gain independent and accurate information on the ET presence meant that MJ-12/PI-40 could put its own spin on the available information to produce policy outcomes in line with MJ-12/PI-40's priorities and needs.

One of these needs was to ensure a degree of autonomy that minimized executive interference in affairs that MJ-12/PI-40 probably decided were outside the experience and abilities of Presidential administrations, viewing them at best only temporary players in the need to politically manage the ET presence. Loss of executive supervision meant that MJ-12/PI-40 became the main player in determining how the ET presence was to be politically managed.[152]

This led to the fourth phase in the political management of the ET presence—The Era of Autonomy and Impunity for Clandestine Organizations.

Phase Four-The Era of Autonomy and Impunity for Clandestine Organizations

President Lyndon Johnson, like Kennedy, was not trusted by MJ-12/PI-40 and was simply denied information concerning the ET presence.[153] MJ-12/PI-40 during the Johnson administration operated without executive supervision and politically managed the ET presence by coordinating among four main constituencies.

The first included the various clandestine organizations embedded in the different military services that were part of the military-industrial complex involved in reverse engineering ET technology for weapons production. The second constituency included the intelligence organizations that attempted to gather information on ET activities; the ET agenda; establish channels of communication with the ETs; and which were embedded in the Central Intelligence Agency, National Security Agency, and the Defense Intelligence Agency.

The third constituency was the President and his senior advisors who, while not fully aware of the scope of the ET presence, were at least aware of the existence of these clandestine organizations and of the policy-coordinating role played by MJ-12/PI-40.[154] The fourth and last constituency was Congress and the general public who were most out of the information loop, and simply unaware of the extent of the clandestine programs set up to deal with the ET presence. At best, Congressional leaders were verbally informed of "waived" Special Access Programs that were focused on the ET presence. It is likely, however, that even this perfunctory gesture was not always followed in order to hide the true cost and extent of programs dealing with the ET presence.

The Air force investigation begun at the end of the Truman administration, Project Blue Book, had been, according to Col. Phillip Corso, who served in the Eisenhower administration and was also briefly the head of a secret Pentagon project to reverse engineer ET technology, "pure public relations from the start," that was designed to keep the general public focused on debating whether or not there was sufficient evidence for the existence of ET piloted UFOs.[155]

Termination of Project Blue Book in 1969 represented the confidence of those politically managing the ET presence that numerous UFO sightings and public reports of contact with ETs no longer represented a threat to the official policy of non-disclosure of the ET presence.

In its role as the key policy coordinating body in the web of clandestine organizations that dealt with the ET presence, MJ-12/PI-40 now assumed firm control over how the ET presence was to be politically managed. Identifying the chief function of MJ-12/PI-40 and its key players is therefore central to understanding how the erosion of executive supervision of the ET presence and the autonomy of MJ-12/PI-40 would impact future Presidential administrations.

Organizational function of MJ-12/PI-40 can be likened to that of a chess player who has to manage a whole range of pieces with different functions, values and strengths in order to achieve an ultimate goal—victory. This meant MJ-12/PI-40's primary role was that of developing a grand strategy to deal with the ET presence in terms of the variety of ET races, their varying agendas and activities, and foreign national governments and clandestine governments on one side of the chess board (the opponent); and on the other side, the four different constituencies that made up the pieces of one's own side of the chess board.

Architect of this strategic role for MJ-12/PI-40 was Nelson Rockefeller, and the Council on Foreign Relations essentially designed the institutional rules by which MJ-12/PI-40 would interact with other constituencies involved in various aspects of the ET presence. There is strong evidence from whistleblower sources that the master strategist of the Special Studies Group that made up the outer layer of MJ-12/PI-40, was Dr. Henry Kissinger, a key Rockefeller protégé, whose experience in managing the ET presence went further back than is commonly appreciated.[156]

The Prominence of Henry Kissinger as PI-40's Master Strategist

There is significant evidence that Nazi Germany had partially succeeded in reverse engineering downed extraterrestrial craft that had been discovered by Nazi authorities in the mid 1930s [this will be examined more closely in Chapter Three].[157] Partly successful efforts by top Nazi scientists in understanding and reverse engineering this ET technology was a major factor in Nazi Germany's advanced weapons technology program and prolongation of the war effort in order to fully deploy these new weapons systems.

At the conclusion of the Second World War, a top secret effort to repatriate the same Nazi scientists in order to utilize their expertise was begun by US Army's Counter Intelligence Corps. "Operation Paperclip," as this secret effort was called, involved the removal of hundreds of Nazi scientists to the well-funded military-scientific laboratories created to produce weapons for the war effort.[158] A little known figure in "Operation Paperclip" was a young German-speaking US Army intelligence officer with a German Jewish background—Henry Kissinger.

Kissinger was born in Fuerth, Germany on May 27, 1923, and served in the Army Counterintelligence Corps from 1943–46.

At the close of World War II, he stayed on active duty in occupied West Germany. He was assigned to the 970th Counter Intelligence Corps Detachment, among whose "official" functions included the recruitment of ex-Nazi intelligence officers for anti-Soviet operations inside the Soviet bloc.[159] Kissinger's detachment, in reality, was playing a key role in "Operation Paperclip"—a role that would mark him out in military intelligence circles as someone who had the keen intellect and strategic thinking abilities that could handle the most important strategic policy issue facing the US—how best to respond to the ET presence.[160]

Kissinger returned to the US, and in 1947 began his university education as an undergraduate at Harvard University. Kissinger, however, retained his ties to the military, as a Captain in the Military Intelligence Reserves. This enabled him to continue to play a role in issues pertaining to the ET presence during the time that the policy at the highest level of the Truman administration was being developed.

By 1950, Kissinger was now a graduate student and was working part time for the Department of Defense. He regularly commuted to Washington—as a consultant to its Operations Research Office, which was under the direct control of the Joint Chiefs of Staff. The Operations Research Office "officially" conducted highly classified studies on such topics as the utilization of former German operatives and Nazi partisan supporters in CIA clandestine activities.

Kissinger's official duties were once again a cover for his role in coordinating the recruitment and utilization of former Nazi scientists in clandestine projects involving the reverse engineering of ET technology, behavior modification projects (mind control), and dealing with a range of intelligence and strategic issues surrounding the ET presence.

In 1952, after completing his PhD, Kissinger became a consultant to the director of the Psychological Strategy Board, an operating arm of the National Security Council for covert psychological and paramilitary operations. Thus, Kissinger's role expanded to dealing with the extensive policy issues surrounding the ET presence. Kissinger's inside knowledge of Operation Paperclip and the ET presence, combined with his strategic thinking abilities, marked him as someone who would rapidly assume a prominent position in the decision making hierarchy surrounding the ET presence.

As a member of the Council on Foreign Relations, Kissinger would undoubtedly have come to the attention of its most prominent members as someone who could provide leadership on how to respond to the ET presence.

In 1954, President Eisenhower appointed Nelson Rockefeller his Special Assistant for Cold War Planning, a position that officially involved the "monitoring and approval of covert CIA operations." This was a cover for Rockefeller's true role as head of MJ-12; and most important, directing US foreign policy in the wake of a "secret treaty" signed between an ET race from or near the Orion Constellation and the US.[161] The "treaty" has been a source of much speculation but its existence and content have been revealed by a number of former military and government intelligence "whistleblowers."[162]

In 1955, Kissinger became a consultant to the National Security Council's Operations Coordinating Board—the highest policy-making board for implementing clandestine operations against foreign governments. Kissinger's analytical and strategic skills were used not only for coordinating US policy in clandestine operations against foreign governments, but also for the clandestine operations against ET races.[163] Kissinger's role in the clandestine operations, his close relationship with Nelson Rockefeller, his intellectual abilities, all combined to lead to a steady increase in his influence.

Rockefeller and others running clandestine organizations understood the danger in not coordinating clandestine policy towards ET races and reverse engineering, with the more conventional foreign policy issues that were the focus of public attention.

Addressing the extensive range of issues and problems would require someone with the strategic thinking abilities to coordinate these two arenas. Rockefeller, the Executive Committee of the Council on Foreign Relations, and military intelligence, chose Kissinger as the person best qualified for this critical role. Rockefeller was instrumental in appointing Kissinger as one of the two Directors of PI-40, the Study Group that would provide policy advice to MJ-12 in response to the Treaty signed with the ET race from Orion in particular, and the ET presence in general.[164]

As a Director and key strategist of PI-40, Kissinger would certainly have been aware of the need to politically manage the ET presence through ensuring the autonomy of MJ-12 and PI-40 and to render efforts of executive supervision ineffective. More important, MJ-12/PI-40 had steadily grown in institutional authority and power to the extent that it could now exert political influence over the executive branch of government. Strong influence if not outright control of successive Presidential administrations was viewed to be a critical part of how the ET presence had to be politically managed; effectively dismantling the executive supervision that was such a prominent feature of the Roosevelt and Truman administrations.

What contributed to this need for MJ-12 to control/influence future administrations is the irony that although most national security officials, politicians, the news media and the public believed the Soviet Union was the primary threat to US Security, in fact the US was secretly cooperating extensively with the Soviet Union in responding to the ET presence. This meant that beneath the official Cold War rhetoric and armed conflicts that consumed public attention and resources, clandestine cooperation was occurring against what was perceived to be a common threat.[165]

In short, the US and USSR were strategic allies as far as addressing the ET presence was concerned, while simultaneously being strategic competitors in the geo-politics of the Cold War. This meant that much of the animosity that characterized the Cold War was a charade that helped divert the general public away from what was really happening. Such a charade could only work if the most senior officials within the Presidential administration were familiar with the ET presence, in order to neutralize more bellicose policy makers who believed the Cold War was for real, and who were fully ready to use nuclear weapons against the Soviet Union in response to a perceived attack.

Influencing successive Presidential administrations could be achieved by embedding key PI-40 members in senior policy positions in each administration, thereby ensuring non-disclosure of the ET presence and moderating Cold War hostilities. For the Kennedy/Johnson administrations, this individual was McGeorge Bundy, one of the original members of PI-40, who upon becoming National Security Advisor would have become the chair of MJ-12.[166] In the case of the future Nixon administration, this would be achieved by embedding within it an even more prominent PI-40 member who could control President Nixon when necessary.

For the Nixon administration, this person would be no other than Henry Kissinger who was plucked out of public obscurity in 1968 to be appointed National Security Advisor of President-elect Nixon. The instrumental figure in Kissinger's appointment was Nelson Rockefeller who had lost to Nixon in the 1968 Republican convention, and subsequently arranged for his protégé to become part of Nixon's team.[167]

Kissinger was intent on centralizing foreign policy making in the White House and the National Security Council, thereby ensuring him a central role in shaping not only US foreign policy, but also clandestine policy towards ET races in his new role as Director of MJ-12. Given his long history as a Director of the Special Studies Group/PI-40 since its formation, Kissinger would have been the most experienced and powerful head of MJ-12 since Nelson Rockefeller.[168]

In Seymour Hersh's critical biography of Kissinger's political managerial style during the Vietnam era, what emerges is that Kissinger was intent on amassing as much power as possible in managing international affairs.[169] Kissinger systematically undermined the positions of others who could pose a threat to his control of international affairs, especially that of the new Secretary of State, William Rogers, and other key policy makers in the Nixon administration.[170]

Kissinger emerges in Hersh's biography as a political figure paranoid about ceding power to others who in his view lacked the subtlety and acumen in dealing with critical foreign policy issues. Kissinger's managerial style was to ensure that all information passed through him as the principal filter for shaping Nixon's priorities and thinking on foreign policy.

A passage from a former Kissinger aide, Morton Halperin, reveals Kissinger's political managerial style:

On January 25, 1969, five days into the administration, the NSC was convened for its first meeting. The issue was Vietnam, and Halperin, now clearly Kissinger's top aide, was assigned to summarize all the papers and prepare a covering memorandum for the President. He carefully listed the various options in the two- or three-page summary, leaving boxes for the President to initial his choices. The idea was to reduce the President's workload: If Nixon chose not to read the attached documents, he could merely review Halperin's summary (which, of course, came with Kissinger's imprimatur) and make his decision. Henry loved the summary and thought it was terrific. But, "Mort," he said, "you haven't told the President what options we should choose."

"I thought to myself," Halperin recalls, "we're not supposed to be giving positions; we're just supposed to send summaries of the options." Years later, Halperin would realize how naïve he had been: "Henry had been publicly saying that we were just going to sort out the issues for the President. I didn't know that Henry wanted to give him the decisions he should take. I was surprised—because I still believed what Henry had said." The Kissinger summary papers, with their recommendations, would become the most secret documents in the Nixon White House.[171]

Kissinger's political managerial style while in government is very significant since it provides insight into how decision making in PI-40 was conducted under Kissinger as the Study group director, and later in MJ-12 when he become its head during the Nixon/Ford administrations.[172]

Kissinger's role in guiding US foreign policy was dictated by his philosophy of "realpolitik." Realpolitik was modeled after his favorite international statesman, 19th century German Chancellor, Otto Von Bismark, who skillfully managed international alliances and limited wars to transform Prussia/Germany into a great power without provoking an international alliance against Germany.[173]

For Bismark, international politics was a grand chess board where morality and sentiment played at best a secondary role. What really mattered was the skillful use of one's resources in achieving one's strategic objective of maximizing power.[174]

"Realpolitik" dominated Kissinger's approach to international politics as evidenced in places such as Laos, Cambodia, Chile and East Timor where morality and sentiment played no role in these countries' treatment as pawns. In this grand game of international chess, the US competed with the Soviet Union to maximize its geo-political power, while simultaneously cooperating strategically in responding to the ET presence.

Little known to the general public, however, Kissinger adopted the same role in steering US policy in how it would respond to the ET presence. Morality and sentiment would play at best a secondary role as the US gradually improved its resources in order to increase its strategic position vis-à-vis the ET races visiting Earth. The moral orientation of these ET races that interacted with humanity and the clandestine organizations that were aware of ET activities were not given great emphasis in Kissinger's realpolitik concerning the ET presence.

What mattered was the extent to which ET races would provide resources for US clandestine organizations to improve their weapons technology and thus improve the US's strategic position vis-à-vis different ET races. Kissinger's realpolitik was the way in which the complex political, social, economic and environment issues would be managed vis-à-vis the ET presence.

Kissinger's role would be similar to his 19th century hero, Bismark. Kissinger would play a key role in transforming the US into the dominant global power that could deal with ET races as an equal, without sparking a damaging interplanetary war with one or more of the ET races that would spell the end for US sovereignty and freedom. Kissinger's close association with the Rockefeller family ensured that Corporate America would continue to play a prominent role in the political management of the ET presence.

With Kissinger, during the Nixon administration, simultaneously playing prominent roles in US foreign policy and its clandestine "interplanetary policy" through MJ-12/PI-40, what emerges is that the political management of the ET presence was dominated by a few individuals intent on amassing as much institutional power as possible, and not delegating authority to those outside of MJ-12/PI-40 who were viewed to lack the necessary experience, political sophistication and intellect in dealing with the complexities of the ET presence. Eisenhower's warning that the political management of the ET presence was "not in the best hands" now appeared prophetic.

Political Impotence of the Carter and Clinton Administrations and the Threat posed by Reagan

The election of Jimmy Carter in 1976, brought in a new Democratic President who had declared that he would reveal the truth about the ET presence once in office. Carter was the first US President who was on the public record as having witnessed a UFO.[175]

Carter, however, would find that as President, he would be unable to determine the full extent of US clandestine programs focused on the ET presence, nor would he have any power to influence political management of the ET presence. Even though his National Security Advisor, Zbigniew Brzezinski was one of the first directors of PI-40 and would have now taken over the chair of MJ-12 from Kissinger, Carter and his principal advisors found they were simply denied necessary information about the ET presence. Thus, making it painfully clear that executive supervision of the ET presence was non-existent.[176]

Confirmation for such a denial comes from Daniel Sheehan, a famed constitutional attorney who served as general and co-counsel for the *New York Times* in the Pentagon Papers case:

> In 1977, I was contacted by the director of the Science and Technology Division of the Congressional Research Service. She informed me that President Carter had held a meeting with the director of the CIA, George Bush, Sr.,

and demanded that he [Bush] turn over to the President
the classified information about UFOs and the information that was in the possession of the US intelligence
community concerning the existence of ET intelligence.
This information was refused to the President of the
United States by the director of the CIA. The DCI
[Director of Central Intelligence] suspected that the
president was preparing to reveal this information to
the American public.[177]

Further confirmation of Carter's inability to get information
on ETs/UFOs came from John Maynard:

I'm a retired intelligence analyst . . . was in the military
for 21 years and started off with the Army Intelligence
Security Agency as an analyst. I went on to work for several different organizations with the military and ended
up with the DIA . . . in charge of . . . the documents for
the Requirements and Evaluation division. In Europe, I
researched these UFO reports and we got quite a bit of
information about the sightings . . . drawings of what the
vehicles looked like, whether they landed or not,
whether they saw any . . . extraterrestrials . . . it made for
an exciting career. They [the reports] were going to
the CIA . . . the DIA . . . the Air Force Office of Special
Intelligence . . . But as far as UFO and intelligence and
extraterrestrial matters go, it's right at the top—and I
would say that the president has limited knowledge of
it. I know that Carter did not have any knowledge what-
soever. And I worked there with . . . President Carter's
organization.[178]

A project funded by the Carter administration in May 1977
through the Stanford Research Institute (SRI) to explore
Extraterrestrial Communication was terminated four months
later through Pentagon pressure. The Pentagon simply threatened the directors of the SRI that it would end projects the
Pentagon funded for SRI if the later went ahead with the White
House Center.[179]

After the refusal by the CIA to hand over ET/UFO files and the debacle over its Extraterrestrial Communication project, Carter and his senior advisors [those outside the official loop] quickly recognized they were "minor players" as far as the ET presence was concerned. Indeed, this lack of ability to politically manage ET affairs may well have been a critical factor in the Iranian revolution that did so much to undermine Carter's reelection chances.[180]

The Republican electoral campaign of 1980 brought with it a new dimension to the political management of the ET presence. Ronald Reagan came into the campaign as a crusading anti-communist with fixed views that only negotiating from a position of military strength was the means of countering the Soviet threat to global democracy.

Privately, however, Reagan had a similar perspective on the ET presence and what he viewed as the need to negotiate from a position of strength vis-à-vis the "ET threat to humanity."[181] Like his predecessor, President Carter, Reagan had an encounter with UFOs.[182]

Unlike Carter, however, he developed a strong belief that the ET presence was a threat to humanity that had to be militarily contained. In contrast, his opponent in the Republican Primaries, former CIA Director George Bush, brought with him a more moderate Republican ideology—one that was more consistent with the views of MJ-12/PI-40, of which Bush had previously been a member, and of Henry Kissinger who was by now the undisputed master strategist for MJ-12/PI-40 with nearly 40 years experience in dealing with the ET presence.

The election of Reagan over Bush would certainly have come as a disappointment to Kissinger and MJ-12/PI-40 not only in terms of bringing in another "outsider" who impacted the ability of MJ-12/PI-40 to politically manage the ET presence, but also because it allowed a dangerous element to emerge in the clandestine effort to manage this presence.

MJ-12/PI-40, under Kissinger, was fully aware of the complexities of the ET presence in terms of different races and orientations, and ensuring that interaction with the numerous clandestine organizations embedded in the different military organizations and intelligence agencies coordinated in a way that maintained a "global balance of power."

What Kissinger and MJ-12/PI-40 were most concerned about was the danger of clandestine organizations in the US military and/or intelligence services engaging in a dangerous confrontation with ET races that could degenerate into large-scale hostilities leading to a "war of the worlds." As the master "Bismarkian" strategist, Kissinger was concerned to maintain the "balance of power" while simultaneously advancing the strategic position of the US vis-à-vis ET races.

PI-40, again under the leadership of Kissinger after having served his full term as head of MJ-12, was therefore intent on containing any "military adventurism" on the part of clandestine organizations in the US military that were at best too confrontational, or at worst infiltrated by ET races intent on initiating global confrontation.[183]

What most concerned MJ-12/PI-40 was the possibility that a Presidential administration could be unduly influenced by clandestine military organizations that either were prone to military adventurism and/or had been infiltrated by ET races [this topic will be addressed in Chapter Four].

Soon after his election, Reagan demonstrated a rigid belief of the nature of the ET threat, and laced many of his public statements referring to the ET presence and its threat to humanity.[184] According to Dixon Davis, one of the two CIA agents appointed to brief Reagan when he was President-elect: "The problem with Ronald Reagan was that all his ideas were fixed. He thought that he knew about everything—he was an old dog."[185]

Reagan's anti-communist rhetoric and massive buildup of military forces was a cover for Reagan's true desire to militarily confront ET races.[186] His first major public comment on an ET threat occurred at a 1985 US-Soviet Summit meeting with Mikhail Gorbachev at Geneva when he said:

> I couldn't help but—when you stop to think that we're all God's children, wherever we live in the world, I couldn't help but say to him (Gorbachev) just how easy his task and mine might be if suddenly there was a threat to

this world from some other species from another planet outside in the universe. We'd forget all the little local differences that we have between our countries and we would find out once and for all that we really are all human beings here on this Earth together. Well I guess we can wait for some alien race to come down and threaten us, but I think that between us we can bring about that realization.[187]

If his unscheduled comment at a US-Soviet Summit were not itself a provocative enough expression of Reagan's views on the possible threat of an ET presence, then his speech to the Forty-Second UN General Assembly of the United Nations on September 21, 1987, was even more provocative and disturbing in its implications:

In our obsession with antagonisms of the moment, we often forget how much unites all the members of humanity. Perhaps we need some outside, universal threat to make us recognize this common bond. I occasionally think how quickly our differences worldwide would vanish if we were facing an alien threat from outside of this world. And yet I ask—is not an alien force already among us?[188]

For Colonel Phillip Corso and other conservative military officers, Reagan was a hero who knew how to best respond to the ET presence—a global defensive shield that could shoot down ET craft anywhere around the planet.[189] The Strategic Defense Initiative had little to do with shooting down ballistic nuclear missiles, and really was part of a planetary shield desired by clandestine organizations in the military who wanted to militarily confront the ET presence.

Reagan's conservative political philosophy and public statements on the need for a massive military build up to the Soviet threat were allusions to the perceived danger of an ET invasion. Reagan and his political advisors were considered by Kissinger, Brzezinski, and others in MJ-12/PI-40, as a threat to the political management of the ET presence and to the tenuous peace that existed between clandestine organizations around the planet and ET races.

Given the gravity of Reagan's fixed views and the implications for managing the ET presence, it is very likely groups responsive to the concerns of PI-40 played a role in attempting to have Reagan removed from public office and replaced by an MJ-12/PI-40 member, George Bush, the Vice President and former head of the CIA.

The Hinkley assassination attempt in 1981 was possibly an attempt by organizations loosely linked with PI-40 to either remove or intimidate Reagan so as to prevent what could have been a disastrous unraveling of the covert global cooperation in managing the ET presence.[190] According to a researcher into the infamous mind control program called "Project Monarch," Hinkley along with Lee Harvey Oswald, Sirhan Sirhans and Timothy McVeigh, was subjected to severe mental and physical abuse which made him an unwilling tool of his programmers.[191] The eventual result of the assassination attempt was that the Reagan administration's militaristic impulses were sufficiently restrained so as to ensure that no military confrontation with ET races would spiral out of control.

The 1988 election of George Bush once again allowed MJ-12/PI-40 to dominate the strategic thinking of a Presidential administration. As a former member of MJ-12/PI-40, Bush was all too aware of the need to politically manage the ET presence in the mould dictated by Kissinger during the Nixon administration.

Indeed, Kissinger's support was critical in the appointment of Bush to become the Director of the CIA in 1975, and his "promotion" to MJ-12 from PI-40, not long after the Watergate scandal had begun to subside.[192] Public secrecy, monopolizing decision making power in MJ-12/PI-40, maintaining the balance of power, continuing to reverse ET technology for weapons acquisition, and maintaining the prominent role of Corporate America in dealing with the ET presence, were the keys to politically managing the ET presence.

MJ-12/PI-40 was certainly content with its influence under the Bush administration and there is evidence that international events were managed in a way that would support the 1992 reelection of President Bush. The "End of the Cold War" was certainly a "gift" to the Bush administration that normally would have ensured a second election victory for an administration enjoying such a tremendous foreign policy success.[193]

The successful outcome of the Gulf War in 1991 was similarly an event that would have normally secured a successful reelection campaign. The outcome of the 1992 Presidential election appeared so certain, prominent Democrats decided not to run and viewed 1996 as the best time for a Presidential campaign.

The election of President Clinton was certainly a surprise development for MJ-12/PI-40 and once again had the effect of placing an "outsider" in the White House. Clinton, like Carter before him, soon found out that he had minimal influence over the political management of the ET presence. Even more disturbing, his senior political officials including the Director of Central Intelligence, James Woolsey, and Secretary of Defense, William Cohen, had little knowledge of the ET presence.[194] Stephen Greer narrated the following exchange he had with a famous astronaut:

> Recently I was in Washington meeting with a very famous astronaut. Everyone would know this person's name . . . This particular astronaut had during his career been in possession of a very specific piece of incontrovertible piece of evidence related to UFOs. It is something that if disclosed would be clear and definitive. This astronaut described how he had approached and worked directly with President Clinton's Secretary of Defense William Cohen to look into and retrieve from classified projects this specific piece of evidence—of that which he had all the specific details . . . the words used by this astronaut to me were "there was an inordinate large amount of money and personal time by the Secretary of Defense William Cohen was spent to locate this evidence, and he was never given access to it."[195]

This suggested that many of those sitting in MJ-12/PI-40, were hangovers from the Bush administration, and Clinton's political appointments were not trusted to maintain secrecy.

Clinton's efforts to extract information from clandestine organizations proved fruitless as evidenced in the following quote from William Laparl, who worked with the CIA in the early days of the Clinton Administration:

> It was known among the high CIA people, and the people who had contact with these people, that the Clintons were on the prowl for UFOs. Bill Clinton had been asking anyone who would listen to him, to tell him the secret. You know, he would get some Admiral in there, and say "By the way, tell me the UFO secret." They would just look at him like "What planet are you from?"[196]

Clinton's interest and efforts to gain information on the ET presence and clandestine projects were a threat to MJ-12/PI-40 insofar as Clinton's initiatives threatened the veil of secrecy that had existed since the 1940s. More important, Clinton's efforts may well have been viewed as the initial stages of an attempt to re-establish executive supervision. It is not too difficult to surmise that many of Clinton's political problems were a result of clandestine efforts to distract the Clinton administration, and ensure minimal support for his domestic policies.

Clinton became resigned to serving his term with only minimal knowledge of the ET presence, and without having any serious impact on how to politically manage the ET presence. His remarks to a question from a Northern Ireland teenager in November 1995 testify to his political impotence on the ET presence:

> I got a letter from 13-year-old Ryan from Belfast. Now, Ryan, if you're out in the crowd tonight, here's the answer to your question. No, as far as I know, an alien spacecraft did not crash in Roswell, New Mexico, in 1947. (Laughter.) And, Ryan, if the United States Air Force did recover alien bodies, they didn't tell me about it, either, and I want to know. (Applause.)[197]

The election of George W. Bush in 2000 once again led to an insider, or at least an insider's loyal son, to be in the White

House. George Bush, Sr., would henceforth play a key role in steering his son, who lacked the kind of intellectual qualities to be a member of PI-40 or Council on Foreign Affairs in his own right, but served as a useful figurehead that could gain the loyalty of the American public in ways that the more urbane and sophisticated George Bush Sr., and Nelson Rockefeller before him, never could.

This set the stage for a new phase in the political management of the ET presence: the takeover of a foreign country for purposes exclusively relating to the strategic advantage this would provide in politically managing the ET presence.

Phase Five-The Political Management of Iraq and Its Ancient ET Technology

In the 2000 Presidential election campaign, George Bush jokingly responded to a question concerning the ET presence by saying it was Richard Cheney's area of expertise.[198] Cheney served as Secretary of Defense in the first Bush administration and according to the formula first used during the Eisenhower administration to determine the members of MJ-12, Cheney would have been a former active member of MJ-12, and was very likely a current member of PI-40.

Bush would have been briefed at some point by Cheney and/or his father about the ET presence, and was simply deferring to the clear expertise Cheney had in the area. Other key administration figures in the new Bush administration such as Donald Rumsfeld, Secretary of Defense during the Ford administration, also would have served on MJ-12 according to the Eisenhower era formula, and would have subsequently sat on PI-40, before finding himself elevated once more to MJ-12.

Other new Bush administration officials such as Paul Wolfowitz and Richard Perle, both of whom had earlier held prominent positions in the Department of Defense, were probably briefed on the ET presence during their tenures.

What distinguished this senior group of officials in the Bush administration with backgrounds in the Department of Defense was their "hawkish" Republican worldview that espoused such novel international theories as preemptive military intervention against rogue states, and creating a global defensive shield against them.

Although such a theory ostensibly was focused on the threat such states posed if they possessed Weapons of Mass Destruction, the knowledge these officials had concerning the ET presence, suggested that they were merely continuing the threat based assessment of the ET presence that had earlier dominated the Reagan administration. The global defensive shield against rogue states using ballistic nuclear missiles against the US, was again a convenient cover for the true intent to be able to militarily intervene against ET craft anywhere on the planet. Aside from the close ties this group of Bush administration "hawks" had with the Department of Defense, some of them also had extensive ties with corporate military contractors that worked on various clandestine projects concerning the ET presence.

The professional background and policies of the Bush administration "hawks" suggests they formed the public head of a "cabal" of senior military officials based in clandestine organizations that promoted a militaristic response to the ET presence.[199] Such officials would no doubt have been aware of clandestine organizations of other countries with whom they cooperated/competed in terms of gaining maximum strategic advantage vis-à-vis the ET presence. They would have also been aware of the strategic significance of different rogue states in the tenuous balance of power that existed on the planet between different ET factions and clandestine government organizations. A key rogue state in such a strategic struggle was Iraq under Saddam Hussein.

There is evidence that Iraq once hosted an advanced civilization that interacted extensively with ET races.[200] The likelihood that this interaction led to the development of technology either left behind by these ETs or was based on ET technology that lay buried in the Iraqi desert, will be argued in Chapter Five as the primary motivation for the US-led military intervention in the 2003 Gulf war.

Once the need to invade Iraq emerged for reasons that primarily concerned political management of the ET presence and the strategic importance of Iraq, it became important to deal with this in a way that would minimize global chaos. This was especially important since clandestine organizations in the US were competing with similar organizations in France, Germany, Russia and even China that presumably already had established some understanding of precisely what was available in Iraq, and its strategic significance for the global balance of power. [201]

The influence of key "hawks" in the Bush administration, Donald Rumsfeld, Paul Wolfowitz, Richard Cheney, Richard Perle and others, was likely viewed by MJ-12/PI-40 as a useful political tool for gaining access to Iraq's strategic ET resources. This had to be managed in a way, however, that would maintain global consensus and not precipitate a conflict that could easily spiral out of control and lead to the intervention of ET races.

Like the Reagan administration before it, the more militaristic impulses of the Bush administration needed to be restrained by MJ-12/PI-40, if Iraq's ET resources were to be gained over the objections of clandestine organizations based in France, Germany, Russia and China.

In August of 2002 when debate over a preemptive US attack was at its height, Kissinger released a significant policy statement that cautioned the Bush administration about alienating its historic allies in dealing with Iraq. He argued that "the notion of justified pre-emption runs counter to modern international law which sanctions the use of force in self defense only against actual rather than potential threats."[202]

This combined with key statements from other former officials from Republican administrations, such as former Bush Sr. National Security Advisor and a likely PI-40 member, Brent Scowcroft, led to President Bush moving towards a more internationalist agenda that embraced the role of the UN.[203]

This culminated in Bush making a speech before the UN a day after the anniversary of September 11 in which he emphasized the importance of confronting Saddam Hussein and the key role of the UN in containing the threat posed by rogue states.[204]

Kissinger and Scowcroft represented a visible initiative by MJ-12/PI-40 to rein in the Bush Hawks insofar as the importance of global consensus was recognized as a primary ingredient for the strategic goals of militarily intervening in Iraq, removing the

Saddam regime, and gaining access to whatever ET technology was hidden in Iraq.

The Republican hawks within the Bush administration had been temporarily outflanked by Kissinger, other Republican moderates and MJ-12/PI-40 members. Clandestine organizations in France, Germany and Russia, therefore had more time to reach an accommodation with the Bush administration. Security Council Resolution 1441 was a triumph for Kissinger's approach to politically managing the ET presence.

By February of 2003, it had become clear that Germany, France and Russia were maneuvering to block the US intervention. Rather than this being purely an altruistic desire to preserve global peace in the face of an unjustified US attack to destroy "non-existent" weapons of mass destruction, these European states desired to keep the US out of Iraq due to the increased strategic power this would give to US-based clandestine organizations.

Kissinger's role is indicative of the strategic struggle occurring behind the scenes over ET technology in Iraq, and the shifting alliances this caused. Kissinger subsequently came out with a key policy speech criticizing France and Germany as threatening the NATO alliance.[205] His speech indicated that the time was ripe for a US military invasion.

Kissinger and MJ-12/PI-40 had given the blessing for an invasion, which was now inevitable. Rather than regional devastation as was first feared, what occurred instead was a rapid collapse of the Saddam regime. US clandestine organizations had achieved their military objectives without precipitating regional and global chaos. The passage of a new UN Security Council resolution in May 2003 by a margin of 14-0 endorsing US administration and reconstruction of post-war Iraq by the UN, marked a decisive victory for the Bush administration, and the influence of MJ-12/PI-40 in politically managing the ET presence.

What was significant in the post-conflict administration of Iraq was the speedy departure of the Pentagon appointed civil administrator, Jay Garner, and his replacement by Paul Bremer, a former State Department Ambassador at Large for Terrorism, and someone with strong connections to Kissinger, formally in charge of the civil administration of Iraq.

This indicated that the more moderate policies backed by Kissinger in dealing with the ET presence, had prevailed over the more confrontational policies of the Bush hawks. A power struggle between moderate and hawkish factions of MJ-12/ PI-40 was occurring behind the scenes, and the Kissinger backed moderates had been successful.

Policies implemented by Bremer in terms of setting back the schedule for the election of an interim Iraq administration, indicate that the US is set to remain in military control of Iraq for a number of years. Iraq's role in terms of being a host to ancient ET technology and analyses, which suggests it plays a significant role in the possible return of ET races that sponsored Iraq's ancient Sumerian civilization, makes Iraq a significant actor in the political management of the ET question.

Conclusion: Politically Managing the ET Presence and the Challenge to Democracy and Liberty in America

Political management of the ET presence has evolved considerably since the Second World War era. Starting initially as a process firmly controlled by Presidential administrations that exercised executive overseeing, thereby making it part of the democratic process despite its secrecy and lack of congressional participation, political management evolved to the point where Presidential administrations were not fully informed of and had no executive control over many aspects of the ET presence.

This meant the political management process had dubious constitutional validity and was controlled by a few actors who could be tied to the Rockefeller-Kissinger axis, and their respective ties to US corporations and elite foreign policy bodies such as the Council on Foreign Relations.

The US-British-Australian intervention in Iraq suggests that political management of the ET process has evolved to yet another level. Now the US and its allies are prepared to militarily intervene in other countries in order to gain strategic goals vis-à-vis the ET presence. The most important of these goals are to maintain official secrecy of the ET presence, withhold from the general public the true nature of the historic role played by ETs in ancient civilizations, and gain whatever military advantage possible from the reverse engineering of ET technology found in countries that, like Iraq, have been prominent sites hosting an ET presence.

According to whistleblowers' sources, numerous ancient ET bases are being increasingly discovered around the planet.[206] Consequently, it is likely that the intervention in Iraq will set a precedent for similar interventions elsewhere across the planet for reasons that increasingly have to do with the political management of the ET presence.

The strategic thinking of organizations such as MJ-12/PI-40 is based on the perception that the best analytical minds and strategic thinkers are employed in managing the ET process, and although this may not be acceptable from a democratic standpoint which emphasizes executive or congressional supervision of all government activities, it is acceptable from a national security perspective.

What can be concluded here is that the view that indeed the "best minds" are in charge of the political management of the ET presence is misplaced. Information of the ET presence has been increasingly controlled and spun in a way that suggests that real decision making power has been inexorably restricted to fewer and fewer individuals who reflect conservative political philosophies typically associated with the Republican party.

Although it is impossible to say exactly how many individuals exercise real influence in politically managing the ET presence, the history of the Rockefeller-Kissinger involvement and the prominent roles played by Corporate America and the Council on Foreign Relations, suggest that this influence is restricted to very few.

Eisenhower's warning about the "best minds" not being in control suggests that the elite club of "experts" that dictates how the political management of the ET presence is to be conducted, is overly influenced by Corporate and elite interests sympathetic to world views associated with the military-intelligence communities. Introducing greater transparency into all aspects of managing the ET presence will make it possible to expand the restricted circle of power and influence that controls information concerning the ET presence in a way that does indeed make it possible for the best minds to be formally in charge of politically managing the ET presence.

The erosion of executive control over the political management of the ET presence has reduced Presidents to at best, rubber stamps of MJ-12/PI-40 policies (this appeared to be the case in the Nixon, Ford, Reagan and both Bush administrations), or, at worst, to political impotence as appears to have occurred in the cases of the Carter and Clinton administrations.

Policies of the present Bush administration indicate that the US presidency is reduced to little more than a vehicle for the realization of questionable policies concerning the management the ET presence. When combined with the blanket of secrecy that has prevented the US Congress and American public from playing a meaningful role in the political management of the ET presence, the current situation is a profound problem for those truly committed to principles of democratic governance and liberty in the US and elsewhere on the planet.

President Eisenhower demonstrated he became all too aware of the true problem confronting the US as a nation in dealing with the ET presence—a de facto political *coup* by interests closely allied with Corporate America and the military-intelligence communities.

It is time for the American public to understand the true nature of his warning and to begin comprehensive political reforms that address the threat to liberty to which Eisenhower was alluding.

Notes

117. I am very grateful to Susan Burton, aka Elizabeth O'Rourke, for her editorial assistance and suggestions in proofreading and editing an earlier version of this chapter.

118. For more discussion of such a political *coup*, see Steven Greer, *Extraterrestrial Contact: The Evidence and Implications* (Crossing Point Publications, 1999).

119. An online copy of Truman's letter authorizing creation of Majestic 12 is available at: http://209.132.68.98/pdf/truman_forrestal.pdf.

120. See Richard Dolan, *UFO's and the National Security State: Chronology of a Cover-up 1941–1973* (Hampton Roads, 2002) pages 1–3.
121. See "Quotations from Chairman Wolf": http://www.drboylan.com/wolfqut2.html; and Neruda, Interview #1. http://www.wingmakers.com.
122. See Jim Marrs, *Alien Agenda: Investigating the Extraterrestrial Presence Among Us* (HarperPaperbacks, 1997) pages 92–95; and Richard Dolan, *UFO's and the National Security State*, pages 5–6.
123. See Stewart Swerdlow, *Montauk: The Alien Connection* (Expansions Publishing Co. 2002); Preston Nichols & Peter Moon, *Montauk Revisited: Adventures in Synchronicity* (Sky Books, 1991); Wade Gordon, *The Brookhaven Connection* (Sky Books, 2001).
124. An online copy of Truman's letter is available at: http://209.132.68.98/pdf/truman_forrestal.pdf.
125. This report can be found in Robert and Ryan Wood, *The MJ-12 Documents Book*. The Report and book available online at: http://www.majesticdocuments.com/products.html.
126. See Dolan, *UFOs and the National Security State*, pages 16–35; and Marrs, *Alien Agenda*, pages 132–49.
127. See Kevin Randle and Donald Schmitt, *The Truth About the UFO Crash at Roswell* (Avon Books, 1994).
128. For extensive discussion of these projects and their policy implications, see Dolan, *UFOs and the National Security State*.
129. See Cooper, *Behold a Pale Horse*, pages 198–99.
130. For discussion of events surrounding Forrestal's "breakdown" and "suicide," see Dolan, *UFO's and the National Security State*, pages 70–76.
131. See "Testimony of Master Sergent, Dan Morris," *Disclosure*, ed., Greer, 359; and Cooper, *Behold a Pale Horse*, pages 198–99.
132. Theresa deVeto, "From Disinformation to Disclosure," *Surfing The Apocalypse* (October, 2001). Available online at: http://www.surfingtheapocalypse.com.
133. See Marrs, *Rule By Secrecy*, p. 46.
134. For discussion of the Rockefeller's support for liberal internationalism, see Will Banyan, "Rockefeller Internationalism," *Nexus* magazine, May-June 2003, 19–22, p. 74. *Nexus* magazine's homepage is: http://www.nexusmagazine.com.
135. See Corso, *The Day After Roswell*. See also a number of whistleblowers testimonies on top secret corporate military projects focused on reverse engineering ET technology in Greer, *Disclosure*.
136. Phil Schneider, "MUFON Conference Presentation, May 1995" available online at: http://www.geocities.com/Area51/Shadowlands/6583/coverup044.html.
137. Fitts has a website at: www.solari.com with a host of resources, reports, interviews and press stories detailing her claims.

138. See Banyan, "Rockefeller Internationalism," *Nexus* magazine, p. 22; and Jim Marrs, *Rule by Secrecy* (Harper Collins, 2000) pages 31–38.

139. Marrs, *Rule by Secrecy*, p. 36.

140. See Cooper, *Behold a Pale Horse*, pages 207–10. See also Michael Wolfe, *Catchers of Heaven: A Trilogy* (Dorrance Publishing Co., 1996).

141. Cooper, *Behold a Pale Horse*, pages 209–210. Another source for Kissinger's leadership position is former Air force Colonel Steve Wilson, who described Kissinger as the overseer of MJ12/PI-40. See online interview with Dr. Richard Boylan, at: http://www.drboylan.com/mj12org2.html.

142. *Behold a Pale Horse*, p. 210.

143. For this reason, William Cooper claims that in the documents he witnessed, this body was called Majority 12. *Behold a Pale Horse*, p. 208.

144. Cooper, *Beyond a Pale Horse*, pages 208–10. For Hoover's knowledge of ETs/UFO's, see Marrs, *Alien Agenda*, pages 180–81.

145. Eisenhower Presidential Departure Speech, January 1961.

146. Stephen Greer is a leading advocate of the view that the lack of congressional/executive supervision of clandestine military projects and decision making processes, is evidence that a silent coup has occurred. See Greer, *Extraterrestrial Contact*.

147. Quoted in "Testimony of Brigadier General Steven Lovekin," in *Disclosure*, ed. Greer, 235.

148. Available online at: http://www.presidentialufo.8m.com/johnf.htm.

149. See document, "TOP SECRET Memorandum for CIA Director, from President John F. Kennedy," November 12, 1963. Available online at: http://www.majesticdocuments.com. See also, "CONFIDENTIAL National Security Action Memorandum No. 271 for NASA Administrator (James Webb) from John F. Kennedy, November 12, 1963." Source: National Archives. This document is cited in Linda Moulton Howe, "JFK, MJ-12 and Outer Space," at: http://www.presidentialufo.8m.com/kennedy&1.htm.

150. Cooper, *Behold a Pale Horse*, p. 215. For further references to Kennedy's ultimatum and documentary sources supporting that this had indeed occurred, see Linda Moulton Howe, "JFK, MJ-12 and Outer Space." Available online at: http://www.presidentialufo.8m.com/kennedy&1.htm.

151. One of the strongest advocates for such a view is Cooper, *Behold a Pale Horse*, pages 215–20. For similar views from government/military insiders, see Linda Moulton Howe, "JFK, MJ-12 and Outer Space." Available online at: http://www.presidentialufo.8m.com/kennedy&1.htm.

152. For whistleblower testimony from a military contractor on the loss of executive oversight, see "Testimony of A.H. Boeing Aerospace," *Disclosure*, ed. Greer, p. 401.

153. See "President Lyndon Johnson, 1963–69" at: http://www.presidentialufo.8m.com/presiden2.htm.
154. For Steven Greer's description of various administrations not having this information, see "Extraterrestrial Contact."
155. Corso, *The Day After After Roswell*, p. 290. See also, "Testimony of Master Sergeant Dan Morris, US Airforce," in *Disclosure*, ed., Stephen Greer, p. 358.
156. As mentioned earlier, Cooper believes Kissinger was one of the two directors of PI-40. *Behold A Pale Horse*, p. 210.
157. See Richard Dolan, *UFO's and the National Security State*, pages 4–15. Marrs, *Alien Agenda*, pages 98–107.
158. See Dolan, *UFO's and the National Security State*, pages 4–15. See also "Testimony of Master Sergeant Dan Morris," *Disclosure*, ed., Greer, p. 363. For online information on Operation Paperclip, see "Secrets of the Third Reich," available at: http://www.violations.dabsol.co.uk/secrets/secretspart2.htm.
159. For a brief biographical summary of Kissinger, see Seymour Hersh, *The Price of Power: Kissinger in the Nixon Whitehouse* (Summit Books, 1983) pages 25–27.
160. For evidence of the relationship between the Army's Counterintelligence Corp and the ET presence, see the following declassified report from 22 July 1947 concerning the Roswell incident: http://209.132.68.98/pdf/ipu_report.pdf.
161. See Cooper, *Behold a Pale Horse*, p. 207.
162. See Cooper, *Behold a Pale Horse*, pages 202–04; Richard Boylan, "Official Within MJ-12 UFO-Secrecy Management Group Reveals Insider Secrets": http://www.drboylan.com/wolfdoc2.html; Phil Schneider, MUFON Conference Presentation, 1995, available online at: http://www.ufocoverup-conspiracy.com/20.htm; See Neruda Interview #1: http://www.wingmakers.com; Boylan gives a more extensive coverage of events surrounding the Treaty signing in "Extraterrestrial Base On Earth, Sanctioned By Officials Since 1954": http://drboylan.com/basespst2.html; See also Corso, *The Day After Roswell*, p. 292.
163. See "Testimony of A.H. Boeing Aerospace," *Disclosure*, Greer, p. 400; Cooper, *Behold a Pale Horse*, p. 210.
164. See "Testimony of A.H. Boeing Aerospace," *Disclosure*, Greer, 400; Cooper, *Behold a Pale Horse*, p. 210.
165. See Phillip Corso, *The Day After Roswell*, pages 287–95.
166. Cooper, *Behold a Pale Horse*, p. 210.
167. See Seymour Hersh, *The Price of Power*, p. 18.
168. For discussion of the Secret Studies Group, see Richard Boylan: http://www.boyland.org.
169. Seymour M. Hersh, *The Price of Power*.
170. See Hersh, *The Price of Power*, pages 32–34.

171. Hersh, *The Price of Power*, p. 36.
172. According to former Col Steve Wilson, Kissinger was the overseer of MJ-12/PI-40. See online interview with Dr. Richard Boylan, at: http://www.drboylan.com/mj12org2.html.
173. For Kissinger's fondness of Bismark and realpolitik, see Kissinger, *Diplomacy* (Simon and Schuster, 1994). See also Kissinger, *Does America Need a Foreign Policy: Toward a Diplomacy for the 21st Century* (Touchstone, 2002).
174. Both Kissinger and Bismark admired the work of the Renaissance scholar, Nicholo Machiavelli, who espoused this view concerning morality in his famous work, *The Prince*.
175. For a copy of Carter's report, see Greer, ed., *Disclosure*, pages 448–50.
176. See "Testimony of A.H. Boeing Aerospace," in *Disclosure*, ed. Greer, pages 400–01; and "Testimony of Mr John Maynard, (ret) Defense Intelligence Agency," in *Disclosure*, ed. Greer, p. 426; and "Testimony of Phillip Corso, Jr.," in *Disclosure*, ed. Greer, p. 469.
177. "Carter White House Denied UFO Info," *Disclosure Project* (March 12, 2002) available online at: http://www.disclosureproject.com; see also http://www.100megsfree4.com/farshores/ufotdp2.htm.
178. "Carter White House Denied UFO Info," *Disclosure Project* (March 12, 2002) available online at: http://www.disclosureproject.com; see also: http://www.100megsfree4.com/farshores/ufotdp2.htm.
179. See "Testimony of Dr Alfred Webre, Senior Policy Analyst," in *Disclosure*, ed. Greer, pages 441–44.
180. See Chapter Six for further discussion of Iran and ET geopolitics.
181. For references to Reagan's anti-ET rhetoric, see "Ronald Reagan, 40th President, January 20, 1981-January 20, 1989." Online article at: http://www.presidentialufo.8m.com/reagan_ufo_story.htm.
182. See "Ronald Reagan, 40th President, January 20, 1981-January 20, 1989." Online article at: http://www.presidentialufo.8m.com/reagan_ufo_story.htm.
183. For discussion of ET infiltration of clandestine organizations, see Chapter Four.
184. For a revealing insight into the rigidity he adopted in his thinking, see his response to a CIA briefing on the Palestinian issue when he was President-elect: "Ronald Reagan, 40th President, January 20, 1981-January 20, 1989." Online article at: http://www.presidentialufo.8m.com/reagan_ufo_story.htm.
185. "Ronald Reagan, 40th President, January 20, 1981-January 20, 1989." Online article at: http://www.presidentialufo.8m.com/reagan_ufo_story.htm.
186. See "Ronald Reagan, 40th President, January 20, 1981-January 20, 1989." Online article at: http://www.presidentialufo.8m.com/reagan_ufo_story.htm.

187. "Ronald Reagan, 40th President, January 20, 1981-January 20, 1989." Online article at: http://www.presidentialufo.8m.com/reagan_ufo_story.htm.
188. "Ronald Reagan, 40th President, January 20, 1981-January 20, 1989." Online article at: http://www.presidentialufo.8m.com/reagan_ufo_story.htm.
189. Corso, The Day After Roswell, pages 291–93.
190. See Glenn Krawczyk, "Mind Control and the New World Order," Nexus magazine (Feb/March 1993) excerpts available online at: http://www.projectfreedom.cng1.com/mc_nwo.html.
191. For discussion of the infamous Project Monarch, see Ron Patton, "Project Monarch: Nazi Mind," The Conspiracy Reader: From the Deaths of JFK and John Lennon to Government-Sponsored Alien Cover-Ups, eds., Al Hidell & Joan D'Arc (Citadel Press, 1999) pages 197–213. Available online at: http://www.aches-mc.org/monarch.html.
192. See Webster G. Tarpley & Anton Chaitkin, George Bush: The Unauthorized Biography, published online at: http://www.kmf.org/williams/bushbook/bush15.html.
193. For analysis of factors for why the Cold War ended, see Ralph Summy and Michael Salla, ed., Why the Cold War Ended (Greenwood Press, 1995).
194. This certainly is Stephen Greer's view after interviewing/briefing various senior officials in the Clinton administration. Extraterrestrial Contact.
195. "Dr. Steven Greer Interview with Art Bell," August 30, 2001, available online at: http://www.presidentialufo.8m.com/part5.htm.
196. Available online at: http://www.presidentialufo.8m.com/part5.htm.
197. "Remarks by the President and the First Lady at "The Lighting of the City Christmas Tree," Belfast City Hall, Belfast, Northern Ireland, November 1995. Published online at: http://www.presidentialufo.8m.com/part8.htm.
198. For transcript of a CNN interview where Bush acknowledges Cheney's expertise on the ET/UFO issue, go to: http://www.rense.com/general3/ufobush.htm.
199. Michael Wolf discusses the influence of such a cabal in Catchers of Heaven, 382–83; see also his interview with Richard Boylan, in Boylan and Boylan, Labored Journey To The Stars. Available online at: http://www.boylan.com/wlfk2a.html.
200. See Zecharia Sitchin, The 12th Planet (Avon Books, 1976); William Bramley, Gods of Eden (Avon, 1989); & R. A. Boulay, Flying Serpents and Dragons: The Story of Mankind's Reptilian Past (Book Tree, 1999).
201. This will be examined more closely in Chapter Six. An earlier version of this chapter was printed as Michael Salla, "America's Triumph &

Europe's Angst—The Secret Race to Control Iraq's ET Technology," *Study Paper* No. 3: www.exopolitics.org.
202. Kissinger "Calls for Policy Outline," ABC News, Australia, August 13, 2002: http://www.abc.net.au/am/s647064.htm.
203. See Brent Scowcroft, "Don't Attack Saddam: It would undermine our antiterror efforts." *Wall Street Journal*, August 15, 2002: http://opinionjournal.com/editorial/feature.html?id=110002133.
204. President George Bush, "Address to the United Nations General Assembly," New York, NY, September 12, 2002. Available online at: http://www.cfr.org/publication.php?id=4834.xml.
205. See "Transatlantic anger." *Daily Telegraph*, 11/02/2003, Available online at: http://www.telegraph.co.uk/news/main.jhtml?xml=/news/2003/02/11/wirq211a.xml.
206. See "Testimony of A.H. Boeing Aerospace," *Disclosure*, p. 401.

Chapter 3

Foundations for Globally Managing Extraterrestrial Affairs—The Legacy of the Nazi Germany-Extraterrestrial Connection

Introduction[207]

There is compelling evidence that in the early 1930s, the technology and presence of one or more extraterrestrial (ET) races became known to the leaders of Nazi Germany who embarked on an ambitious effort to communicate with these races for the purpose of acquiring their advanced technology. Using communication techniques that would be widely dismissed today as "psychic channeling," there is evidence that the Nazi sponsorship of occult societies that specialized in this form of communication with these ET races, was successful in gaining information that produced rapid technological breakthroughs that eventually came to the attention of the intelligence services of Britain, France, USSR and the USA.

Although predictably dismissive of such esoteric practices by the Nazi regime, each of the intelligence services of these major states initiated efforts to attain whatever intelligence information they could, on the purported Nazi communication methods with an ET race(s) while monitoring the "ET inspired" technology being developed by Nazi Germany.

At a time of growing international tension, with another major European war (World War 2) looming on the horizon, major global powers would have been concerned about the ramifications of Nazi Germany seeking to acquire advanced technology through esoteric forms of communication with

ET races. Although sightings of ET/UFO craft were relatively rare in the 1930s, historically there had already been a sufficient number to raise the possibility of an ET presence on the planet.[208] Not only was Nazi Germany actively developing technology that was inspired through such communication; it had also learned of remote locations around the planet where it could retrieve ET artifacts. The Nazis sponsored numerous expeditions to remote locations, the results of which were largely unknown to Western intelligence services.[209]

There is also evidence that Nazi Germany was able to eventually retrieve an operational "ET craft," which suggested the Nazis were being assisted by one or more ET races.[210]

In this chapter I analyze how global management of what can be defined as "Extraterrestrial Affairs"—government policies dealing with the existence of ET races and ET inspired technology—has as its foundations events that occurred during the 1930s when ETs first began to communicate with the leadership of a major world government. The fact that it was Nazi Germany that began a campaign to establish military dominance in Europe, is significant in terms of the way the ET presence would later be globally managed by the victorious Allied powers that emerged from the carnage of the Second World War.

I begin by analyzing Nazi Germany's "success" in communicating with ET races and gaining information for the development of ET inspired technology that would be used to build offensive weapons for the Nazi war effort. I will argue that the "successful" conclusion of the Second World War led to a rude awakening on the part of the Allied powers of the full ramifications of the Nazi successes in developing ET technology.

Not only had Nazi Germany successfully developed and/or reverse engineered ET technology through questionable psychic channeling methods, discovered of ET artifacts and retrieved an ET craft, but there is evidence that a significant number of the Nazi elite had escaped with the most advanced of their ET inspired technology to hidden locations in Antarctica and South America.

This meant that contrary to public perceptions of a successful conclusion to the Second World War, a significant portion of Nazi Germany's most advanced technological assets and military-scientific elite were outside the reach of the victorious Allied powers.

What compounded the serious policy dilemma confronting the Allied Powers with the continuation of remnants of the Nazi regime in Antarctica and South America was the physical intervention of ET races that seriously impacted on the need to manage the ET presence globally. Even more disturbing was the possibility that the elite remnants of the Nazi regime were being assisted by one or more ET races, thereby making it impossible for a complete eradication of the Nazi presence.

What follows is an effort to identify the main policies used by major states to globally manage the acquisition and development of ET technology, respond to the ET presence, and deal with the policy consequences of Nazi elites hidden in secret bases in the Antarctic and South America.

Nazi Germany's Pre-War Programs to Develop ET Inspired Technology

Adolph Hitler's fascination with Occult Sciences, Esoteric philosophies and exotic technologies led him to exploit whatever avenues he had in gaining access to and developing weapons technologies that would allow Nazi Germany to gain its rightful place, in Hitler's view, as a leading global power.[211] As a follower of occult sciences, Hitler was well aware of the possibility of communicating with extraterrestrial races through methods such as "psychic channeling" whereby an individual could establish communication with non-physical and/or distant life forms and transmit information.

Such communication was well known among the Occult societies scattered throughout Northern Europe who studied the work of mystics such as Helena Blavatsky. They wrote extensively of her esoteric communications with other "life forms" and how to develop these communication abilities.[212]

Although the general public today dismisses such phenomena as ludicrous, there is compelling evidence that not only did Hitler take it seriously, but he also devoted considerable resources of the Nazi state into converting information gained from such efforts into technology development and weapons production.[213] Much of the information gained in such "psychic communications" led to Nazi expeditions in the period before the Second World War to remote locations such as Tibet, Antarctica, South America, Iraq and elsewhere in search of buried ET artifacts from earlier civilizations.

Vril Society, one of the principal Nazi Occult societies supported by Hitler, "was allegedly 'channeling' messages from an alien civilization in the Aldebaran solar system and planned to develop a craft that could make physical contact with the civilization there."[214] Another significant Occult Group was the Thule Society that was similarly claiming to be in communication with an advanced race. Instead of an off-world ET race, however, this was an advanced human race with Nordic features from an ancient Earth civilization that inhabited subterranean territories accessible from the polar regions and other secluded areas around the planet.[215]

The seriousness and support given by Hitler to such communications is evidenced by the scientific resources given to these Occult societies for developing their "ET inspired" technologies. By 1934, for example, "the Vril Society had apparently developed its first UFO shaped aircraft, known as the Vril 1, which was propelled by an anti-gravity effect."[216]

Although there was predictable skepticism by more traditional branches of the German military of the viability of such "channeled" information, the Nazi SS were at the forefront of efforts to develop this "exotic" technology. Later in the Second World War, the Nazi SS would take over complete control of Hitler's "scientific-military-occult complex" ensuring the highest level of secrecy in developing and operationalising ET-inspired technology.

Hitler viewed such technologies as part of a "natural order" he wished to establish as revealed in an interview he had in 1934 with the son of a German scientist, Viktor Schauberger, a pioneer in aviation technology based on anti-gravity propulsion:

> In June of 1934 my father was invited by the Reich's Chancellor Adolph Hitler to discuss his work. Hitler

wanted to know about his discoveries and talk about the various possibilities and what his great plan was. And he said "yes, I'm looking for a new technology that must once again harmonize with the natural order of things and that is my real program."[217]

Hitler gave powerful material support to Schauberger suggesting the pattern by which technologies, which harmonized with Hitler's occult/naturalistic worldviews, would be supported:

Schauberger was given a team of scientists to help him with his work . . . they perfected the "flying disc" powered by Schauberger's turbine which rotated air into a twisting type of oscillation resulting in the build-up of immense power causing levitation [anti-gravity propulsion]. Schauberger's prototype was then developed into a vehicle known as the Belluzzo-Schriever-Miethe Diskus, a machine built up to 22 ft in diameter. These craft traveled at over 2000 km/hr and were planned to go over 4,000 km/hr. By 1945 they could reach 1300 mph and gain an altitude of 40,000 feet in less than three minutes. The craft was also noted to glow blue-green as it rose and left a silvery glow.[218]

A number of US intelligence sources testified that Nazi Germany had indeed developed technology that resembled modern day UFOs. According to Virgil Armstrong, a former CIA agent:

We know that in the early parts of the war there were certain factions of the Allied forces that did not believe he [Hitler] had a secret weapon and it wasn't until the Americans made much emphasis of this that they began to look at it seriously and indeed did discover that Hitler not only had a secret weapon, he had what we would call today a UFO or spacecraft.[219]

Another prominent US military official who testified about the Nazi supported technologies was Captain Ed Ruppelt, who was the initial Chief Investigator for US Air Force Project Bluebook: "When WWII ended, the Germans had several radical types of aircraft and guided missiles under development. The majority were in the most preliminary stages, but they were the only known craft that could even approach the performance of objects reported to UFO observers . . ."[220] Astronaut Edgar Mitchell also confirmed in 1991 that much of the ET cover up dated from the Second World War.[221]

There have also been reports that Nazi Germany had retrieved a "crashed" ET craft.[222] Colonel Phillip Corso, who was a senior officer in charge of reverse engineering ET technology during the Eisenhower and Kennedy administrations, gave support to such an event in an interview:

> There were crashes elsewhere, and they [the Germans] gathered material too. The Germans were working on it. They didn't solve the propulsion system. They did a lot of experiments on flying saucers. They had one that went up to 12,000 feet. But where all, we and they, missed out was on the guidance system. In R&D we began to realize that this being [an ET] was part of the guidance system, part of the apparatus himself, or itself, as it had no sexual organs."[223]

If such a crash had indeed occurred, on top of whatever information was gained from the Nazi Occult Societies communication with ET races, then this would have considerably boosted Nazi Germany's efforts to develop ET technology for a campaign of military conquest in Europe.

It is very likely that at some stage in the time before the onset of the Second World War in 1939, military intelligence officials from the Western democracies and the Soviet Union guessed there had been a crash, from the available evidence: intelligence assessments of Nazi sponsored occult societies, Hitler's support of esoteric philosophies and practices, fully funded Nazi expeditions to remote locations around the planet, and the technological innovations supported in Nazi scientific laboratories. It appeared that Nazi Germany was serious in developing technology that Hitler and his senior officials gained from occult communications with ETs.

The scientific cultural traditions of both the Western democracies, based on "scientific rationalism" developed in the European Age of Enlightenment; and of the Soviet Union where a Marxist Historical Materialism was dominant, would have led to the military intelligence communities of the Western democracies and the Soviet Union, dismissing the relevance of Hitler's occult communications. Nevertheless, the fact that Hitler was actively supporting such communications with the scientific assets of the Nazi state would have warranted close monitoring of the situation.

As more information about the UFO presence emerged in the late 1930s, predictably Western and Soviet intelligence services would have been concerned that Hitler's occult communications with ETs might give Nazi Germany an important military advantage in any future war.

More disturbing from the perspective of Western intelligence sources was the possibility that Nazi Germany was tacitly being given assistance from an ET race in these communications despite Hitler's militaristic policies in Europe. That Nazi Germany received assistance from ETs was suggested by the father of modern rocketry, Hermann Oberth, who confirmed a Nazi-ET connection when he stated, "We cannot take credit for our record advancement in certain scientific fields alone. We have been helped." When asked by whom, he replied, "the peoples of other worlds."[224] The likelihood that Nazi Germany had come into possession of a "crashed" ET craft may have been evidence of some form of tacit assistance given to Nazi Germany by one or more ET races.

From the perspective of an ET race communicating and even visiting the Earth in the 1930s, Nazi Germany would have been a logical choice for such "assistance." Hitler's receptiveness to esoteric practices and technologies meant that such an ET race had a means of communicating with a major world power at a time when other governments would have been suspicious of the policies of visiting ET races and of opening up unfamiliar channels of communication with one or more of them.

The idea of establishing communication through esoteric practices such as "psychic channeling" would have been dismissed as ludicrous or even dangerous by Western and Soviet policy makers who were still attempting to discover as much as they could about the ET presence through more conventional military intelligence sources and scientific methods. Much later, the US and other Allied states developed their own protocols and standards for establishing communication with ET nations through similar psychic channeling techniques pioneered by the Nazi Occult societies.

Former Air force Sergeant, Dan Sherman, revealed his own training in telepathic/psychic communication by the National Security Agency, which is the premier US organization for communicating with ET races.[225]

In giving whatever limited assistance it could to Nazi Germany, assuming protocols exist for advanced races communicating with the governments of worlds not yet possessing a unified global government, ET races in communication with Nazi authorities possibly received benefits in return that would have been a cause for concern by the future Allied powers. The possibilities of a tacit alliance between Nazi Germany and an ET race, even if this only went as far as Nazis using psychics to communicate with such a race, would certainly have given rise to an important question by the future Allied powers.[226]

Would Hitler risk the best interest of global humanity in exchange for what would facilitate Germany's re-emergence as a major world power?[227] They most likely answered yes and played for time in deciding how to deal with Hitler's aggressive nationalist policies; the technology developed by Hitler's "military-scientific-occult" complex; and to the nature of the "threat," if any, posed by the ET presence to human sovereignty on the planet.

The possibility of Nazi success in developing some form of communication with an ET race and even having direct access to ET technology would have contributed to the eagerness of Britain to accommodate Germany's concerns in redressing inequities from the Versailles Peace Agreement. Any political and diplomatic dialogue to address these matters, even if it upset Britain's main European ally, France, would give Britain much needed time to gauge the security threat posed by Hitler's regime and his exotic weapons acquisition programs.

The Munich agreement struck between the British Prime Minister, Neville Chamberlain, and Hitler in resolving the 1938 crisis over German populated areas of Czechoslovakia, meant Czechoslovakia lost territory and its important defense assets. From the perspective of Britain and France, such a strategic gamble was necessary if indeed Nazi Germany were to be persuaded that it could benefit greatly if it chose to cooperate with the West in responsibly dealing with the ET presence and technology.

Cooperation with the West in terms of financial support and investment from Western corporations had already provided the bulk of Nazi Germany's re-industrialization efforts. Major US and British corporations invested heavily in Nazi German industries and established important relationships with senior Nazi leaders.[228]

Rather than merely being a temporary phenomenon made possible by the brief period when major Western states such as Britain and the US had considerable sympathy for Nazi efforts to remove the inequities of the Versailles Peace Treaty,[229] there is compelling evidence that such relationships continued even during the war period itself. Rockefeller-controlled Standard Oil Co., for example, had extensive dealings with the German petrochemical giant I.G. Farben in oil and chemical sectors, and their relationship continued even after the US entered the war in December 1941.

In May 1942, criminal charges were initially brought against Standard Oil executives and later dropped, but its deals with I.G. Farben became subject to a Senate Special Committee Investigating the National Defense Program chaired by Harry Truman.[230]

The Second World War, the Nazi-ET Connection and the Covert Nazi Exodus

The 1939 deal struck between Nazi Germany and the Soviet Union to divide Poland between them was the action that triggered the Second World War. For Britain and France, it meant that Nazi Germany was fixed on a campaign of European domination regardless of any political concessions made by the former for the sake of peace in Europe.

If it were true that Germany had indeed received tacit assistance from an ET race and/or had acquired ET inspired technology, Germany's invasion of Poland had profound implications. This meant Germany would have to be quickly defeated before it could fully operationalize whatever ET inspired technology or information it had in its possession for offensive weaponry.

Nothing was spared in the main war objective of defeating the Axis powers who constituted a long term threat not only for European democracies, but also for the sovereignty of global humanity vis-à-vis one or more ET races tacitly assisting Nazi Germany. Winston Churchill, the British Conservative Prime Minister, rebuffed all efforts to strike a peace deal with Nazi Germany despite the generous terms offered by Hitler.[231]

After the rapid military defeat of France in 1940, Britain was desperate to engage the US in the war as soon as possible, to assist in the defeat of Germany. Although this would undoubtedly have been a logical policy for Britain or any nation embroiled in a desperate military struggle with a formidable military opponent, the nature of Germany's technological programs and the likely ET connection required immediate action by major non-belligerents such as the US.

In the early stages of the War, President Roosevelt, was informed of the ET presence and the likelihood that Nazi Germany was rapidly developing offensive weapons based on ET technology and assistance. According to Dr. Michael Wolf, who claims to have been a member of the secret National Security Council body that oversees ET affairs in the US, "The first UFO came down in 1941 into the ocean west of San Diego, and was retrieved by the Navy."[232] Another date for this discovery given by the now deceased Colonel William Brophy was Feb 25, 1942.[233]

None of these justifications for entering the war, however, could be revealed to the general public or the US Congress. This made necessary an alternative course of action by US policy makers. It is likely that President Roosevelt and the British Prime Minister, Winston Churchill, contrived political events in the Pacific so it would be inevitable that Imperial Japan would attack the American Pacific Fleet based at Pearl Harbor.[234] Such a contrivance would have been necessary, given that Hitler had taken all the steps he could in ensuring that the US would not enter the war on the side of Britain.

When for example, President Roosevelt lent fifty destroyers to Britain in 1940 without consulting Congress, Prime Minister Churchill remarked: "This was a decidedly unneutral act by the United States" and should, "according to all the standards of history have justified the German Government in declaring War."[235] Hitler, however, remembered well the lesson from World War I and did not even bother to make an official protest.[236]

Essentially, there was no way of persuading the American public of the need to side with Britain if Nazi Germany was clearly avoiding its error from the First World War—when its unrestricted submarine warfare brought the US into the war.

Evidence of the US recovering a downed ET craft in 1941/42, may have been a means of ETs leveling the playing field in terms of providing similar ET technologies to the respective sides in the World War. Germany's invasion of the Soviet Union in 1941 was testimony to Hitler's confidence that his secret weapons technology programs would be successful in producing the offensive weapons required for Nazi victories in Europe.

At the end of the war, the superiority of Nazi Germany's technology was starkly revealed by correspondence between Major General Hugh Knerr, Deputy Commanding General for Administration of US Strategic Forces in Europe, and Lieutenant General Carl Spatz in March 1945:

> Occupation of German scientific and industrial estab-lishments has revealed the fact that we have been alarmingly backward in many fields of research. If we do not take this opportunity to seize apparatus and the brains that developed it and put this combination back to work promptly, we will remain several years behind while we attempt to cover a field already exploited.[237]

This suggests that the years in which Nazi Germany were developing ET inspired technologies, while the Allied powers were skeptical of the communication techniques used by the Nazi's sponsorship of occult societies, produced a serious gap.

At the time it became known that Nazi Germany's offensive weapons capabilities were derived from its communications with ET races and likely recovery of ET technology, Britain, the US and even the Soviet Union, were already far behind the technological discoveries made by the Nazis. Even the discovery and retrieval of ET craft by the US in 1941/42, would not have enabled the Allies to bridge the technological gap with Nazi Germany.

The Nazi Retreat to Antarctica, "Operation High Jump" and ET Assistance

The official defeat of Nazi Germany and Imperial Japan in 1945 was in fact a tactical victory that masked a major strategic defeat for the "victorious Allies" that was kept from the general public. A significant proportion of Nazi Germany's political elite, their most advanced ET technology and fully operational "saucer ships" had escaped from Allied occupation forces.[238] According to Richard Wilson and Sylvia Burns:

> The Germans in the scientific community knew the war was lost as early as 1942. They decided to establish a plan for continuing the dream of the Third Reich despite the war. They decided that the establishment of a separate society founded on Nazi principles of genetic purity was the answer. The development of gravitational technology aided that plan. On February 23, 1945, the newest engines of the Kugelbitz were tested and then extracted from the craft. The Kugelbitz was blown up by SS personnel and the scientists, plans and engines were shipped out of Germany to the South Polar regions, where the Germans had maintained underground construction activity since 1941. Two days later, on February 25, 1943, the underground plant at Khala was closed

and all the workers sent to Buchenwald and gassed. The Germans also sent their "aryan elite" children and other elements of their society to the underground base. General Hans Kammler, who disappeared in April 1945, was instrumental in the evacuation operation, as was General Nebe. There, the Germans developed a eugenic society that apparently is limited to a specific number of people. They're still there. Apparently they also maintain technical colonies in South America.[239]

What remained of Nazi Germany's advanced weapons programs was disturbing enough in terms of the overall technological advances achieved by the Nazis in many fields of weapons production.[240] The fact that the Nazis had removed their most advanced secrets, technology and personnel directly before the final defeat of Germany would have been a huge shock to Allied leaders once it became clear what had occurred.[241]

A megalomaniac Nazi leadership that could not accept inevitable defeat was in fact a holding action for a methodically well planned extraction of the Nazis' most valuable resources and personnel to well prepared remote locations in the Antarctic and South America. This allowed the Nazis to continue their unique social system, and plan to eventually play an important, if not dominant role in global affairs.

The Nazis had sufficient time and resources to prepare for such an exodus given their extensive business links, front companies, and connections with South American governments and companies. The well equipped expeditions to the Antarctic in the pre-war period allowed the Nazis to familiarize themselves with the Antarctic terrain and lay the foundations for any post-war role to be played by these territories.

The most ambitious Nazi expedition occurred in 1938 when extensive portions of the Antarctic were claimed by Captain Alfred Ritscher on behalf of the Nazi government. The aircraft carrier, *Schwabenland*, sent planes to perform extensive aerial surveillance of the region claimed by Nazi Germany, which was called Neuschwabenland.[242] During the war itself, extensive submarine activity in the region of Antarctica suggested that Nazis could have been building bases. Such a possibility was fueled by a comment made by the commander of Nazi Germany's submarine fleet, Admiral Karl Donitz in 1943, when he claimed that his fleet had built "in another part of the world a Shangri-La land—an impregnable fortress."[243]

After Germany's unconditional surrender on May 8, 1945, Nazi submarine activity in the Antarctic region continued as evidenced by the following report by the *Agence France Press* on September 25, 1946: "The continuous rumors about German U-boat activity in the region of Tierra del Fuego ['Feuerland' in German] between the southernmost tip of Latin America and the continent of Antarctica are based on true happenings."[244]

What compounded this realization of a Nazi elite exodus to Antarctica for the Allies was the now irrefutable evidence that ET races were indeed visiting the Earth. The ET presence would now be a factor in the Allies pursuing and eradicating the remnants of Nazi Germany that had relocated to Antarctica and South America, and who were now using their fully operational "saucer ships" to move around the planet and even fly into deep space.

Many of the UFOs witnessed in the immediate post war era, according to reports from a number of military officials aware of the advanced nature of the Nazis' technology, were fully operational Nazi space craft.[245]

A little known effort to once and for all end the Nazi threat occurred with a Naval military expedition led by Admiral Richard Byrd to the Antarctic in 1946/47. Byrd's military expedition was named "Operation High Jump" and consisted of "4700 military personnel, six helicopters, six Martin PBM flying boats, two seaplane tenders, fifteen other aircraft, thirteen US Navy support ships and one aircraft carrier; the *USS Philippine Sea*."[246]

Among the commands issued to Admiral Byrd from the Commander of the US Navy, Admiral Chester Nimitz were: "(b) to consolidate and extend American sovereignty over the largest practical area of the Antarctic continent; (c) to determine the feasibility of establishing and maintaining bases in the Antarctic and to investigate possible base sites."[247] Ironically, it was Admiral Byrd who had earlier addressed Captain Ritscher's Nazi expedition before it departed for Antarctica in 1938/39.

Now Admiral Byrd was leading a US Naval Expedition to seek out and eliminate the Nazi elite who escaped to bases created or "discovered" during the *Schwabenland* expedition.

The Antarctic summer of 1946/47 was the first opportunity to mount such a large military expedition to the frigid regions of Antarctica. Coming so soon after the end of the Second World War, it was a puzzle why such a large armada would travel to Antarctica at a time of increasing Cold War tension and decommissioning of Naval personnel, unless the expedition was sent to militarily deal with some unresolved issues from the War itself—remnants of the Nazi elite hidden in an underground base or bases established or "discovered" in the pre-war era.

Hitler had authorized a number of military missions to the Antarctic in the pre-war era making it possible that one or more underground bases had been established or discovered.[248] The Byrd mission was scheduled to last up to six months but ended in a mere eight weeks because it had, according to Chilean Press reports, "run into trouble" and there had been "many fatalities."[249] If the true goal of the mission was to locate and eradicate any Nazi bases, press reports and early end to the mission indicated dismal failure and a rude awakening for the US Navy.

A March 5, 1947 Chilean press interview of Admiral Byrd, after the premature end of Operation High Jump, suggested there had indeed been a military failure and a new threat was located at the South Pole:

Adm. Byrd declared today that it was imperative for the United States to initiate immediate defense measures against hostile regions. The Admiral further stated that he didn't want to frighten anyone unduly but it was a bitter reality that in case of a new war the continental United States would be attacked by flying objects which could fly from pole to pole at incredible speeds.[250]

It was clear that the best the US Navy could muster was no match for the small but well armed Nazi elite that survived the war in their remote Antarctic location. Again, the possibility that the Nazis were receiving ET assistance in fending off the US attack could not be discounted. Nazis efforts through occult groups such as the Thule Society to communicate with an advanced subterranean humanoid civilization, "Thule," may have resulted in the elite Nazis being assisted in relocating to the hidden Antarctic base and possibly receiving significant ET support from any attack by the US and its allies.

A little known expedition of Admiral Byrd to the North Pole at the same time of Operation High Jump where he supposedly came into contact with an advanced subterranean race with Nordic physical characteristics suggests that the Thule Society had indeed been correct in its assessment of the existence of such a race. Admiral Byrd disclosed the circumstances of this encounter in a posthumously published entry in his diary. The leader of this advanced subterranean race greeted him:

> "We have let you enter here because you are of noble character and well-known on the Surface World, Admiral" . . . you are in the domain of the Arianni, the Inner World of the Earth . . . Admiral, I shall tell you why you have been summoned here. Our interest rightly begins just after your race exploded the first atomic bombs over Hiroshima and Nagasaki, Japan. It was at that alarming time we sent our flying machines, the 'Flugelrads,' to your surface world to investigate what your race had done . . . You see, we have never interfered before in your race's wars and barbarity, but now we must, for you have learned to tamper with a certain power that is not for man, namely, that of atomic energy. Our emissaries have already delivered messages to the powers of your world, and yet they do not heed. Now you have been chosen to be witness here that our world does exist. You see, our Culture and Science is many thousands of years beyond your race, Admiral."[251]

The veracity of Byrd's dairy continues to be debated, but Byrd's comments to the Chilean Press suggests he was sufficiently unnerved by events related to his polar expedition(s) in 1946/47 for such an encounter to have occurred. Subsequent reports of extensive UFO activity in the Antarctic region were confirmation that Antarctic was being used as a base of operations for the new enemy that so unnerved Admiral Byrd—either Nazi Germany and/or one or more ET races.[252]

Foundations for Global Management of Extraterrestrial Affairs

The "victorious" Allied powers (who called themselves the United Nations, eventually becoming the official name of the new international organization to replace the League of Nations in 1945) formed the foundations of a post-World War II order in response to events that had preceded and occurred during the War. The most important event aside from the visitation of ET races themselves was the rapid technological advances achieved by Nazi Germany's scientists as a result of sponsoring esoteric communication techniques with ET races. Primary lessons learned from the Nazi-ET connection were the following:

- ET races were visiting the Earth and eager to establish ongoing communications with the political leaderships of major national governments.
- Psychic communication techniques with ET races played a significant role in Nazi Germany's rapid technological advancements.
- ET artifacts dating from antiquity could be found in remote locations around the planet, and had a potential for rapid technological advances by their discoverers.
- One or more ET races tacitly supported Nazi Germany's weapons acquisition programs.
- ET races would not directly intervene in violent national conflicts and appeared to play an even handed role in assisting belligerent states to develop ET technologies for either offensive or defensive purposes.
- Nazi Germany's elites survived the war in remote locations in Antarctica and South America and would play a continued role in regional/world affairs.

The foundations for globally managing ET affairs after the Second World War were a number of policies based on the lessons learned from the Second World War era. There is considerable evidence to suggest that the major Allied powers of the US, USSR, Britain, and France have "cooperated" in observing and implementing these global management policies despite powerful rivalries and diverging interests. Much of the cooperation between the US and the USSR was due to the shared perception of the need to cooperate in dealing with the ET presence and the continued Nazi bases, and the profound lessons learned from Nazi experience when a major state embarked on military adventurism based on its confidence that it could use ET technology for offensive purposes.

In spite of desired and necessary global cooperation, it was not possible primarily because of ideological differences between the Western and Soviet bloc nations concerning their visions of how to best organize society, and the planet. This meant that each bloc, respectively led by the US and USSR, was simultaneously cooperating to effectively respond to the ET presence and existence of Nazi bases, while competing to maximize their respective zones of influence around the planet.

The US and USSR took the lead in creating the political, military and economic structures that each ideological bloc would use in dealing with its own members, and with the rival bloc of nations. Each ideological bloc would deal with the various policy issues emerging from the existence of ET races and technologies using the structures it set up specifically for dealing with this issue.

However, each bloc would cooperate in coordinating policy on the ET presence through the regular summit meetings between their political leaderships and the channels of communication established by their respective military and intelligence communities.

Eventual recognition of the Peoples Republic of China as a Permanent member of the Security Council in 1972, signified its emergence as a major state that would also play a significant role in globally managing ET affairs by asserting a regional zone of influence in pursuing and acquiring ET technology and responding to the ET presence. Indeed, the assertion of complete Chinese control over Tibet from 1959, suggests that the US and other major powers recognized China's sphere of influence over Tibet which, based on evidence of Nazi expeditions, had significant ET artifacts.[253]

There is little evidence that the non-Aligned Group of nations that emerged in the 1960s played a significant role in globally managing ET technology and the ET presence. Based on the institutional structures, relationships, and cooperative agreements reached by the Allied powers in dealing with ET technology and the ET presence around the planet, five main policies adopted by the Allied powers for globally managing ET affairs.

1. Non-Disclosure of Extraterrestrial Affairs

Non-disclosure to the general public and most elected officials of the major allied states, would be enforced until some time in the future when policy consequences of the ET presence and ET technology were clearly determined.

In the case of the US, President Roosevelt adopted the decision for non-disclosure after the US confirmed the reality of the ET presence and of ET technology. This was later institutionalized by the Truman and Eisenhower administrations in a manner that would allow the non-disclosure to be continued for an indefinite period.[254]

Each of the Western democratic nations playing a prominent role in the global management system set up to deal with ET affairs, would form their own institutional structures responsible for coordinating ET policies and ensuring non-disclosure.[255] Each of the national governments would give all ET related projects and information a sufficiently high security classification to make it a federal/national crime for military and intelligence officials to come forward to reveal their participation in projects concerning the ET presence and technology.[256]

This would be a highly effective means for restricting public debate and media investigation of ET related issues as evidenced by the continued media blackout of the ET presence.[257]

Success of the strategy of non-disclosure required strict enforcement of national security laws, and pressure on other states not privy to all aspects of ET affairs, to turn over any information, artifacts or technologies in their possession to one or more of the major powers in accord to the spheres of influence initially set out at the February 1945 agreement at Yalta between Franklin D. Roosevelt, Winston Churchill, and Joseph Stalin.

The Yalta agreement is significant since it not only established spheres of influence for dealing with the territories liberated by the Allies, but it was also likely to have sanctioned a non-disclosure policy of the ET presence and the Nazi-ET connection. This suggested the Allied states would cooperate to ensure that ET affairs would remain a national security issue, with severe penalties for disclosure by public officials. In the case of the Soviet bloc of nations, and later China, even more draconian national security laws were set in place to ensure non-disclosure. Even the bravest of those public officials who were aware of government/military projects concerning ET technology and the ET presence, cooperated in the policy of non-disclosure.

National political leaderships of states not playing a prominent role in globally managing ET affairs, were only sufficiently informed of the ET presence, in order to delegate the matter to their respective national security bodies. It appears that in cases where ET artifacts were discovered, ET craft landed or retrievals of craft occurred, and/or where ET contact occurred, these would be dealt with through the national security organs of the state that would cooperate with the major states that had influence over the host nation.

The secret global recovery system operating for countries in the US sphere of influence is called "Project Pounce." Colonel Steve Wilson, a former leader of this clandestine group of specialists from different branches of the US military revealed the activities of this secret Project in a series of interviews:

> Project Pounce is an elite group of Air Force Black Berets and military scientists who rush to the scene of any UFO crashes, cordon off the area, retrieve the extraterrestrial

spacecraft and any occupants, then "sanitize" the crash site back to its pre-crash appearance, and intimidate any outside witnesses into silence.[258]

In an interview, a former Army/CIA officer revealed having witnessed in a secret US base, ET "craft we have picked up and captured in different parts of the world."[259] More possible confirmation of a secret global recovery system comes from Dr. Jamisson Neruda,[260] who claims to be a defector from a clandestine organization embedded within the National Security Agency organization that specializes in ET communication and technology; he describes the circumstances surrounding the retrieval of an ET piloted craft discovered by his father in 1956, who he claims served in the Bolivian Army:

> My father discovered a damaged spacecraft in the jungles of Bolivia during a hunting trip. It was a triangular vessel about seventy meters from end-to-end, nearly equilateral . . . My father recovered a specific technology from the ship, and then contacted a military official within the Bolivian government that was a trusted friend. Initially, my father was interested in selling the craft to the Bolivian military, but it quickly became a concern of the U.S. military—specifically the SPL [Special Projects Laboratory]. A director from the SPL met with my father, ascertained the ship's location, and performed a complete salvage operation in the span of three days.[261]

The victorious Allies that formed the United Nations and whose principal members became the permanent members of the UN Security Council, would cooperate in ensuring non-disclosure of the ET presence to their respective general publics and other national governments. This suggested that the United Nations Security Council provided an important forum for the permanent members to coordinate their respective national policies on ETs and also ensured non-disclosure of the ET presence and/or discovery of ET technology.

2. Non-Disclosure of the ET-Nazi Connection and Countering Nazi Influence in South America

The ET connection with Nazi Germany, and the survival of the Nazi elite in remote locations in Antarctica and South America would not be disclosed to the general public and most elected public officials by those national governments aware of the Nazi exodus.

This was to ensure that there would be no reemergence of the Nazi ideology as the basis of new national government anywhere in the world, and of Nazi elites capturing a major state for promoting their Nazi belief systems. This posed considerable difficulties in South America where many governments had strong pro-Nazi sentiments and had provided material support and safe havens for the Axis powers. Countries such as Argentina, Paraguay, Chile and Brazil were carefully watched due to strong pro-Nazi sympathies among political elites, and potential for these states to be vehicles for the spread of Nazism/Fascism in the South American continent.[262]

Indeed, much of the Cold War struggle that occurred throughout South America was an effort to contain the spread of Nazism/Fascism and the need to rein in the influence of Nazi enclaves that influenced governments in this continent. The fear was that South America could one day become a vehicle for a renewed effort by the remaining Nazi elites for regional, if not global, domination. The Cold War struggle in South America was a covert means for the US and USSR to minimize the threat posed by the escaped Nazi elite, by exhausting South American states in a series of political and economic crises.[263]

These perennial crises would ensure that no South American state could ever achieve the kind of economic potential that would enable it to develop the industrial capacity and technological base that would provide the Nazi elite a vehicle for achieving a leadership role in regional and/or world affairs. For example, the 2002 decision by the International Monetary Fund not to provide additional funds to Argentina, led to an easily predictable economic meltdown that resulted in the closing of banks, cut back in government services, and rapid increase in unemployment.[264] Rather than this being a result of different macro-economic philosophies by the Bush administration as compared to the Clinton administration, it may be suspected that the real reason was to deny Argentina the resources with which it could play a major political role in the region.

The final result would be the denial of an increase in the power of Nazi elites who continue to exert a powerful behind the scenes influence over the Argentine political system and other states in South America. Significantly, the individual in charge of establishing Cold War strategy in Latin America during the Truman administration was Nelson Rockefeller, who was later secretly appointed by Eisenhower to take charge of ET affairs.[265]

3. Repatriation of Nazi Scientists/Technologies and Continuing Nazi Sponsored Mind Control Projects

All ET inspired technology left by Nazi Germany was divided among the victorious powers of the US, Britain, France, and the Soviet Union in terms of who had possession of the technology or scientists in their respective zones of control in Occupied Germany and former Nazi occupied territories. Each Allied state incorporated this technology into their respective clandestine military efforts aimed at weapons development and intelligence acquisition.

Each of the major Allied states had its own version of "Operation Paperclip," in which the US sponsored the removal of Nazi scientists to the US, even in cases where they had strong pro-Nazi records thereby violating US immigration laws.[266] These efforts of recruiting Nazi scientists were distinguished by the continuation of many Nazi sponsored projects in the US and USSR.

The expatriation of former Nazi scientists was particularly important in a number of areas in which the Nazis used slave labor and/or unwilling human subjects in testing and developing advanced "behavior modification" and mind control techniques.[267] Restrictions on such experiments in the US and other democratic nations meant that these Nazi scientists had a "wealth of experience" that could not be easily replicated in the US and elsewhere. Most notorious of these Nazi Scientists was Josef Mengele who, contrary to common perceptions of living in exile in South America, reportedly participated in and/or led clandestine US mind control projects such as MK-Ultra and Project Monarch that involved severe human rights abuses on children in particular.[268]

Project MK-Ultra was subject to a review by the US Senate's Select Committee on Intelligence which examined the abuses committed in the behavior modification programs used by the government/military agencies involved in MK-Ultra.[269]

Areas of special interest to Western nations aware of the ET presence were genetic and mind control experiments aimed at optimizing human performance in extreme conditions. These experiments were secretly continued in the US and other former Allied states for the purpose of bioengineering "super soldiers" who could display the kind of genetic and mental qualities for extremely high military performance in outer space, and for advanced time/interdimensional travel technology. Testimonies of former participants of these experiments suggest that many of these former Nazi sponsored genetic and mind control programs were indeed used for producing "super soldiers."[270]

One individual who claims to have been a participant of these genetic and mind control experiments, Andy Pero, gave an interview revealing the background of these experiments in which he was involved:

> After WW2 many Nazi scientists were brought over to the US through our own Intelligence community who formerly worked in mind control research in the concentration camps. I believe they are a remnant of the Nazi party working in conjunction with different branches of the US government and the military. Much of my training and torture sessions were done right at the University of Rochester, NY. They used to take me to a private room in the attic or top floor of the library. The big lab where I had most of the programming done to me was at the Rome National Air Base in Rome, NY.

I have also been used in the Montauk chair while at Camp Hero, Montauk, L.I. and also in a chair in Atlanta, GA at Dobbins Air Force Base . . .

The trainers would put me into a trance whereby I'd be told I could jump off a ladder of minimal height. In my mind, I believed that I was only jumping off a footstool or a short ledge. In actuality, I was progressively led to jump higher and higher heights to the point of successfully jumping off buildings and even out of planes without a parachute. When under mind control, I could do whatever I was instructed to do as long as I believed them. I would do 200 or more push ups in perfect form, sometimes as long as a half hour straight, or until I was told to stop. I weight lifted 545 lbs. on a barbell and squats while attending college and much more (500–1500 lb.) while I was under the mind control in the training laboratory not far from Rochester, NY.[271]

Other areas of experimentation involved psychometric weapons development and experiments working with time/dimensional travel.[272] A number of participants in these highly secret projects sponsored by intelligence and military branches of government have come forward to give testimony of these projects. Preston Nichols, claims to have been a former director of one of these projects and has testified to the use of children, the homeless and other unwilling human subjects in continuing these secret experiments.[273] He outlined the history of Montauk Project as follows:

Over the years, the Montauk researchers perfected their mind control techniques and continued to delve further into the far reaches of human potential. By developing the psychic abilities of different personnel, it eventually got to the point where a psychic's thoughts could be amplified with hardware, and illusions could be manifested both subjectively and objectively. This included the virtual creation of matter. All of this was unparalleled in the history of what we call "ordinary human

experience" but the people who ran the Montauk
Project were not about to stop. They would reach
even further into the realm of the extraordinary. Once
it was discovered that a psychic could manifest matter,
it was observed that it could appear at different
times, depending on what the psychic was thinking.
Thus, what would happen if a psychic thought of a
book but thought of it appearing yesterday? It was
this line of thinking and experimentation which led
to the idea that one could bend time itself. After
years of empirical research, time portals were opened
with massive and outrageous experiments being
conducted.[274]

In a report released on the Montauk Project and its flagrant
violation of the human rights of participants in the experiments,
John Quinn, who believes he was also an unwilling participant
in these, refers to the role played by a prominent psychiatrist
based at McGill University and the Allen Memorial Institute in
Montreal, Canada during the 1950s and 1960s:

[Dr Ewen] Cameron, who had made no secret of his
slavering admiration for the monsters and butchers of
Bergen-Belsen and indeed for the entire Nazi movement in all aspects, rightly viewed his psychotic and
brutal "work" for the CIA and other agencies as a
continuation of the experiments carried out by the
Nazis upon their millions of helpless human victims.
Circumstantial evidence and a number of personal
accounts indicate that similar operations were in fact
also being conducted on Long Island, probably at
Camp Hero, Fort Pond Bay Naval Base in Montauk, and
at Brookhaven Labs during this time period, perhaps
involving Ewen Cameron himself.[275]

The sponsorship of human performance enhancing experiments and mind control was adopted by major governments
interested in applying the work of Nazi Scientists to future requirements for humans in space conditions, time/interdimensional

travel and possible conflict with ET races.[276] These experiments continue today and remain among the most classified projects developed by major states that globally manage the ET presence, ET technology and legacy of Nazi Germany.[277]

4. Managing Extraterrestrial Artifacts Found around the Planet

All ET artifacts found around the planet would be brought under the control of one or more of the "victorious powers" of US, Britain, the Soviet Union, and France. This meant that, in spite of the post-war division of the globe into different "spheres of influence" agreed to at Yalta, most if not all ET technology would eventually find its way into the clandestine military programs of the US, Britain, the Soviet Union and France, or would at least be monitored by these major states.

With the emergence of mainland China as a permanent UN member, this meant that it was also was recognized as having a legitimate sphere of influence wherein it could work to access, control and/or monitor discovered ET artifacts. Maintaining the principle established at Yalta in 1945 to carve up the planet into different spheres of influence would help ensure that there would be no proliferation of ET inspired technology, since a major power would be recognized as having legitimacy to covertly intervene, control and/or monitor ET artifacts.

This would help minimize chances of a repeat of the Nazi experience whereby a discontented regional power could use ET technology for weapons development, and embark on a program of regional military domination that would once again threaten peace and stability in a region or the globe.

This fundamental principle of globally managing ET affairs was particularly important in those parts of the planet where ancient civilizations existed and where ET artifacts were likely to be hidden in inaccessible or yet to be discovered areas. Regions such Tibet, Egypt, Iraq, Afghanistan, Indochina, South and Central America, and elsewhere were all highly valued assets due to the potential ET artifacts possibly located in these countries and regions. Global cooperation among the US and USSR and other permanent members of the UN Security Council members in responding to the ET presence and gaining access to ET artifacts, yielded to intense strategic competition for control of these territories and their hidden treasures.

The Cold War ideological conflict masked the very real struggle for each major state to maximize its power in terms of the technological breakthroughs ET artifacts would provide. There is evidence that the current war in Iraq is but the latest example of a regional military conflict whose ultimate prize is ET artifacts that would impact on the technological programs of the major states managing ET affairs around the planet.[278]

The split between NATO members France and Germany with the US and Britain over the legitimacy and timing of the military intervention in Iraq, suggested that a fundamental realignment in managing ET affairs had occurred with France and Germany siding with Russia and even China, in wanting to restrain the US. This suggested that the post-Second World War cooperation for managing ET affairs was under severe strain, and that very real tensions lay underneath the polite language of international diplomacy.[279]

5. Cooperating to End the Nazi Threat

The major powers would cooperate in responding to the challenge posed both by the remnants of Nazi Germany in their hidden military bases in Antarctica and South America; and to the one or more ET races that had continued to assist Nazi elites. This cooperation was marked by agreements to not disclose this information to their respective general publics or to most elected political officials.

What surely most troubled Allied officials was the success of the Nazi elites to develop fully operational saucer craft that were propelled by antigravity generators and navigational systems that still had not been successfully developed by the US and USSR as mentioned by Col. Corso in an interview reflecting his time in service (he retired from military service in 1963).[280] This Nazi success occurred well before the Allied states were able to develop their own fleets of saucer ships.

According to Col. Steve Wilson, "the first successful U.S. antigravity flight took place on July 18, 1971 at S-4 dreamland [Area 51] wherein light bending capabilities were also demonstrated to obtain total invisibilities."[281] A number of military whistleblowers suggest that the US currently has a fleet of ET reverse engineered ships with antigravity propulsion systems and that manned flights to the Moon and even Mars are regular occurrences by the clandestine organizations developing and using such technology.[282]

If Wilson's date and description are accurate, it suggests that the US had reached a similar technological stage with the Nazis, who presumably had achieved this technological feat sometime towards the end of the Second World War. This was evidenced by the appearance of the legendary Foo fighters, which bewildered Allied airmen on bombing missions over Germany.[283]

After an exhaustive study of this phenomenon, British researcher Mark Birdsall concluded: "Without question, nearly all Foo-Fighter and Ghost Rocket reports can be categorized as advanced technology channeled from . . . various secret German WWII scientific facilities."[284] This suggests that a significant technological gap divided the US/USSR from the Nazi elite who escaped to Antarctica with their prized technological assets and information derived from their occult communications with ET races.

The presence of a significantly well-armed and undefeated Nazi presence in Antarctica and South America would be kept from the general public and most elected officials. Such a non-disclosure policy is evidenced by the secrecy surrounding the true goals of Admiral Byrd's Antarctic mission in 1946/47, and subsequent conflicts in the Antarctic and South America. The level of secrecy even for senior political officials can be gauged by comments from former Congressmen such as Senator Barry Goldwater who served as Chairman of the Senate Intelligence Committee. In response to a question by a UFO researcher he stated: "This thing [ET/UFO affairs] has gotten so highly classified . . . it is just impossible to get anything on it."[285] Goldwater was likely referring to the procedure applying to waived Special Access Programs whereby the chairs of Congressional Defense and/or Intelligence committees, at best, were verbally informed of the existence of a particular "deep black" project without being given any specific details of it, and were not allowed to discuss it with other committee members.

The superior ET inspired technology achieved by Nazi remnants that allowed them to continue to maintain remote bases would surely have disturbed the US and USSR. This helps understand the basis of the cooperation between the major Western powers and the Soviet Union and its satellite states, to globally manage the existence of ET races and technology throughout the Cold War era, and to hide the truth about the threat posed by remnants of Nazi Germany.[286]

Conclusion: Global Management System for ET Affairs and the Legacy of the Nazi-ET Connection

The management system designed by the Allied powers to deal with ET affairs, including the legacy of the Nazi Germany-ET connection, is based on circumstances that stem directly from the Second World War. The desire not to disclose the existence of significant Nazi bases in Antarctica and elsewhere was understandably based on perceptions by the leaderships of Allied states that this would lead to disclosure of the ET assistance received by Nazi Germany.

Due to the potential of this for disclosure of the ET presence more generally, a policy that became a foundation for the global management of ET affairs after the War, the truth about the Nazi bases would not be disclosed. Furthermore, the fact that Nazi bases in Antarctica could not be militarily defeated suggested both the technological superiority of Nazi weapons, and the likelihood that they continued to receive assistance from one or more ET races preventing the eradication of Nazi bases.

Given global public perceptions of "complete victory" in the Second World War, the Allied governments did not want their respective national publics to learn of the major strategic defeat suffered by the Allies with the successful establishment of a Nazi presence in Antarctica and South America, and the Nazi-ET connection. This would mean that these technologically advanced Nazi enclaves would pose a direct threat to the militaries of major world governments.

Perhaps more important: core Nazi principles such as elitist decision making, eugenics and militarism, would be a threat to "democratic" values around the globe, and how ET affairs were to be globally managed.

The chief legacy of the Nazi German-ET connection is that Nazi enclaves continue to influence a key region of the planet, South America, leading to numerous political and economic crises in that continent which continues to seriously impact the lives of South American citizens.

Moreover, a number of researchers claim that Nazism continues to covertly influence government policy at the highest level in countries such as the US and Russia, and, to a lesser extent, Britain and France, through the Nazi scientists expatriated into those countries after the Second World War. These former Nazi scientists assumed prominent leadership positions in the clandestine projects to develop ET inspired technologies. These projects became Trojan horses for Nazi principles and beliefs both in government and corporations, that fulfill numerous contracts to service the military and intelligence communities in the US.

This is especially the case in projects that involve "mind control" and "genetic" experiments that utilize ET inspired technologies for a variety of purposes that are not transparent and are abusive of the rights of human subjects. There is evidence that Nazi infiltration through the "Trojan horse" of former Nazi Scientists into the military-industrial complexes that oversee ET affairs is so significant as to constitute a direct threat to democracy and liberty in the US and other major powers.

There is a need for full disclosure of ET affairs in general, in order to make it possible for humanity to make the transition to the reality of extraterrestrial life, and the political issues that arise with dealing with ET affairs. Not only ethical and political principles motivate full disclosure, but also significant national security principles are at stake. The very survival of the US as a bastion of liberty and democracy—key principles established by the founding fathers of the US—are at stake if clandestine projects dealing with ET affairs and the continued Nazi influence, are not placed under the supervision of the appropriate congressional and executive committees that are transparent in their operations and reports.[287]

A full Congressional inquiry into the true circumstances surrounding the escape of Nazi elites and establishment of bases in Antarctica and elsewhere, by the US Congress and similar parliamentary bodies of other nations, is immediately required.

Such official inquiries are needed to make the public more aware of how Nazi principles have infiltrated into the key national institutions responsible for managing ET affairs, and the threat this poses to democratic values and institutions. Evidence for infiltration of Nazi principles into the key decision making bodies on ET affairs is given by whistleblowers such as Dr. Michael Wolf, who claims that "within the UFO Cover-Up there is a dark, covert renegade organization known as the 'Cabal'. He describes it as a "well-orchestrated conspiratorial bevy of plotters . . . top-heavy with the military, and headed by (a Navy Under-Secretary)." He claims that the "paranoiac Cabal works against, and deliberately undermines, the goals of peaceful negotiations with the extraterrestrial visitors."[288]

At a global level, there is a similar threat that key institutions that manage ET affairs have become infiltrated by Nazi elites and/or Nazi principles. It is imperative that the public becomes fully informed of the variety of ET races in existence, their activities and agendas. It is also imperative to identify those races that have been most active in supporting the Nazi elite and their activities since the end of the Second World War.

Although achieving transparency in the full range of activities, agendas and motivations of ET races are extraordinarily complex, it is certainly worth investigating why one or more ET races assisted in the development in the Nazi's advanced technology, and may be playing a role in the expansion of Nazi principles in the national and global management of ET affairs.

There remains the danger of an unnecessary military confrontation with ET races who, it is claimed in the majority of whistleblower testimonies, demonstrate little hostile intent to global humanity, and indeed have thus far demonstrated remarkable resilience in not retaliating against attacks from clandestine government organizations.[289] Delay in addressing the influence of Nazi elites and/or Nazi principles in the global management of ET affairs may result in a series of events that have tragic consequences for the sovereignty and freedom of humanity for generations to come.

Notes

207. I am greatly indebted to my good friend, Dr. John King, who graciously allowed me to use his holiday home for the writing of this chapter, an earlier version of which was published as "Foundations for Globally Managing Extraterrestrial Affairs—The Legacy of the Nazi Germany-Extraterrestrial Connection," Study Paper #6: www. exopolitics.org July 27, 2003.

208. For discussion of historical UFO sightings, see Richard Dolan, *UFOs and the National Security State: Chronology of a Cover-up* (Hampton Roads, 2002) pages 1–3; and Jim Marrs, *Alien Agenda: Investigating the Extraterrestrial Presence Among Us* (Harper Paperbacks, 1997), pages xxvi–xxx.

209. For discussion of Nazi expeditions, see Christof Friedrich, *Secret Nazi polar expeditions* (Samisdat, 1976); Christopher Hale, *Himmler's Crusade: The Nazi Expedition to Find the Origins of the Aryan Race* (John Wiley & Sons, 2003). For an online article on Nazi Expeditions to Antarctica, see "The Antarctic Enigma": http://www.violations.dabsol.co.uk/ind1.htm.

210. For online references to Nazi Germany's recovery of an ET craft sometime in 1937–38, see Robert K. Leśniakiewicz, "The UFO Crashes in Poland": http://www.notizieufo.com/pol5.htm; and "The Omega File: Nazi History": http://www.think-aboutit.com/Omega/files/omega3.htm.

211. See Peter Levenda, Peter Lavenda, Norman Mailer, *Unholy Alliance: History of the Nazi Involvement With the Occult* (Continuum Pub Group; 2nd edition, 2002); Trevor Ravenscroft, *Spear of Destiny* (Red Wheel, 1987); and Nicholas Goodrick-Clark, *The Occult Roots of Nazism: Secret Aryan Cults and Their Influence on Nazi Ideology: The Arisophists of Austria and Germany, 1890–1935*. For an online article

on Hitler and the Occult, see "Hitler, German Nazi Beliefs and Tibet": http://www.geocities.com/okar_review/hitlertibet.html.

212. See Helena Petrovna Blavatsky, *The Secret Doctrine: The Synthesis of Science, Religion, and Philosophy*, Vol. 1 & 2 (Theosophical University Press, 1999).

213. For discussion of these technologies see Henry Stevens, *Hitler's Flying Saucers: A Guide to German Flying Discs of the Second World War* (Adventures Unlimited Press, 2003); Gary Hyland & Anton Gill, *Last Talons of the Eagle: Secret Nazi Technology Which Could Have Changed the Course of World War II* (Headline Book Publishing Co., 2000). For online discussion of these technologies, see "Secrets of the Third Reich": http://www.violations.dabsol.co.uk/secrets/secretspart1.htm.

214. "Secrets of the Third Reich": http://www.violations.dabsol.co.uk/secrets/secretspart2.htm.

215. See Joscelyn Godwin, *Arktos: The Polar Myth in Science, Symbolism, and Nazi Survival* (Adventures Unlimited, 1996). For an online article on Hitler and the Thule Society, see "Hitler, German Nazi Beliefs and Tibet": http://www.geocities.com/okar_review/hitlertibet.html.

216. "Secrets of the Third Reich": http://www.violations.dabsol.co.uk/secrets/secretspart2.htm. For discussion of anti-gravity technology see David Hatcher Childress, ed., *Anti-Gravity and the Unified Field* (Adventures Unlimited, 1990); and Nick Cook, *The Hunt for Zero Point: Inside the Classified World of Antigravity Technology* (Broadway Books, 2003).

217. "Secrets of the Third Reich": http://www.violations.dabsol.co.uk/secrets/secretspart1.htm.

218. "Secrets of the Third Reich": http://www.violations.dabsol.co.uk/secrets/secretspart1.htm.

219. "Secrets of the Third Reich": http://www.violations.dabsol.co.uk/secrets/secretspart1.htm.

220. "Secrets of the Third Reich": http://www.violations.dabsol.co.uk/secrets/secretspart1.htm.

221. Marrs, *Alien Agenda*, p. 27.

222. For online references to Nazi Germany's recovery of an ET craft sometime in 1937–38, see Robert K. Leśniakiewicz, "The UFO Crashes in Poland": http://www.notizieufo.com/pol5.htm; and "The Omega File: Nazi History": http://www.think-aboutit.com/Omega/files/omega3.htm.

223. Quoted in "Secrets of the Third Reich": http://www.violations.dabsol.co.uk/secrets/secretspart3.htm.

224. Robin Collyns, *Did Spacemen Colonise the Earth?* (Pelham Books, 1974) p. 236. Also quoted in "Secrets of the Third Reich": http://www.violations.dabsol.co.uk/secrets/secretspart3.htm.

225. Dan Sherman, *Above Black: Project Preserve Destiny, Insider Account of Alien Contact and Government Cover-up* (One Team Publishing, 1997). Available online at: http://www.aboveblack.com.

226. For an article claiming that Nazi Germany had reached an agreement with a Reptilian ET species, see "The Nazi-UFO Connection": http://www.angelfire.com/ut/branton/nazi.html.

227. For discussion of ET races described to be hostile/malevolent to human society, see chapter four. First published as "Responding to Extraterrestrial Infiltration of Clandestine Organizations Embedded in Military, Intelligence and Government Departments," Study Paper #4 (May 30, 2003) www.exopolitics.org.

228. For discussion of the role of US corporations in assisting in the industrialization of Nazi Germany, see Charles Higham, *Trading with the Enemy: An Expose of the Nazi-American Money Plot, 1933–1949* (Doubleday Press, 1982); Antony C. Sutton, *Wall Street & the Rise of Hitler* (GSG & Associates, 1976). For an online article, see "Documented Evidence of a Secret Business and Political Alliance Between the U.S. 'Establishment' and the Nazis, Before, During and After World War II, up to the present": http://thewebfairy.com/nwo/.

229. For discussion of the inequities of the Versailles Peace Treaty, see Michael Salla, *The Hero's Journey Toward A Second American Century* (Praeger Press, 2002).

230. Charles Higham, *Trading with the Enemy: An Expose of the Nazi-American Money Plot, 1933–1949* (Doubleday Press, 1982). For online reference, see: http://thewebfairy.com/nwo/standard.html.

231. John Costello, *Ten Days to Destiny: The Secret Story of the Hess Peace Initiative and British Efforts to Strike a Deal With Hitler* (Quill, 1993).

232. Richard Boylan, "Quotations from Chairman Wolf," in Boylan and Boylan, *Labored Journey To The Stars*. Available online at: http://drboylan.com/wolfqut2.html.

233. Personal interview of Colonel's Brophy's son by Dr Richard Boylan, "Air Force Colonel's Son Reveals 1940s U.S.-UFO/Star Visitor Encounters," *UFO facts*, July 21, 2003: http://groups.yahoo.com/group/UFOFacts/message/10345.

234. See George Morgenstern, *Pearl Harbor, The Story of The Secret War* (Cossta Mesa, 1991); see also discussion of events surrounding the entry of the US into the Second World War by controversial British conspiracy theorist, David Icke, *And The Truth Shall Set You Free*, pages 118–22.

235. Quoted in Julius Pratt, *A History of United States Foreign Policy* (Prentice Hall, 1955) p. 638.

236. For discussion of Hitler's efforts to avoid US entry into the War, see Michael Salla, *The Hero's Journey towards the Second American Century*, pages 147–149.

237. "Secrets of the Third Reich": http://www.violations.dabsol.co.uk/secrets/secretspart2.htm.

238. For extensive discussion of such an exodus to Antarctica and South America, see Joscelyn Godwin, *Arktos: The Polar Myth in Science, Symbolism, and Nazi Survival;* Jim Marrs, Alien Agenda, pages 107–13; and also see Branton, *The Omega Files; Secret Nazi UFO Bases Revealed* (Inner Light Publications, 2000). Available online at: http://www.think-about-it.com.

239. Richard K. Wilson and Sylvan Burns, "SECRET TREATY: The United States Government and Extra-terrestrial Entities. Available online at: http://www.fortunecity.com/roswell/prediction/51/text-files/secret.txt.

240. For extensive discussion of the advanced technology left by Nazi Germany, see "Secrets of the Third Reich": http://www.violations.dabsol.co.uk/secrets/secretspart1.htm.

241. For discussion of how senior Nazi began transferring funds and resources through South America, see Marrs, *Alien Agenda,* pages 107–113.

242. See the "Antarctic Enigma": http://www.violations.dabsol.co.uk/ind2.htm.

243. "Antarctic Enigma,": http://www.violations.dabsol.co.uk/ind2.htm.

244. "Antarctic Enigma,": http://www.violations.dabsol.co.uk/ind2.htm.

245. For discussion of Nazi developed Saucers being witnessed during the post-World War period, see "Secrets of the Third Reich": http://www.violations.dabsol.co.uk/secrets/secretspart3.htm.

246. "The Antarctic Enigma": http://www.violations.dabsol.co.uk/ind2.htm. For further references to Operation High Jump, see Branton, *The Omega Files.* Available online at: http://www.think-aboutit.com/Omega/files/omega3.htm.

247. "The Antarctic Enigma": http://www.violations.dabsol.co.uk/ind2.htm.

248. For reference to Nazi expeditions to Antarctica in the pre-war period, see "The Antarctic Enigma": http://www.violations.dabsol.co.uk/ind2.htm. The possibility that the Nazis had "discovered" underground bases in Antarctica suggests that the Thule Society had indeed been successful in establishing communications with an ancient subterranean race of humans from long dead surface civilizations.

249. See "The Antarctic Enigma": http://www.violations.dabsol.co.uk/ind2.htm. For further references to this battle, see also Branton, *The Omega Files.* Available online at: http://www.think-aboutit.com/Omega/files/omega3.htm.

250. Quoted in an interview of Admiral Byrd by Lee van Atta, "On Board the Mount Olympus on the High Seas," *El Mercurio* (Santiago, Chile,

March 5, 1947). See "The Antarctic Enigma": http://www.violations. dabsol.co.uk/ind2.htm.

251. Richard Byrd, *The Missing Diary of Admiral Richard Byrd* (Inner Light Publications, 1992). Admiral Byrd's Diary is available online at: http://www.v-j-enterprises.com/byrdiar.html.

252. See Raymond W. Bernard, *The Hollow Earth: the greatest geographical discovery in history made by Admiral Richard E. Byrd in the mysterious land beyond the Poles—the true origin of the flying saucers* (Bell Publishing Co.). For online discussion of ET sightings in Antarctica region, see "Antarctic Enigma": http://www. violations.dabsol.co.uk/ind2.htm.

253. For the CIA's involvement in the Tibetan uprising and subsequent abandonment of Tibet, see Roger McCarthy, *Tears of the Lotus: Accounts of Tibetan Resistance to the Chinese Invasion, 1950–1962* (McFarland & Company, 1997). For an account of the Nazi-Tibet connection, see Peter Moon, *The Black Sun: Montauk's Nazi-Tibetan Connection—Montauk Series, Bk. 4* (Sky Books, 1997).

254. For analysis of US non-disclosure policy, see Chapter Two. See also Greer, *Disclosure*; & Dolan, *UFOs and the National Security State*.

255. For discussion of the institutional structure of the US, see Chapter Two. See also Greer, *Disclosure*; & Dolan, *UFOs and the National Security State*.

256. For a detailed discussion of a global cover-up of the ET presence and technology, see Timothy Good, *Above Top Secret: The Worldwide UFO Coverup* (Acacia Press, 1989); and Dolan, *UFO's and the National Security State*.

257. For discussion of the media blackout, see Terry Hanson, *The Missing Times* (Xlibris Corporation, 2001).

258. Richard Boylan, "The Man Who "Outed" the U.S. Saucer Program: Colonel Steve Wilson," in Boylan and Boylan, *Labored Journey To The Stars*. Available online at: http://www.drboylan.com/ colbirb2.html.

259. Linda Moulton Howe, "UFOs and EBEs: More Insider Evidence," *Nexus* magazine (August-September, 1998): http://www.nexusmagazine. com/ufosebes.html.

260. [Authors note:] The actual existence of Dr. Jamisson Neruda as a defector from a clandestine NSA organization is controversial and is almost impossible to verify. There is a possibility that 'Dr Neruda' is used as a pseudonym for someone who actually does fill a position similar to that described by Neruda who is part of an acclimation program approved by senior officials. Another possibility is that the website is disinformation. The extensive information on the website, ostensibly created by Dr. Neruda (www.wingmakers.com), has philosophical depth, coherence, clarity, detail and consistency with

other sources, and leads me to conclude that it is not disinformation. Despite questions over the actual existence of a Dr. Jamisson Neruda, I believe much of the website material is accurate and worth referencing as a valid source.

261. "Neruda Interviews": http://www.wingmakers.com/neruda3.html.
262. Sources on Nazism in South American countries include: Ronald C. Newton, *The Nazi Menace in Argentina, 1931–1947* (Stanford University Press, 1992; Uki Goni, Yuki Goni, *The Real Odessa: Smuggling the Nazis to Peron's Argentina* (Granta Books, 2002); and Graeme Stewart Mount, *Chile and the Nazis: From Hitler to Pinochet* (Black Rose Books, 2001).
263. For an account of clandestine subversive operations by six Latin American intelligence agencies influenced by the CIA, see John Dinges, *The Condor Years: How Pinochet and His Allies Brought Terrorism to Three Continents* (New Press, 2004).
264. For an online description of the Argentine Financial Crisis, see "A Rich Country Goes Bust Again: Those Who Ruined Argentina," *World Press Review* (March 2002): http://www.worldpress.org/americas/0302observateur.htm.
265. For a critical account of Nelson Rockefeller's links with Nazism and how this effected his leadership of the Cold War struggle in Latin America, see "Rockefeller: A Traitor For President": http://home.att.net/~m.standridge/rocky.htm. For a more neutral online description of the Cold War struggle in Latin America, go to: http://www.csupomona.edu/~jmvadi/454/The%20Cold%20War.html.
266. For detailed discussion of Project Paperclip, see Linda Hunt, *Secret Agenda: The United States Government, Nazi Scientists, and Project Paperclip, 1945 to 1990* (St Martins Press, 1991); and Clarence G. Lasby, *Project Paperclip: German Scientists and the Cold War* (Scribner 1975). For online discussion of Operation Paperclip, see "Secrets of the Third Reich": http://www.violations.dabsol.co.uk/secrets/secretspart2.htm.
267. For an overview of Nazi mind control experiments, see Ron Patton, "Project Monarch: Nazi Mind," *The Conspiracy Reader: From the Deaths of JFK and John Lennon to Government-Sponsored Alien.* Available online at: http://www.aches-mc.org/monarch.html.
268. Ron Patton, "Project Monarch: Nazi Mind," *The Conspiracy Reader,* pages 197–213. Available online at: http://www.aches-mc.org/monarch.html.
269. For the Select Committee's report which was released by an FOIA request by John Greenewald, see "Project MKUltra: The CIA's Program of Research in Behavior Modification," Joint Hearing Before the Select Committee on Intelligence and the Subcommittee on Scientific Research, August 3, 1977. Available

online at: http://www.blackvault.com/documents/remoteviewing/hearing/hearing0.htm.

270. A number of interviews of these Super solider experiments are available online at: http://www.hostileinvader.com/CampHero.html. For discussion of Mind-Body technology, see Thomas Beardon, *Excalibur Briefing: Explaining paranormal Phenomena, the interaction of mind and matter* (Cheniere Press). Available online at: http://www.cheniere.org/books/excalibur/index.html.

271. Interview with Andy Pero, "Project Superman": http://www.hostileinvader.com/ProjectSuperman.html. For an interview with "Jared," another individual who claims to have been programmed as a super solder, see Eve Lorgen, "Secret Project Super Warrior Gone Rogue" *Alienlovebite* (August, 2001). Available online at: http://www.alienlovebite.com/secret_project_super_warrior_gon.htm.

272. For discussion of these various technologies and how they were conducted at the famed Montauk Airforce/Naval facility, see Preston Nichols, *Montauk Project: Experiments in Time* (Sky Books, 1999); Al Bielak and Brad Steiger, *The Philadelphia Experiment And Other UFO Conspiracies* (Innerlight Publications, 1991); Stewart Swerdlow, *Montauk: The Alien Connection* (Expansions Publishing Co., 2002); Wade Gordon, *The Brookhaven Connection* (Sky Books, 2001). For online interview with Al Bielak, go to: http://psychicspy.com/montauk1.html. For online reference to time travel, see Richard Boylan, "Colonel Steve Wilson, USAF (ret.) Reveals UFO-oriented Project Pounce": http://www.drboylan.com/swilson2.html.

273. For extensive discussion on the use of children in these experiments, see John Quinn, "Phoenix Undead: The Montauk Project and Camp Hero Today," (NewsHawk Inc, 1998). Available online at: http://vs03.tvsecure.com/~vs030f1/monew.htm.

274. Preston Nichols & Peter Moon, *Montauk: Explorations in Consciousness* (Sky Books, 1995). Available online at: http://psychicspy.com/montauk1.html.

275. John Quinn, "Phoenix Undead: The Montauk Project and Camp Hero Today,"(NewsHawk Inc, 1998). Available online at: http://vs03.tvsecure.com/~vs030f1/monew.htm. For further discussion of Dr. Cameron and other prominent mind control "specialists," see Ron Patton, "Project Monarch: Nazi Mind," *The Conspiracy Reader*, pages 197–213.

276. For history of mind control experiments, see Jim Keith, *Mind Control, World Control* (Adventures Unlimited Press, 1999); see also John Marks, *The Search for the Manchurian Candidate: The CIA and Mind Control* (Norton and Co., 1991).

277. For a report detailing with how these experiments continue up to the present, see John Quinn, "Phoenix Undead: The Montauk Project

and Camp Hero Today,"(NewsHawk Inc, 1998). Available online at: http://vs03.tvsecure.com/~vs030f1/monew.htm.

278. Chapter Five discusses how Iraq possesses ET artifacts that lie behind the 2003 US led military intervention in Iraq.

279. For discussion of the shifting alliances in managing the ET presence, see Chapter Six.

280. Quoted in "Secrets of the Third Reich": http://www.violations. dabsol.co.uk/secrets/secretspart3.htm.

281. Quoted in Richard Boylan, "Colonel Steve Wilson, USAF (ret.) Reveals UFO-oriented Project Pounce," available online at: http://www.drboylan.com/swilson2.html.

282. See Richard Boylan, "Quotations from Chairman Wolf," in Boylan and Boylan, Labored Journey To The Stars. Available online at: http://www.drboylan.com/wolfqut2.html. See also Richard Boylan, "Secret Air Force Mach-50 Plane, Other Exotic Classified Aerospacecraft, And the U.S. Antigravity Fighter Discs Deployed With Star Wars Weapons To Fight In the Gulf War," in Boylan and Boylan, Labored Journey To The Stars. Available online at: http://www.drboylan.com/xplanes2.html.

283. Jim Marrs, Alien Agenda, pages 95–97, and Dolan, UFOs and the National Security State, pages 5–11.

284. Quoted in Marrs, Alien Agenda, p. 114.

285. Marrs, Alien Agenda, p. 201.

286. For an account of US-Soviet cooperation in dealing with UFOs, see Linda Moulton Howe, "UFOs and EBEs: More Insider Evidence," Nexus magazine (August-September, 1998): http://www.nexusmagazine. com/ufosebes.html.

287. For an extensive discussion on how US foreign policy has evolved in terms of the key principles of democracy, liberty and rule of law, see Michael Salla, The Hero's Journey Toward the Second American Century.

288. Interview with Dr Richard Boylan, "Official Within MJ-12 UFO-Secrecy Management Group Reveals Insider Secrets," available online at: http://drboylan.com/wolfdoc2.html.

289. For discussion of the benevolent intentions of ETs, see Steven Greer, Extraterrestrial Contact: The Evidence and Implications (Crossing Point Publications, 1999); and Richard Boylan and Lee K. Boylan, Close Extraterrestrial Encounters: Positive Experiences With Mysterious Visitors (Wildflower, 1994).

Chapter 4

Extraterrestrial Infiltration of Clandestine Organizations Embedded in Military, Intelligence and Government Departments

Introduction[290]

A growing number of individuals who have served in military, intelligence or government institutions testify to the presence of extraterrestrial (ET) races that compete among themselves and with clandestine (human) organizations for influence over global humanity.[291] Dr. Steven Greer has gathered the testimonies of more than 100 of these witnesses in written and/or video format, and made these available for the general public and for a congressional inquiry.

He claims a further 300 are ready to come forward to give testimony, if given legal protection from prosecution for violating their secrecy oaths.[292] The clandestine organizations are groups of individuals embedded within the intelligence and military services of different national governments whose role is to deal with all issues pertaining to the ET presence.

The different ET races span the entire spectrum from non-interventionist ones that have a philosophy based on not interfering with human free will when interacting with and influencing individuals, organizations and societies; to "interventionist" races that intercede in human affairs. These do not necessarily respect human free will for motivations that range from a "self-serving" desire to "harvest" the resources of global humanity, to an altruistic desire to assist global humanity in developing to its highest species potential.

The most credible sources providing evidence of these clandestine organizations and the different ET groups are "whistleblowers" that participated in various clandestine military/intelligence projects.[293] Another important source are individuals who have directly experienced contact with different ET factions and/or have been unwilling subjects of clandestine/ET projects.[294]

These former participants in projects run by clandestine organizations have testified to the relationships between humanity and various ET races in terms of the latter's motivations, activities and moral philosophy, and the alliances they form with "clandestine organizations" embedded within intelligence and security forces that interface with different ET races. The nature of these alliances appear to be very fluid in terms of how ETs and elites interface, and the various elites that come to the pinnacle of these organizations.

It appears that a struggle between different factions of ETs who share interventionist and non-interventionist approaches to human affairs have been reflected in the various clandestine organizations that interface with them and dictate global policy. These factional differences appear both in terms of the relationships between these clandestine organizations, and also in the internal dynamics of clandestine organizations.

This chapter describes the dynamics of the interactions between clandestine organizations and various ET races. Emphasis will be on describing the different intervention philosophies and activities of ET races, and in identifying how this impacts the decision making and organizational structure of clandestine organizations embedded within military and intelligence departments of the US and other national governments.

Finally, the chapter will finish by describing the extent to which clandestine organizations have been infiltrated by different ET factions and the threat this poses to the sovereignty of humanity.

Evidence used in framing the analysis provided in this chapter is primarily drawn from the testimonies of participants in clandestine government organizations that serve as the strongest evidentiary source for analysis of the ET presence.[295] All of these individuals participated in "black projects" that have the highest security classifications in the US and other countries, and carry severe penalties for divulging to the general public.

The fact that many of these witnesses have been able to make these testimonies public in various lectures, videos, websites or books, suggest that an "acclimation program" is occurring whereby the general public is being prepared for the more disturbing aspects of the ET presence.[296] The recommendations made at the conclusion of this chapter are designed to assist in developing an adequate response to the infiltration of clandestine organizations by various ET factions.

Understanding the Dynamics of Interaction between Different ET factions and Humanity

The controversial Sumerian translator, Zecharia Sitchin describes in great detail the nature of the struggle between two factions of ETs whom the Sumerians called the Anunnaki.[297] He describes how this ET race provided the biological material for the genetic engineering of the human species that was created out of a fusion of the biological material of primates with the genetic material of this ET race.[298]

Sitchin describes how the faction led by the ET/god Enlil was self-serving towards a humanity that was basically viewed as an expendable resource created to provide a variety of resources for use by the Anunnaki. The other ET faction led by the ET/god Enki had a far more altruistic view of humanity characterized by a deep affection that was oriented towards the development of humanity as a species.

The ancient Sumerian factional struggle between ETs over how humanity was to be viewed and treated is reflected in the mythological belief systems of later civilizations and their respective warring pantheons. This suggests that the ancient "war of the gods" is an archetypal event that has been long embedded in the collective human consciousness from racial memories of an intense historical conflict between different ET factions.[299]

The historical conflict between different ET factions has most often been given expression in a dualist moral framework in which these ET factions or "gods" are respectively either "benevolent" or "malevolent" in motivation and activities. In the Sumerian records, the god Enlil could certainly be viewed as having a malevolent orientation towards humanity as opposed to his brother Enki who had a benevolent attitude.

This is certainly the scenario described by Sitchin in his translation of the "great flood" where Enlil commanded that humanity should not be forewarned of the great flood due to the belief that humanity was corrupt and expendable, as opposed to Enki who forewarned the most enlightened members of humanity, Utnapishtim/Noah.[300]

A similar story appears in the ancient Greek myth of Prometheus and Zeus suggesting that a factional conflict between ETs over how to interact with humanity was deeply embedded in the collective unconscious of humanity.

In the religious arena this perceived factional struggle between the creator gods of humanity has given rise to dualistic religions such as Zoroastrianism and Manicheaism where a supreme god of Light is locked in a great cosmic struggle against a god of Darkness. In Judeo-Christian-Islamic traditions, this struggle is depicted in terms of the confrontation between two competing angelic hosts led respectively by the archangels Michael and Lucifer.

The apocryphal Book of Enoch comes closest to describing the ET origins of this religious struggle in how the rebellious Angels/Nephilim led by 'Semjasa' corrupted the Earth, and how they were expelled by the Archangel Michael and his angelic host, while the Earth was purged by the great flood.[301]

A dualistic moral framework, however, is not an accurate basis for understanding ET efforts to influence and/or control human affairs through alliances with clandestine organizations. The complexity of the ET interactions described by different sources suggests that a more multifaceted dynamic between different ET factions exists, and simple moral categories such as benevolent/good and malevolent/evil are misleading. For example, according to Jamisson Neruda who claims to be a defector from a clandestine organization embedded within the

National Security Agency, for a number of ET races with multiple agendas that are intervening on the planet, simple moral categories are insufficient to fully understand the consequences of their activities and influence.[302]

Consequently, a "triadic framework" that doesn't use misleading moral categories is necessary so as to more accurately reflect the dynamics of the ways ETs interact with one another, the rules of intervention that are set and observed by ET races, and the "political philosophies" of these ET races.

The main factors influencing the dynamics of this three-pronged ET influence are the interventionist philosophies of these races in terms of respecting human free will, the degree to which the ET "political philosophy" dismisses or accepts the idea that humans have reached the necessary "species maturity" to evolve and flourish without being controlled by advanced ET races; and the degree to which ET interaction with humanity is self-serving from the perspective of the ETs or serving the interests of humanity.

These factors give rise to three models that will be used to describe the main characteristics of how ETs control and/or influence the development of human societies and clandestine organizations that interface with the ET races. These models are the "good shepherd," "protective parent" and "wise mentor."

Although the list of ET races described in the following categories is not exhaustive when compared to some of the classification systems that are circulating on the internet by those claiming to be communicating with or "channeling" ET races, it does cover the most significant races in whistleblower testimonies, whose influence is most felt in the policy making process.

The "Good Shepherd" ETs

ET races that have an interventionist approach, share a "pessimistic" view in their assessment of humanity's "species maturity," and are self-serving in moral orientation. They can be viewed in terms of the analogy of the "good shepherd." "Good shepherd" ETs hold views similar to the shepherd tending to a flock of sheep.

The sheep and shepherd have different intrinsic value whereby the right of the shepherd to use their flock as they please is accepted by the shepherd as self-evident and a natural part of existence. There is therefore no moral reservation on the shepherd's part in controlling and using their sheep as a resource.

The "good shepherd" may develop an affectionate relationship with some members of their flock, especially those who exhibit qualities prized by the shepherd such as intelligence or physical appearance. These "members of the flock" may be generously rewarded for their prized qualities with the best feeding pastures and mating opportunities, but less endowed members of the flock are viewed as little more than an expendable resource that serves the interest of the good shepherd and their community. For the shepherd, it is inconceivable that the "sheep" could be expected to tend to themselves since they could be stolen and/or exposed to predators, thereby diminishing the shepherd's resource base.

If the "good shepherd analogy" is extended to humans it can be concluded that "good shepherd" ETs have as part of their belief system the view that humans are too "immature" as a species to be allowed to develop without being closely scrutinized in how humanity governs itself and uses the planet's resources. The overly pessimistic view of human nature leads to the desire to control human institutions so that "good shepherd" ET races can monitor and limit the evolutionary growth of humanity in order to "harvest" humanity and/or the biosphere (Earth) as a renewable resource for ET races.

According to Sitchin's translations of Sumerian cuneiform texts and various religious traditions, there is evidence supporting a biological connection between humanity and the "good shepherd" ETs, and the fact that the latter played a key role in the creation or bioengineering of the human race. The "good shepherds" correspond in the Sumerian records to the Enlil faction of the Anunnaki.

In terms of the different ET races described by whistleblowers, the "good shepherd" ETs include the Grays from

Zeta Reticulum, Tall Grays (from Orion), Reptilians (Earth based), Draco-Reptilians from Orion, and the Anunnaki (giant humanoids from Nibiru).[303]

The most common strategy used by "good shepherd" ETs to exercise control over humanity is to create the illusion of "wolves" in the form of dangerous individuals, organizations or other contrived threats which allows individuals and communities to delegate their sovereign power to political institutions. This essentially duplicates the political process described by the 17th century English philosopher, Thomas Hobbes in *Leviathan*, where individuals in a "state of nature" (an anarchical/ lawless environment) will surrender their individual sovereignty to a sovereign ruler in order to protect themselves from potential aggression, theft and rape.[304]

Similarly, good shepherd ETs create sufficient "illusionary wolves" who threaten law and order, to persuade individuals to surrender their individual sovereignty to powerful political institutions. Authors such as David Icke argue, for example, that the 9/11 attacks on New York and Washington were effectively an attempt to depict Islamic terrorists as "wolves" in order to scare the global general public to surrender more freedom to government authorities.[305]

Subsequently, "good shepherd" ETs enter into a collection of "Faustian bargains" with political elites who directly benefit if they agree to cooperate with these ET races in controlling all sectors of national life: political, religious, economic and military.[306] Such a "Faustian" process is alluded to in the writings of ancient historians such as the Manetho who chronicled the 30 human dynasties in Egypt that emerged after the gods/ demigods surrendered their direct rule over humanity.[307]

The motivation of these human elites is similar to collaborationists in occupied countries. They see themselves as simply recognizing political reality and getting on with life in the hope that conditions improve in the future. Historical agreements/ alliances between human elites and "good shepherd" ETs have been the subject of investigation by conspiracy theorists such as Jim Marrs and David Icke.[308]

The "good shepherd" faction of ETs has three sub-groups that are strategic competitors, but also cooperate to minimize the influence of the other two dominant ET factions that are dedicated to the evolution of the human species. The first are the Earth based "Reptilian" ETs who have been hidden on the planet for millennia, and have managed humanity as a resource in a way that doesn't deplete the planet's resources and threaten the integrity of the biosphere.[309]

Strictly speaking, this sub-group is not extraterrestrial, but is an advanced non-humanoid race that inhabits subterranean realms. Some authors claim this Reptilian/non-humanoid race inhabited the Earth's surface long before humanity but had to abandon the surface after severe environmental catastrophe and/or interplanetary warfare. The well-known journalist, Linda Moulton Howe, interviewed an individual who had a remarkable encounter with a group of these "Reptilian beings," and reveals some significant facets about this ancient race and their approach as "good shepherds":

> I understood better their nature and agenda. They are neither benevolent nor evil. They have been among us in secret for thousands of years, maybe longer. But the length of time isn't as much the issue as why they have been among us. I believe they have been farming us for raw materials. We humans have been a self-perpetuating crop, a crop that doesn't need much tending and continues to reproduce, at least up to now . . . Thank goodness they don't kill us; they just use us.

> This system has worked well for the aliens for a long time. But now there's a problem and their investment is in trouble. They have spent a lot of time, travel and effort to farm us. But we are on an almost irreversible path of self-destruction. Nuclear and biological weapons and their waste have polluted the air, land and water. Forests, jungles and trees are being cut down or are dying. Now there are breakdowns in the food chain and the rest of the food chain is contaminated. Over-population, disease and viruses beyond our grasp, with new and more complicated illnesses cropping up every day. These are just a few of the problems we humans have created.[310]

This Earth based Reptilian race, due to its long presence on Earth and efforts to restrict humanity's more destructive tendencies, has historically acquired the myth of being a "guardian race."[311] In the Gothic architecture of many European cathedrals and American buildings, one can witness the numerous sculptures of "Gargoyles" that symbolize a protective force in humanity's violent history and search for religious truth.[312]

This sub-group therefore partly corresponds to the Enki faction of the Anunnaki described by Sitchin. It does not wish to share control of the human race with other ET races and tries to prevent off-world ET intervention (which constitutes a threat to Earth based Reptilians' ability to manage humanity) by assisting humanity in dealing with a range of problems such as the environmental degradation, the threat of nuclear war, and overpopulation—all of which threaten the resources of this sub-group of "good shepherds."

This sub-group therefore assists in the development of a one-world government that centralizes political power and restricts human sovereignty and freedom without eliminating it altogether. Giving credence to this scenario, Phil Schneider, a civil engineer contracted to build secret underground facilities for clandestine organizations, described the evidence he encountered that ETs would be the true rulers of a one world government. This is why he and many others left the "service" of US-based clandestine organizations.[313]

A second sub-group of the "good shepherd" ETs are an off-world race that has entered into agreements with clandestine organizations in which advanced technology is exchanged for the right to establish a presence on the planet and to collaborate on joint ET/human projects.

A secret Treaty signed in 1954 between the Eisenhower administration and an ET race has been disclosed by William Cooper and other "whistleblowers."[314] Cooper narrates the events surrounding this Treaty from classified documents he had to read when he served in Naval Intelligence as part of the briefing team to the Commander of the Pacific Fleet:

[I]n 1954 the race of large nosed Gray Aliens which had been orbiting the Earth landed at Holloman Air Force

Base. A basic agreement was reached. This race identified themselves as originating from a Planet around a red star in the Constellation of Orion which we called Betelgeuse. They stated that their planet was dying and that at some unknown future time they would no longer be able to survive there. This led to a second landing at Edwards Air Force Base. The historical event had been planned in advance and details of the treaty had been agreed upon. Eisenhower arranged to be in Palm Springs on vacation. On the appointed day the President was spirited away to the base and the excuse was given to the press that he was visiting a dentist. President Eisenhower met with the aliens and a formal treaty between the Alien Nation and the United States of America was signed.[315]

Alluding to the same treaty signed by the Eisenhower administration, Col. Phillip Corso, a highly decorated officer who served in Eisenhower's National Security Council, wrote: "We had negotiated a kind of surrender with them as long as we couldn't fight them. They dictated the terms because they knew what we most feared was disclosure."[316]

The technology exchange directly aids the development of highly advanced weapons systems that US-based clandestine organizations desire in order to maintain influence, to contend with and limit the ET presence, and to compete against one another for strategic advantage around the globe. This sub-group is typically described as comprising "small Grays" from Zeta Reticulum and/or "tall Grays" from Orion who desire to use the resources of humanity and the biosphere for reestablishing the genetic integrity of their race.

According to Col. Corso, the Grays "weren't benevolent alien beings who had come to enlighten humans. They . . . were harvesting biological specimens on Earth for their own experimentation."[317] This sub-group loosely cooperates with the first sub-group in encouraging the development of a centralized world government that would enter into agreements with this sub-group where it could better utilize human and planetary resources.

The first sub-group desires a one world government because of the greater efficiency it provides for their management of global humanity. The second sub-group desires it since it is more consistent with their philosophical belief that the interests of the individual are subsumed by the needs of the collective.

The third sub-group comprises two races that share a more pessimistic view concerning human capabilities for being in charge of the planet's resources. Historically they have formed an alliance in controlling humanity. The first is a very large humanoid race that is described in the book of Genesis as the Nephilim (literally giants) who impregnated human females who then gave birth to giants.[318]

This race is reported to originate from the constellation of Lyra and inhabits the mysterious planet Nibiru (Sumerian for 'planet of crossing') that, according to Sitchin's translations of Sumerian documents, returns every 3,600 years to this vicinity of the solar system.[319]

The second race is described as a Reptilian species from the Draco system of Orion who are genetically related to Earth based Reptilians but are more dominant and advanced technologically.[320] The two races of this sub-group correspond to the Enlil faction of the Anunnaki described by Sitchin in his translations of Sumerian texts. This sub-group of "good shepherd" ETs is very hierarchical in nature and views the domination of one species over others as being the most natural and efficient way of managing planetary resources.

Their racial world view is very similar to that held in Nazi Germany and it is argued that this "good-shepherd sub-group" assisted some of the elites of Nazi Germany to escape from the allied invasion to Antarctica and other regions in the South Atlantic, where they established secret bases.[321]

The self-serving agenda of this third sub-group of "good shepherd" ETs is to encourage militaristic responses among different clandestine organizations that destabilize global humanity by channeling resources and influence into the military-industrial complexes of different nations, causing these clandestine organizations to overextend themselves by sparking overt military conflict with the Gray Zeta ET race (second sub-group of "good shepherd" ETs).

Such a scenario is evident in Col. Corso's revelation that for "over fifty years, now, the war against UFO's [Zeta Grays] has continued as we tried to defend ourselves against their intrusions."[322] An escalating military confrontation between Zeta ETs and clandestine organizations could eventually culminate in intervention by the third sub-group of "good shepherd" ETs—Draco Reptilians/Giant humanoids who correspond to the Enlil faction of the Anunnaki.

The intervention by Anunnaki-Enlil faction of "good shepherd ETs" would occur as global environmental upheavals and/or military conflict with the Zetas occur to the extent that this provides these two ET races the opportunity to intervene as "saviors" of humanity and the "returning Elohim."[323]

With the advanced holographic, time travel and shape shifting abilities that have been reported to belong to this ET race, it could contrive a "Second Coming" comprising a genetically manufactured "Jesus" accompanied by the "Ascended Masters" and the "Angelic Host" that would be celebrated by religious adherents as the start of the Kingdom of God.[324] Posing as saviors, these two allied ET races, Draco Reptilians/giant humanoids, would essentially take over a weakened global humanity after a series of catastrophic environmental and military events and usher in an "era of peace" under a united world government whose leadership is overtly controlled by this sub-group of the "good-shepherd" ETs. They would be helped by the other two losing "good shepherd" sub-groups in preventing other ET factions from assisting global humanity in its predicament.

In general, ETs in the first and third sub-groups of the "good shepherd" category desire non-disclosure of the ET presence and go to great lengths to intimidate, silence and eliminate individuals who have participated in clandestine organizations from revealing the full extent of their activities. The main goal of all sub-groups in the "good shepherd" ET category is to "harvest" the resources of humanity without comprising the integrity of the biosphere and ET control over the evolution of global humanity.

Thus the moral orientation of the "good shepherd" ET in general is analogous to the historical way in which colonial governments dominated and assimilated indigenous communities. Although the three sub-groups of the "good shepherd" faction are strategic competitors over who exercises control over global humanity, they share a common interest in restricting the sovereignty and independence of the human species so that it can be used as a global resource. The first two sub-groups (Earth based Reptilians & Zeta Grays) would lose some of their influence in controlling humanity if the Draco Reptilians/Giant Humanoids were to assume outright control of humanity, but they would lose even more of their ability to influence and control humanity if the next ET faction were to intervene. This motivates a loose alliance between these three sub-groups of the "good shepherd" ET faction.

Protective Parent ETs

The second analogy to be used to describe the motivations and activities of a distinct category of ET races is the "protective parent" model. The "protective parent" ET category wishes to shield humanity as an "adolescent race" as far as possible from the dangers that exist for humanity as a maturing race. ETs in this category have a moral orientation of helping humanity become aware of the presence of other ET races throughout the galaxy and to cooperate with these races in an alliance often described by whistleblowers and other sources as the Galactic Federation.[325]

The Galactic Federation depicted in the Star Trek series is a fairly close approximation of how these ET races are organized. There is a respect for the sovereignty of humanity and a desire to help humanity unite and integrate advanced technology in order for it to be ready for accession to the Galactic Federation as explained by Jamisson Neruda, who claims to be a defector from a clandestine organization embedded in the National Security Agency:

> Each galaxy has a Federation or loose-knit organization that includes all sentient life forms on every planet within the galaxy. It would be the equivalent of the United Nations of the galaxy. This Federation has both

invited members and observational members. Invited members are those species that have managed to behave in a responsible manner as stewards of their planet and combine both the technology, philosophy, and culture that enable them to communicate as a global entity that has a unified agenda. Observational members are species who are fragmented and are still wrestling with one another over land, power, money, culture, and a host of other things that prevent them from forming a unified world government. The human race on planet earth is such a species, and for now, it is simply observed by the Federation, but is not invited into its policymaking and economic systems.[326]

These ET races do not enter into agreements for providing advanced technology for weapons programs by clandestine organizations. This places them at a considerable disadvantage to "good shepherd" races. It has been recorded, for example, that a meeting between President Eisenhower and representatives of these races in 1953 (before the 1954 Treaty with the Zeta/Orion ET group) did not lead to an agreement since these ET races believed humanity was too immature for the technology desired; and that nuclear weaponry, for instance, should be destroyed.[327] William Cooper describes in some detail the events surrounding this meeting:

> In the meantime a race of human looking aliens contacted the U.S. Government. This alien group warned us against the aliens that were orbiting the Equator [those who Eisenhower eventually signed a Treaty with] and offered to help us with our spiritual development. They demanded that we dismantle and destroy our nuclear weapons as the major condition. They refused to exchange technology citing that we were spiritually unable to handle the technology which we then possessed. They believed that we would use any new technology to destroy each other.
>
> This race stated that we were on a path of self destruction and we must stop killing each other, stop polluting the

Earth, stop raping the Earth's natural resources, and learn to live in harmony. These terms were met with extreme suspicion, especially the major condition of nuclear disarmament. It was believed that meeting that condition would leave us helpless in the face of an obvious alien threat . . . Nuclear disarmament was not considered to be within the best interest of the United States. The overtures were rejected.[328]

The protective "parent ET" races spend considerable time assisting various human organizations to counter the agendas of "good shepherd" ET races that are actively trying to control global humanity for the purpose of harvesting the resources of humanity and the planet. This category of ETs promotes an agenda of full disclosure of the ET presence, and is dedicated to serving the best interests of humanity as viewed from the lens of a "protective parent" that served as a biological source for humanity.[329]

Thus the "protective parent" ETs correspond more closely to the Enki faction of the Anunnaki described in Sitchin's translations of Sumerian cuneiform texts. Some of the ET races that fall into this category are typically described as the Nordics (Lyra), Sirians (Sirius B), Pleiadians, Altairians, and Alpha Centaurians.[330]

Two sub-groups can be identified in the testimonies of those having had contact or witnessed evidence of ETs in the Protective Parent category. The first is an on-world presence of humanoid races that have historically assisted humanity in its evolutionary development. Such a race has been argued by a number of authors to be the remnants of the ancient Lemurian and Atlantean civilizations that established large crystalline cities inside the Earth's crust after abandoning their cities/civilizations established on the Earth's surface.[331]

In a secretive flight to the Artic Ocean in 1947, Admiral Richard Byrd reported in his diary—whose veracity continues to be debated[332]—of his encounter with an ancient humanoid race in a subterranean city under the North Pole:

The radioman and I are taken from the aircraft and we are received in a most cordial manner. We were then

boarded on a small platform-like conveyance with no
wheels! It moves us toward the glowing city with great
swiftness. As we approach, the city seems to be made of
a crystal material. Soon we arrive at a large building that
is a type I have never seen before. It appears to be right
out of . . . a Buck Rogers setting!! We are given some
type of warm beverage which tasted like nothing I have
ever savored before. It is delicious. After about ten minutes, two of our wondrous appearing hosts come to our
quarters and announce that I am to accompany them. I
have no choice but to comply. I leave my radioman
behind and we walk a short distance and enter into what
seems to be an elevator. We descend downward for
some moments, the machine stops, and the door lifts
silently upward! We then proceed down a long hallway
that is lit by a rose-colored light that seems to be emanating from the very walls themselves! One of the beings
motions for us to stop before a great door . . . I step
inside and my eyes adjust to the beautiful coloration that
seems to be filling the room completely. Then I begin to
see my surroundings. What greeted my eyes is the most
beautiful sight of my entire existence. It is in fact too
beautiful and wondrous to describe. It is exquisite and
delicate. I do not think there exists a human term that can
describe it in any detail with justice![333]

Strictly speaking, this sub-group is not extra-terrestrial in
origin but simply a sub-terrestrial humanoid race that is genetically linked to humanity. A number of archeologists/historians
believe these ancient advanced races are the basis of numerous myths concerning the intervention of mysterious "white
brothers/gods" in the development of civilization around the
planet.[334] The Aztecs and Incans, for example, at first believed
the Spanish Conquistadors were their returning "white brothers/
gods."[335] These sub-surface Lemurian cities continue to interact with ET races, have advanced technology and assist humanity in dealing with its myriad of social, economic, political and
environment problems. Sources describe the psychotronic

crystal technology used by these Lemurian sub-surface cities, and the efforts to promote this technology for peaceful purposes.[336]

This sub-group race loosely cooperates with the first sub-group of the "good shepherd" ET faction (Earth based Reptilians) in ensuring that humanity doesn't destroy its surface habitat. However, they are strategic competitors when it comes to the evolutionary development of humanity which this sub-group (Lemurians/Atlanteans) supports but which the Earth based Reptilians restrict.

It is this loose alliance of Earth based ET races that influences/controls the leadership of the secret societies that have historically dominated humanity. Thus the leadership of Freemasons, Illuminati, Knights Templars, etc., all reflect a loose cooperation by terrestrially based ET races that share common interests in preventing global catastrophe on the planet, but differ profoundly over the evolution of the human species and whether "off-world" ET races should intervene on Earth.[337]

The second sub-group in the Protective Parent model is off-world ETs that intervene to assist humanity in dealing with off-world ET races. This category is commonly described as "Nordics" and "Semites" that come from Sirius B, Pleiades, Altair, Alpha Centauri, and Andromeda. They are humanoid in appearance, between 7–8 feet in height, and have an interventionist strategy in dealing with the destabilizing strategies of the second and third ET sub-groups from the "good shepherd" faction. In an interview with Dr. Michael Wolf, a former National Security Council consultant who became part of the new "acclimation" program, Dr. Richard Boylan reports as follows:

Wolf was nonchalant about such human-extraterrestrial interactions, having himself worked side by side in classified government laboratories with a human-appearing ET from the Altair system and a "Grey" humanoid scientist from the Zeta Reticuli system. "Altair's fourth and fifth planets are inhabited. In fact, the people from Altair colonized the Pleiades system long ago. The human-looking Pleiadean extraterrestrials some people meet are actually ancestrally Altairians. There are two variants, the Semitic-looking ones and the Nordic-looking ones. The 'Semitics' are the race which landed at Holloman Air Force Base (New Mexico) in the '60s, and conversed with some generals there."[338]

Some of the ways in which these "Nordic/Semite" ETs assist humanity is, for example, to counter the harmful environmental effects of advanced weapons technology developed and deployed by clandestine organizations. Also, significant terrorist actions sponsored by the "good shepherd" ET faction, are presumably mitigated or prevented by Nordic/Semite races.[339]

For instance, terrorist actions subsequent to the September 11, 2001 attack may have been prevented by covert assistance from these races to security forces around the planet, thereby helping to stabilize Earth's security situation.

These Nordic/Semite off-world ETs do not enter into agreements with clandestine governments in terms of weapons technology, but do assist in encouraging the development of advanced technology which does not have a military application. Dr. Wolf, for example, witnessed a tall "Nordic/Semitic" race in joint ET/Clandestine government facilities that presumably worked on non-weapons related technology.[340] Individuals describe the positive experiences they have in interacting with these ET races as opposed to the more intimidating experiences with the "good shepherd" ET races.[341] This sub-group is essentially a strategic counter weight to the influence of the off-world elements of the "good shepherd" faction. The "off world good shepherd" sub-groups view the off-world "protective parent" ET sub-group as its mortal enemy, since the latter presents a threat to the ability of the former to intervene and control humanity as a resource.

Wise Mentor ETs

The third analogy to be used to describe ET control and influence is the "wise mentor" category. These races have a hands-off approach to global humanity and only offer assistance if it is in the best interest of all concerned in such an intervention. They promote "consciousness raising" and have a moral orientation that is deeply spiritual insofar as they present the unity of all life, and the importance of honoring the role of all forces in the evolutionary development of humanity.

They do not offer technology in the conventional sense but a highly advanced "language of light" technology consisting of sacred geometrical forms that are simultaneously found throughout the universe, in the atom, and the human energy field. They teach that understanding the sacred geometrical light patterns in all life will lead to the emancipation of individuals and life on the planet.[342]

Wise mentor ETs do not directly confront and counter the influence of "good shepherd" ET races, which differentiates this category from the "protective parent." Indeed, "wise mentor" ETs warn against the implicit dangers of intervention since this may retard the evolutionary growth of humanity.

Put simply, the wise mentor ETs view the hard knocks of humanity's encounter with "good shepherd" ETs as part of the evolutionary process for a species and thus do not intervene. In contrast, protecting humanity from the "hard knocks" of humanity's encounter with "good shepherd" ETs is an important goal of "protective parent" ETs.

The philosophical issues here are the same confronting an "energy healer" in preventive medicine. If the alternative medical practitioner healed the illness without active collaboration by the patient, then the patient recovers but would be susceptible to future recurrences. The accomplished alternative medical practitioner, however, simply demonstrates to the patient how to heal themselves, thereby minimizing the chances of future recurrences.[343]

Two sub-groups of the "wise mentor" faction are generally described as direct off-shoots of non-physical beings from a higher dimensional reality who projected form into the dimension/density that humanity occupies.[344] The first are non-humanoid races that are claimed to derive from Arcturus, Sirius A and parts of the Orion constellation. According to Dr. J.J. Hurtak, these beings form a hierarchy similar to that described in religious texts concerning angelic orders of the Seraphim and Cherubim.[345]

The second are described by Lyssa Royal and Jamisson Neruda as the "Founding" or "Central" Race that seeded the Galaxy untold millennia ago.[346]

The first sub-group, according to Hurtak, comprises "Councils" that interact with receptive humans and organizations to offer assistance and guidance when requested.[347] Most evidence for the existence of such ET Councils comes from reports of telepathic communications with these beings who typically are described as having a mixture of humanoid features and birdlike or catlike heads. It appears that these beings may have been the inspirational source for ancient Egyptian sculptures depicting humans with animal heads such as the "god" Thoth, who had the head of an Ibis (a native Egyptian bird).

The second sub-group is described variously as the "Founding" or "Central Race" that presumably gave humanity its original genetic form. According to Lyssa Royal and Keith Priest, the "Founding Race" plays the role of "parental archetypes" for humanity's expression in male and female forms, and originally seeded humanity in the constellation of Lyra.[348]

According to Neruda, the Founding/Central race inhabits a region within the central galaxies of the universe and seeded the galaxies many billions of years ago. They left "subtle fingerprints" of their presence which if interpreted correctly, opens the door for different species to reestablish communication with them.[349]

Royal, Priest and Neruda all equate the Founding/Central Race with the Elohim of ancient religious texts, and argue that they act as silent helpers in the evolution of humanity for those who choose to "re-connect" with them. The idea of root races that seeded the Galaxy is found in "advisory bodies" such as the "Council of Nine" that offers spiritual counseling for the evolution of the human species according to individuals claiming to be in communication with them.[350]

Table 1. Summary of Motivations and Activities of Extraterrestrial Races

Category	Factions—Subgroups	Primary Agenda	Alliances/Conflicts
Good Shepherd	Earth Reptilians	Harvests human emotional energies	'Loose alliances' with Draco Reptilians and Gray races. Also cooperate with subterranean human races to prevent ecocide
	Grays—Zeta/Orion	Harvests human genetic material	Works with Earth based Reptilians. Zeta Grays often in conflict with Draco Reptilians
	Draco Reptilians (Orion)	Establishes control over Earth's resources	Exercises control over 'subordinate races' (humans and Earth based Reptilians). Often in conflict with Zeta Grays
	Giant Hominoids from Lyra/Nibiru	Most efficient use of Earth's resources	Cooperate with Draco Reptilians in ensuring most efficient use of Earth's resources
Protective Parent	Subterranean Humanoid Civilizations (Lemuria/Atlantis)	Assist surface humans to evolve as a species & deal with Earth based Reptilians	Conflict with Earth based Reptilians over evolution of (surface) human race, but cooperate with Reptilians in preventing destruction of ecosphere
	Humanoid ET Races (Sirius, Pleiades, Altair, etc.)	Assist surface humans to evolve as a species & deal best with ET races	Opposes efforts by Grays (short and tall) and Draco Reptilians in gaining control over humanity and earth
Wise Mentor	Non-humanoid races (Arcturus, Sirius A, Orion)	Offers advice to humanity in how to best deal with its evolutionary challenges	Encourages integrative solutions to human problems stemming from conflict between different ET races above, below and on the Earth's surface
	Humanoid—Formless (Central Race—center of Galaxy)	Provided initial genetic material for emergence of humanoid races in the planet Lyra and elsewhere	Seeds advanced technology/knowledge within planets whose discovery enables species to evolve in harmony with the biosphere

© Michael Salla, PhD, 2003.

The Structure of Clandestine Organizations

The key to understanding how the above ET categories influence clandestine organizations is that the latter are generally aware of the political, moral and philosophical orientations of the different ET races and of other clandestine organizations. Clandestine organizations therefore try to steer a cause through these various ET intervention philosophies and strategies. At the same time they cooperate and compete with one another in a way that maximizes the power of the clandestine organizations, without being unduly compromised by "infiltration" by the different ET factions/subgroups.

Thus for the respective leaders of clandestine organizations, a three dimensional chess game is occurring involving multiple players, theaters and goals that influence the dynamics within and between them.

Clandestine organizations focused on the ET presence first became established when various intelligence and military organizations became aware of the ET presence, at least from 1941, when a downed ET spacecraft was found in low ocean water west of San Diego.[351] The Navy took charge of the investigation and assumed a leading role which it continues to play up to the present.

This is supported by the testimonies of those claiming to have participated in clandestine experiments surrounding time/interdimensional travel as it first began to emerge into the public arena concerning the Philadelphia Experiment and later at Montauk, Long Island.[352] Subsequently, there emerged a need for public secrecy while an adequate policy response could be developed by the US government.

This led to the emergence of clandestine organizations embedded within various military, intelligence, and policy making branches of government, each of which have different though overlapping functions according to the larger goals of the department.

Members of the "parent department" are not aware of the full extent of activities and influences of these embedded clandestine organizations, even though they share the same overarching function.[353] For example, the three main branches of the US military—Navy, Army and Air force—have their own weapons development and intelligence departments all designed to ultimately protect the national security of the US.

Within each of these specialized departments is embedded a clandestine organization that is responsible for reverse engineering ET technology for the purpose of weapons development, and for gaining intelligence concerning ET operations on the planet, in order to develop an adequate defense policy.[354]

Thus the clandestine organization embedded in the US Navy, for example, will be unknown to other Naval units focused on broader issues concerning weapons development and intelligence gathering, and whose lower secrecy classification would make it a crime for Navy personnel to gather information about these clandestine organizations.[355] This effectively leads to clandestine organizations embedded in the Navy that are compartmentalized and have a degree of autonomy, power and resources unknown to personnel of the wider Navy even at senior leadership levels.

Former Air force Sergeant Dan Sherman describes the way clandestine organizations are embedded in various military/intelligence organizations without being discovered by prying congressmen. In recalling a Captain's briefing to him, Sherman wrote:

> Black missions, which we call Level 2, are what the alien projects are effectively hidden behind. The existence of black missions is only known by a handful of Congressmen and the President. These black missions are the last line of defense for the alien projects. Wherever an alien project is located there *must* be a black mission to cover its existence from prying eyes. It creates a highly sophisticated shield designed to mask the gray project's existence from high level officials who have no need-to-know. Otherwise, the alien project would eventually come under scrutiny by *someone* within official channels. As it stands under the current system, if a nosy Congressman starts looking where he has no need-to-know, he can be briefed on the black mission, be made to feel important and thereby squelching any further digging. It's an extremely effective

method of hiding alien missions and is the reason they have been hidden so effectively for so long.[356]

The National Security Agency was created in 1952; intelligence gathering was its primary responsibility. Within the NSA there is embedded a clandestine organization responsible for intelligence gathering on ET races and establishing communication with them.

According to Jamisson Neruda, the clandestine organization in the NSA is called the "Advanced Contact Intelligence Organization" (ACIO) and is embedded within the Special Projects Laboratory. As in the case of the US Navy, the larger membership of the NSA will be unaware of the true activities of ACIO due to its higher secrecy classification.

Sergeant Sherman recalls how when briefed by his captain that he was part of a secret NSA project called "Project Preserve Destiny" in which he was a result of an experiment designed to enhance telepathic communication with the "Gray" ET species:

> The experiment that I'm referring to was, and still is, named "Project Preserve Destiny." It started in 1960 and was fully operational by 1963. It was a genetic management project with the sole purpose of cultivating human offspring so that they would have the ability to communicate with the grays.[357]

The most important of all the clandestine organizations embedded in US government agencies is the one contained within the National Security Council (NSC). President Truman established the NSC in 1947 and its function was to coordinate policy recommendations from different branches of government, military and intelligence communities into a coherent set of policy recommendations from which Presidents can choose.[358]

This coordinating function played by the NSC in general is replicated in the clandestine organization embedded in the NSC, which has been known by a number of names, including Majestic-12 derived from a document signed by President Truman in 1947.[359]

Created by Truman as a Presidential policy coordinating committee on the ET presence, MJ-12 was formally incorporated into the NSC in 1954 with an NSC edict creating the parent organization in which MJ-12 would be embedded. The "official" version pertaining to this part of NSC history is as follows:

In 1954 NSC 5412 provided for the establishment of a panel of designated representatives of the President and the Secretaries of State and Defense to meet regularly to review and recommend covert operations. Gordon Gray assumed the chairmanship of the "5412 Committee" as it was called, and all succeeding National Security Advisers have chaired similar successor committees, variously named "303," "40," and "Special Coordinating Committee," which, in later Presidential administrations, were charged with the review of CIA covert operations.[360]

The 5412 Committee contains a subcommittee called PI-40 whose role is to coordinate information from all other clandestine organizations focused on the ET presence so those policy makers comprising PI-40 can develop a coherent set of policy choices for deliberation.[361] Clandestine organizations embedded in private organizations such as the Council of Foreign Affairs provide the best personnel and resources for recruitment and policy discussion in PI-40.

In describing the early composition of MJ-12, William Cooper, noted the reliance on a group from the Council on Foreign Relations he dubbed the "wise men":

The "Wise Men" were key members of the Council on Foreign Relations. There were 12 members including the first 6 from Government positions thus Majority Twelve. This group was made up over the years of the top officers and directors of the Council on Foreign Relations and later the Trilateral Commission. Gordon Dean, George Bush and Zbigniew Brzezinski were among them. The most important and influential of the "Wise Men" who served on MJ-12 were John McCloy,

Robert Lovett, Averell Harriman, Charles Bohlen, George Kennan, and Dean Acheson. Their policies were to last well into the decade of the 70s. It is significant that President Eisenhower as well as the first 6 MJ-12 members from the Government were also members of the Council on Foreign Relations.[362]

In theory then, PI-40 should be at the pinnacle of power when it comes to the ET presence employing the best minds for a coordinated response to the ET presence. In reality, however, due to bureaucratic resistance, separate agendas and "rogue individuals," different clandestine organizations are reluctant to share information that could compromise their power, resources or influence. This is illustrated in Jamisson Neruda's discussion of how the clandestine organization he claims to have been a member of, refuses to share its most important information with the parent organization, the NSA, in which it was embedded.[363]

As might be imagined, these problems are magnified even more at the global level when the chief clandestine organizations at the national level meet to discuss and coordinate global policy on the ET presence.

According to "whistleblower" testimony, the annual "Bilderberg group meeting" has embedded within it a clandestine organization whose express goal is to coordinate national policies concerning the ET presence. Dr. Richard Boylan outlines the origins and functions of Bilderberg based on his interviews with various whistleblower testimonies as follows:

Bilderberg was conceived in response to the 1952 ET repeated overflights of Washington, DC and the following year's meeting between President Eisenhower and ET representatives at what is now Edwards Air Force Base, CA. It is no coincidence that Walter Bedell Smith, President Eisenhower's CIA Director, was also his designee to the 1954 inaugural meeting of the Bilderberg Council. Bilderberg is an attempt for world leaders to draw together in concerted action to create a unified policy in world matters of peace, democracy, and coordinated preparation of world institutions and the populace for the massive changes which public disclosure of extraterrestrial presence will bring.[364]

Such a claim is given greater credence by the role played by Nelson Rockefeller in starting the annual Bilderberg group meetings. In 1954, President Eisenhower appointed Rockefeller his "Special Assistant for Cold War Planning," a position that officially involved the "monitoring and approval of covert CIA operations."

This was merely a cover for Rockefeller's true role in directing US foreign policy in the wake of the "secret treaty" earlier discussed between the Zeta/Orion ET race and the US. Rockefeller's main concern was to design, implement and monitor the extensive military and intelligence programs set up in response to the ET presence in general, and the formal treaty with the Zeta/Orion ET race.

Rockefeller played a key coordinating role in the clandestine organization, Majestic 12, embedded within the National Security Council. With the Bilderberg annual meeting, Rockefeller would play a similar role in ensuring that different Western bloc national governments would coordinate their resources in meeting both the challenge posed by the Warsaw Pact and the ET presence.

Although clandestine organizations should in theory operate in a similar fashion to their parent departments which coordinate and share resources for the overriding goal of protecting the National Security of the US, the truth is that these clandestine organizations cooperate to a minimal degree. Their cooperation is limited by perceptions of a zero-sum competition against one another for influence, prestige and resources.

For example, clandestine organizations in the Army, Navy and Air force working to integrate ET technology into weapons systems will be in competition over which weapons systems deserve funding and the perceived threats justifying such expenditure. Unlike the intense debate over conventional weapons that emerges into the public arena, debate over ET technology acquisition and deployment is highly classified.

The compartmentalized nature of these organizations, the security classification which puts them beyond congressional/departmental supervision for regular branches of government, the interaction with ET races and their technology, and the fierce interagency rivalries over funding for weapons acquisition, make these clandestine organizations prime targets for ET infiltration.

ET Infiltration of Clandestine Organizations

The infiltration of clandestine organizations occurs through technology exchange/development programs, and intelligence-gathering techniques which supposedly assist them in performing their specific functions, but which in reality make them susceptible to ET infiltration. One common technology used by these organizations which is highly questionable in terms of the degree to which this permits ET infiltration is "Brain Enhancement" Technology which, according to Dr. Wolf, "allows utilization of a vastly-increased percentage of the brain, in order for humans to mentally engage the extraterrestrials in full telepathic mental exchange."

The Treatment involves "a way of opening the brain up, a way to stimulate the neurons. It allows billions of synapses to form."[365] According to Dr. Wolf, he underwent a mental enhancement process where his IQ was raised from 141 to 186.[366] Similarly, Jamisson Neruda describes the Brain Enhancement technology used in the clandestine organization, Labyrinth, embedded in the NSA, and the expectation that all reaching a sufficiently high security classification were "invited to undertake the process."[367]

Al Bielak, a participant in the infamous Montauk program run by the US Navy, also reported the use of Brain enhancement technology by the NSA.[368] Rather than solely increasing IQ and brain capacities, such technology raises serious concerns over its capacity to program recipients in cognitive and behavioral patterns that support ET influence and infiltration into the highest policy making spheres.

The result of these numerous clandestine organizations having different functions and interactions with ET technology, is that this contributes to a high level of distrust and competition among clandestine organizations in the US which superficially cooperate but are suspicious to the degree to which ET infiltration has occurred with "partner" organizations. This ET infiltration problem is alluded to in Col. Phillip Corso's analysis of the relationship between the US military, the CIA and the intelligence services of other countries:

> The CIA, KGB, British Secret Service, and a whole host of other foreign intelligence agencies were loyal to themselves and to the profession first and to their respective governments last . . . Spy organizations like the CIA and the KGB tend to exist only to preserve themselves, and that's why neither the US military nor the Russian military trust them . . . CIA penetration by the KGB and what amounted to their joint spying on the military was a fact we accepted during the 1950s and 1960s . . .[369]

Although Corso was referring to the Cold War struggle, the ET focus of his book, *The Day After Roswell*, implicitly was suggesting this infiltration problem also applied to the ET interaction with different clandestine organizations. A revealing factor in Corso's comments is that institutional culture plays a role in how a clandestine organization may be infiltrated by different ET factions and sub-groups.

The different branches of the US military place an emphasis on loyalty, discipline, hierarchical decision making, and weapons development which makes them susceptible to ET races that share these values. Therefore it is likely that Reptilian sub-groups from the "Good Shepherd" ET category which have been noted to share these military cultures are likely to have infiltrated various branches of the US military.[370] This is supported by testimony by John Maynard, former military intelligence analyst with the Defense Intelligence Agency:

> I came to the conclusion that something was not quite right between the aliens and the people who were in contact with them. Not so much that it was stated

outright, but just something that was said while I was doing background checks on cross-referenced documents. Also, in statements made during conversations with several fellow workers and my friends who worked at Area 51, it became obvious that all was not right at Groom Lake [Nevada Army Facility].

Furthermore, other discreet conversations had indications that there was a confrontation going on between higher authority and those that had daily contact with the aliens. However, I never learned exactly what the problems were. All I could grasp from the conversations was that there definitely was a confrontation of some kind. I have continued my research on this and believe that it is still going on today, but in a more heated sense, such as armed belligerence on both sides, with a much smaller alien presence.[371]

Maynard is suggesting here that rogue clandestine organizations, most likely infiltrated by good shepherd ETs, were operating independent of centralized control by policy coordinating organizations such as MJ-12/PI-40. This sometimes resulted in armed military conflict between different factions of the US military, presumably those under centralized control and those infiltrated by ET races.

Aside from intra-US military aggression, there is evidence that infiltration also manifested itself in extremely aggressive behavior by sectors of the US military towards the Zeta Gray race. That such infiltration has occurred is supported by testimony by Dr. Wolf in an interview by Dr. Richard Boylan concerning a group he calls the "cabal":

Wolf has labeled this conspiratorial group of plotters "The Cabal." Made up of extremist, fundamentalist, xenophobic, racist, and paranoiac officers, the Cabal fears and hates extraterrestrials. And, without any Presidential or Congressional authorization, the Cabal has commandeered Star Wars weaponry to shoot down UFOs, taken surviving extraterrestrials prisoner, and attempted to extract information by force.[372]

Confirmation that a secret war using highly advanced technology is being conducted by sections of the US military against the Zeta comes from Col. Steve Wilson, a highly decorated military officer who claims to have led a clandestine project (Project Pounce) to retrieve downed ET craft.[373] Intelligence services such as the CIA and NSA, which focus on the intelligence gathering, dissemination of information and establishing communication with different ET races, are more susceptible to infiltration by Zeta Grays who share certain aspects of this institutional culture.[374]

The extent to which these clandestine organizations have been compromised by "good shepherd" ETs is evident in whistleblower testimonies such as Phil Schneider's. Schneider witnessed the secret joint underground facilities between humans and ETs, and the key role played by these ETs in the establishment of a New World Order.[375]

Schneider described how the clandestine organization he worked for was compromised by "tall Grays"/"Reptilians" and how they were preparing for a "one world government."[376] There are also testimonies of a number of former participants in clandestine programs that involved joint ET/human collaboration in testing and developing new technologies in organizations embedded in the Navy, Army and Air force.[377]

According to Stewart Swerdlow and other participants in a highly classified series of projects led by the US Navy dubbed the "Montauk Project," clandestine organizations involved in kidnapping US citizens for mind control experiments are collaborating with Gray/Reptilian ETs in trying to learn more about human emotional and behavioral responses and developing advanced time/interdimensional technologies.[378] Finally, Bill Cooper believes that a joint human/ET power structure exists which has an agenda for the total control over human institutions and populations.[379]

The "protective parent" ET races have a distinct disadvantage in dealing with clandestine organizations since their unwillingness to exchange technology that has a military application, and indeed restrictions on the use of advanced weaponry leads to them having limited influence with clandestine organizations. As mentioned earlier, a meeting between

President Eisenhower and this faction of humanoid ETs resulted in failure due to a disagreement over the utility of the US nuclear military program.[380] Subsequently, "protective parent" races focus their efforts on minimizing the chances of global warfare breaking out, minimizing the harmful effects of advanced weapons testing, preventing the destabilizing agendas of "good shepherd" ETs from succeeding; and countering the infiltration of "good shepherd" ETs into key clandestine organizations.[381]

The influence of "wise mentor" races on clandestine organizations is even more limited, since their spiritual counseling has only limited appeal to clandestine organizations as bureaucratic institutions locked into a zero-sum conflict for power, resources and influence. Dr. Neruda claims in his interviews that he was forced to defect from the clandestine organization embedded in the NSA, since the spiritual counseling by the "central race" in the form of philosophy, art and music was deemed to be insufficient for offering the sort of weapons technology necessary for defense against ET intervention.

When Neruda was suspected of being under the influence of this "wise mentor race," he had to defect or risk having invasive memory technologies applied that would remove all knowledge of the interaction he had with this race. The influence of these "wise mentor" races does appear to have a significant impact on those individuals in clandestine organizations that open themselves to the influence of the former.[382] They become progressive forces for public disclosure of the ET presence through a gradual acclimation program, and for a more benign military response to ET interventions, yet they remain in the minority in the policy making process.[383]

Conclusion: Responding to ET Infiltration in Clandestine Organizations

The compartmentalized nature of clandestine organizations with their specialized functions concerning technology exchange, intelligence gathering and development of advanced weaponry, makes them vulnerable to infiltration by ET races that do not serve the highest interest of global humanity as an evolving species. The danger of such infiltration is that policy making at the national and global level concerning the ET presence is skewed to serve the interest of a particular faction of ETs termed the "good shepherd," whose agenda is to utilize humanity and the biosphere (Earth) as a resource base for the agendas of the different ET sub-groups in the "good shepherd" category.

Those ET groups who can play a more supportive role in the development of global humanity ("protective parent" and "wise mentor" ET factions) are marginalized in the policy making process due to the manner in which clandestine organizations are dominated by interests dedicated to technology acquisition and intelligence gathering.

The danger of maintaining such a focus is that it will play into the hands of "good shepherd" ETs intent on "harvesting" humanity as a resource while marginalizing those ET groups that can offer better assistance to global humanity in its evolution as a distinct species. The following policies therefore need to be implemented:

- Full disclosure of the ET presence to allow public awareness of the different ET factions and the extent to which these have influenced clandestine organizations.
- Supervision of all clandestine organizations and operations concerning ETs by specially convened congressional/legislative bodies designed to illicit information on the scope and implications of these technologies and activities.
- Full and open diplomatic relations with ET representatives ensuring peaceful relations and interactions between global humanity and ET races.
- Elimination of clandestine weapons programs infiltrated by "good shepherd" ETs whose intent is to destabilize national governments and encourage military responses to the ET presence.
- Transparency in all global policy making in organizations such as the Bilderberg group that attempts to coordinate global policy on the ET presence.

• Monitoring of mental enhancement technologies in terms of the extent to which they compromise the independence of individuals assuming important leadership positions in dealing with the ET presence.

ET infiltration of clandestine organizations needs to be recognized as a phenomenon that requires immediate response specifically by policy makers and in general by global humanity. Such infiltration makes it difficult if not impossible to effectively coordinate national and/or global policy making concerning the ET presence, regardless of the competency of those playing a coordinating role for all clandestine organizations dealing with this presence.

Hesitation in developing an adequate response to such infiltration threatens the short-term sovereignty of global humanity and indeed the long-term presence of humanity as a resident species on this planet. Truth, transparency and close supervision of all activities concerning ETs is the best course for policy makers and global humanity in the challenges that lie ahead for integrating the technologies, knowledge and possibilities posed by the ET presence.

Notes

290. Many thanks to Susan Burton, aka Elizabeth O'Rourke, for her editorial assistance in proofreading and editing an earlier version of this chapter.

291. See Michael Wolf, *Catchers of Heaven: A Trilogy* (Dorrance Publishing Co., 1996); Dan Sherman, *Above Black: Project Preserve Destiny* (Oneteam Press, 1997); Stewart Swerdlow, *Montauk: The Alien Connection* (Expansions Publishing Co. 2002); Preston Nichols & Peter Moon, *Montauk Revisited: Adventures in Synchronicity* (Sky Books, 1991); Wade Gordon, *The Brookhaven Connection* (Sky Books, 2001). See also Steven Greer, *Military and Government Witnesses Reveal the Greatest Secrets in Modern History* (Crossing Point Pub., 2001). A collection of interviews of an individual who claims to be a high level defector, Dr. Neruda, from a Clandestine Organization embedded within the National Security Agency is available online at: http://www.wingmakers.com. For websites that have links to articles by a number of former government participants go to: http://www.drboylan.com.

292. See Stephen Greer, *Executive Summary of the Disclosure Project* (Crozet, VA.: Disclosure Project, April 2001). Website: www.disclosureproject.com.

293. For a discussion of the different sources of evidence on the ET presence, see Chapter One. For the most detailed online source for whistleblower testimonies, go to: http://www.disclosureproject.com.

294. For an in-depth discussion of this phenomenon of ET experience, see C.D.B. Bryan, *Close Encounters of the Fourth Kind: Alien Abduction, UFOs, and the Conference at M.I.T* (Alfred Knopf, New York, 1995); John E. Mack, *Human Encounters with Aliens* (Ballantine Books, 1994); Linda Moulton Howe & Jacques Vallee, *Alien Harvest: Further Evidence Linking Animal Mutilations and Human Abductions to Alien Life Forms* (Linda Moulton Howe, 1993).

295. For analysis of different evidentiary sources for ETs, see Chapter One.

296. For reference to a secret government acclimation program, see Richard Boylan, "Government's Unacknowledged Acclimation Program," available online at: http://www.drboylan.com/aclmatn2.html. For a 1990 document purporting to describe an official acclimation program, see: http://www.swa-home.de/acclima.htm.

297. Sitchin's translations are compiled in six books called the *Earth Chronicles* (Avon Books).

298. Sitchin, *The 12th Planet: Book 1 of the Earth Chronicles* (Avon Books, 1976) pages 336–61.

299. See Carl Jung, *The Archetypes and the Collective Unconscious: Collected Works of C.G. Jung*, Vol. 9, Pt. 1 (Princeton University Press, 1981).

300. Sitchin, *The 12th Planet*, 381–86.

301. For online version of the *Book of Enoch*, go to: http://wesley.nnu.edu/noncanon/ot/pseudo/enoch.htm.

302. See Neruda interviews: http://www.wingmakers.com.

303. For various lists of ET races, see Richard Boylan, "The Various Kinds of Star Visitors," available online at: http://www.drboylan.com/etraces.html. See also, Boylan, "Official Within MJ-12 UFO-Secrecy Management Group Reveals Insider Secrets," in Boylan and Boylan, *Labored Journey To The Stars*. Available online at: http://www.drboylan.com/wolfdoc2.html; see also Robert Dean, Interview: http://www.extraterrestrial-aliens.com/32.htm; see also: http://www.extraterrestrial-aliens.com.

304. Thomas Hobbes, *Leviathan* (Oxford University Press, 1998).

305. David Icke, *Alice in Wonderland and the World Trade Center Disaster* (Bridge of Love Publications, 2002).

306. Faust was a German professor in plays by Thomas Marlow and Goethe who surrendered his soul to the Devil in order to gain worldly fame. The strongest advocate of this relationship between Good

Shepherd ETs and the global elite view is David Icke, *The Biggest Secret: The Book That Will Change the World*, 2nd ed. (Bridge of Love Publications, 1999).

307. See Manetho, Manetho, tr., Waddell (Harvard University Press, 1940).

308. Jim Marrs, *Rule by Secrecy: The Hidden History that Connects the Trilateral Commission, the Freemasons, and the Great Pyramids* (Perennial 2001); David Icke, *The Biggest Secret*.

309. See William Bramley, *Gods of Eden* (Avon, 1989); and R. A. Boulay, *Flying Serpents and Dragons: The Story of Mankind's Reptilian Past* (Book Tree, 1999). For an online interview of an individual who met a delegation of this sub-group of "good shepherd" ETs, see Linda Moulton Howe, "Interview with Jim Sparx," *Nexus* magazine, 7: 2 (2000). Available online at: http://www.nexusmagazine.com/jimsparx.html.

310. See Linda Moulton Howe, "Interview with Jim Sparx," *Nexus* magazine, 7:2 (2000): http://www.nexusmagazine.com/jimsparx.html.

311. Evidence of ancient warfare that must have destroyed entire civilizations is discussed by David Hatcher Childress, *Technology of the Gods: The Incredible Sciences of the Ancients* (Adventures Unlimited Press, 2000).

312. See Janetta Rebold Benton, *Holy Terrors: Gargoyles on Medieval Buildings* (Abbeville Press, 1997); Darlene Trew Crist & Robert Llewellyn, *American Gargoyles: Spirits in Stone* (Clarkson N. Potter, 2001).

313. Phil Schneider, MUFON Conference Presentation, 1995, available online at: http://www.ufocoverup-conspiracy.com/20.htm. For description of his sighting of 12 tall grays/reptilians, see the *Mars Record*, p. 301, online at: http://www.metatech.org/TheMarsRecords.pdf.

314. See Richard Boylan, "Official Within MJ-12 UFO-Secrecy Management Group Reveals Insider Secrets," available online at: http://www.drboylan.com/wolfdoc2.html; William Cooper, "Origin, Identity and Purpose of MJ-12," in *Behold A Pale Horse* (Light Technology Publications, 1991), available online at: http://www.geocities.com/area51/shadowlands/6583/maji007.html; and Phil Schneider, MUFON Conference Presentation, 1995, available online at: http://www.ufocoverup-conspiracy.com/20.htm; see Neruda Interview #1: http://www.wingmakers.com; Boylan gives a more extensive coverage of events surrounding the Treaty signing in "Extraterrestrial Base On Earth, Sanctioned By Officials Since 1954," in Boylan and Boylan, *Labored Journey To The Stars*. Available online at: http://drboylan.com/basespst2.html.

315. Cooper, "Origin, Identity and Purpose of MJ-12,"—paper delivered at MUFON Conference 1989, available online at: http://www.geocities.com/Area51/Shadowlands/6583/maji007.html.

316. Phillip Corso, *The Day After Roswell* (Pocket Books, 1997) p. 292.

317. Corso, *The Day After Roswell*, p. 292.

318. See "Genesis," Bk. 6, any edition of Holy Bible.
319. See Sitchin, *The 12th Planet.*
320. For discussion of Draco technology, see Stewart Swerdlow, *Montauk the Alien Connection*, pages 137–43; see also Courtney Brown, *Cosmic Explorers: Scientific Remote Viewing, Extraterrestrials, and a Message for Mankind* (Signet 2000), pages 170–202.
321. For information on Operation Paperclip, see Linda Hunt, *Secret Agenda: The United States Government, Nazi Scientists, and Project Paperclip, 1945 to 1990* (St. Martin's Press, 1991); and *Clarence G. Lasby, Project Paperclip: German Scientists and the Cold War* (Scribner, 1975). For online discussion of Operation Paperclip, see "Secrets of the Third Reich": http://www.violations.dabsol.uk/secrets/secretspart2.htm.
322. Corso, *The Day After Roswell*, p. 290.
323. For more detailed discussion of these scenarios, see Michael E. Salla, "Exopolitical Comment #6." Available online at: http://www.exopolitics.org.
324. For discussion on a manufactured Christ, see Stewart Swerdlow, *Montauk: The Alien Connection*, pages 145–52. For discussion of time travel and holographic technologies of ETs and clandestine organizations, see: Preston Nichols & Peter Moon, *Montauk Revisited*; Wade Gordon, *The Brookhaven Connection*; and Neruda Interviews, #3, pages 1–3: http://www.wingmakers.com; see also the following interview with Bob Lazar, which discusses time travel: http://www.swa-home.de/lazar3.htm; and see Dr. Boylan, "U.S. Government, Dimensional Portals and Dr. Wen Ho Lee": http://drboylan.com/wenhlee2.html.
325. See Richard Boylan, "Further Disclosures by Wolf," in Boylan and Boylan, *Labored Journey To The Stars*. Available online at: http://www.drboylan.com/wlflkla.html. See also "Neruda Interview" #1, pages 24–25: http://www.wingmakers.com.
326. #1, pages 24–25; http://www.wingmakers.com.
327. See William Cooper, "The Secret Government: Origin, Identity and Purpose of MJ-12," in *Behold a Pale Horse*, pages 195–238; and available online at: http://www.geocities.com/Area51/Shadowlands/6583/maji007.html. See also Michael Wolf, *The Catchers of Heaven*; and Richard Boylan, "Official Within MJ-12 UFO-Secrecy Management Group Reveals Insider Secrets," available online at: http://www.drboylan.com/wolfdoc2.html.
328. Cooper, *Behold A Pale Horse*, p. 202. Also cited online at: http://www.geocities.com/Area51/Shadowlands/6583/maji007.html.
329. Stephen Greer, director of the Disclosure Project, claims to have made contact with this group of ETs through his efforts in establishing communication protocols for advanced ET races. Go to: http://www.cseti.org.

330. For descriptions of these ET races, see Richard Boylan, "The Various Kinds of Star Visitors," available online at: http://www.drboylan.com/etraces.html; and Boylan, "Official Within MJ-12 UFO-Secrecy Management Group Reveals Insider Secrets," available online at: http://www.drboylan.com/wolfdoc2.html; see also Robert Dean, Interview, http://www.extraterrestrial-aliens.com/32.htm; see also Al Bielak 1991, Interview: http://www.bielak.com; and also: http://www.extraterrestrial-aliens.com.

331. For a history of Atlantis and Lemuria, see Rudolf Steiner, *Atlantis and Lemuria* (Fredonia Books, 2002). See subterranean cities, see Raymond Bernard, *The Hollow Earth: The Greatest Geographical Discovery in History* (Carol Pub Group, 1991). For online information on subterranean cities, go to: http://www.crystalinks.com/agartha.html.

332. For online information on Admiral Byrd, go to: http://www.crystalinks.com/agartha.html. For a critique of the veracity of Admiral Byrd's diary, see Dennis Crenshaw, "The Missing Secret Diary of Admiral Byrd: Fact or Fiction?" *The Hollow Earth Insider*, June 22, 2001. Available online at: http://www.thehollowearthinsider.com/news/wmview.php?ArtID=6.

333. Richard Byrd, *The Missing Diary of Admiral Richard Byrd* (Inner Light Publications, 1992). Admiral Byrd's Diary is available online at: http://www.v-j-enterprises.com/byrdiar.html.

334. See David Hatcher Childress, *Technology of the Gods: The Incredible Sciences of the Ancients* (Adventures Unlimited Press, 2000).

335. See Carlos Mata, *God's Way* (Morris Publishing, 2002).

336. For descriptions of these interactions with ancient Lemurians, see the online material by Don and Carol Croft, http://www.educate-yourself.com.

337. For discussion on the history of clandestine organizations, see Jim Marrs, *Rule By Secrecy*; and David Icke, *And The Truth Shall Set You Free*, pages 221–38. Jamisson Neruda gives extensive discussion of the organization of clandestine organizations in Interview #4 9-40. He divides these into three main groups: Isolationists/Illuminati (economic power—e.g., Bilderbergs); Military power, e.g., Council of Foreign Relations; Tavistock Institute; and the Icunabala (master strategists—secretive).

338. Richard Boylan, "Latest Revelations by NSC Consultant Dr. Michael Wolf," in Boylan and Boylan, *Labored Journey To The Stars*. Available online at: http://www.drboylan.com/wlflk2a.html.

339. For discussion of how Pleiedians intervened during the second world war, see Al Bielak, 1991 Interview: http://www.freezone.org/mc/e_conv02.htm.

340. Richard Boylan, "Latest Revelations by NSC Consultant, Dr. Michael Wolf," in Boylan and Boylan, *Labored Journey To The Stars*. Available online at: http://www.drboylan.com/wlflk2a.html.

341. See Stewart Swerdlow, *The Montauk: The Alien Connection*.
342. The best account of this philosophy and an advanced ET 'light technology' from a government whistleblower is the online "Wingmakers" material released by the "defector," Jamission Neruda. Available at: www.wingmakers.com.
343. See Carolyn Myss, *Anatomy of the Spirit: the Seven Stages of Power and Healing* (Random House, 1997).
344. See Royal & Priest, *The Prism of Lyra*, pages 11–14.
345. See J.J. Hurtak, *The Book of Knowledge: The Keys of Enoch* (Academy of Future Science, 1977).
346. See Royal & Priest, *Prism of Lyra*; and Neruda Interviews, pages 1–4. Available online at: http://www.wingmakers.com.
347. Descriptions of these advanced ET races and various councils can be found in J.J. Hurtak, *Keys of Enoch*.
348. Royal & Priest, *The Prism of Lyra*, pages 11–14.
349. See Neruda Interview #1, pages 10–12ff: http://www.wingmakers.com. Another source of material for the activities of a Central Race is Ashanaya Deanne, *Voyagers: Secrets of Amenti*, Vols. 1–2 (Wildflower Press, 2002).
350. See Phyllis Schlemmer, *The Only Planet of Choice: Essential Briefings from Deep Space*, 2nd ed. (Gateway Books, 1995). See also Hurtak, *Keys of Enoch*; and Deane, *Voyagers*.
351. See "Quotations from Chairman Wolf" in Boylan and Boylan, *Labored Journey to the Stars*, available at: http://www.drboylan.com/wolfqut2.html; and Dr. Neruda, Interview #1: http://www.wingmakers.com.
352. See Brad Steiger, Alfred Bielek, Sherry Hanson Steiger, *Philadelphia Experiment and Other UFO Conspiracies* (Inner Light Publications, 1990); Preston Nichols, *The Montauk Project*.
353. For classification and analysis of these organizations, see Richard Boylan: "The Shadow Government: Its Identification and Analysis," in Boylan and Boylan, *Labored Journey to the Stars*, available online at: http://www.drboylan.com/shadgovt2.html.
354. See Phillip Corso, *Beyond Roswell*, for discussion of his involvement in the Army's clandestine efforts to reverse engineer ET technology.
355. William Cooper served on the briefing team of the Commander of the Pacific Fleet and reported he had to study and report on a number of highly classified reports concerning the ET presence. See Cooper, *Behold a Pale Horse*. Although Cooper was not formerly part of a clandestine organization, the high security classification of the ET material meant only very few Navy personnel could ever learn about the presence.
356. Dan Sherman, *Above Black: Project Preserve Destiny, Insider Account of Alien Contact and Government Cover-up* (One Team Publishing, 1997), Ch. 3. Available online at: http://www.aboveblack.com.

357. Sherman, *Above Black*, Ch 2. Available online at: http://www. aboveblack.com.

358. For online information on the history of the NSC, go to: www.nsc.gov.

359. An online copy of Truman's letter authorizing creation of Majestic 12 is available at: http://209.132.68.98/pdf/truman_forrestal.pdf.

360. See: http://www.whitehouse.gov/nsc/history.html.

361. Other whistleblower sources on the true function of MJ-12 are interviews by Colonel Steve Wilson and Dr. Michael Wolf in Boylan and Boylan, *Labored Journey To The Stars*. Both interviews available online at: http://www.drboylan.com/mj12org2.html and http://www. drboylan.com/wolfqut2.html.

362. Cooper, "Origin, Identity and Purpose of MJ-12," available online at: http://www.geocities.com/Area51/Shadowlands/6583/maji007.html; See also Cooper, *Behold A Pale Horse*, p. 208.

363. See Neruda Interviews, pages 1–4.

364. See Richard Boylan, "Bilderbergers, ETs and World Peace," available online at: http://www.drboylan.com/bldrbg2.html. See also Richard Wilson & Silvia Burns, "The US Government and Extraterrestrial Entities," http://www.extraterrestrial-aliens.com/31.htm.

365. Richard Boylan, "Quotations from Chairman Wolf," in Boylan and Boylan, *Labored Journey To The Stars*. Available online at http:// www.drboylan.com/wolfqut2.html.

366. See Wolf, *Catchers of Heaven*.

367. Neruda Interview #3, pages 38–39; http://www.wingmakers.com.

368. See Al Bielak interview in 1991: http://www.freezone.org/mc/ e_conv06.htm.

369. *The Day After Roswell*, p. 93.

370. For an analysis of the institutional culture of Reptilian species, see Courtney Brown, *Cosmic Explorers*, 178–224.

371. Theresa deVeto, "From Disinformation to Disclosure," *Surfing The Apocalypse* (October, 2001). Available online at: http://www. surfingtheapocalypse.com.

372. "Quotations from Chairman Wolf" in *Boylan and Boylan, Labored Journey to the Stars*, available online at: http://www.drboylan.com/ wolfqut2.html.

373. See Richard Boylan, "Colonel Steve Wilson, USAF (ret.) Reveals UFO-oriented Project Pounce," available online at: http://drboylan.com/ swilson2.html.

374. For an analysis of the institutional culture of Zeta species, see Courtney Brown, *Cosmic Explorers*. pages 243–51. See also *Cosmic Voyage* (Onyx Books, 1997).

375. Phil Schneider, "MUFON Conference Presentation, May 1995," available online at: http://www.geocities.com/Area51/Shadowlands/ 6583/coverup044.html.

376. Video with Schneider's comments about New World Order conspiracy is titled: "Phil Schneider's Last Lecture (1995)" and can be purchased from: http://educate-yourself.org/products/pslastlecturedescrip.shtml.

377. See Stewart Swerdlow, *Montauk: The Alien Connection*; Preston Nichols & Peter Moon, *Montauk Revisited*; and Wade Gordon, *The Brookhaven Connection*. For an overview, see John Quinn, "Phoenix Undead: The Montauk Project and Camp Hero Today." (NewsHawk Inc, 1998). Available online at: http://vs03.tvsecure.com/~vs030f1/monew.htm.

378. See Stewart Swerdlow, *Montauk: The Alien Connection*; Preston Nichols & Peter Moon, *Montauk Revisited: Adventures in Synchronicity*; and Wade Gordon, *The Brookhaven Connection*.

379. Cooper, *Behold a Pale Horse*. See also Cooper, "Origin, Identity and Purpose of MJ-12": http://www.geocities.com/Area51/Shadowlands/6583/maji007.html.

380. See William Cooper, *Behold a Pale Horse*; and Cooper, "Origin, Identity and Purpose of MJ-12": http://www.geocities.com/Area51/Shadowlands/6583/*maji007*.html. See also Michael Wolf, *The Catchers of Heaven*; and Richard Boylan, "Official Within MJ-12 UFO-Secrecy Management Group Reveals Insider Secrets," available at http://www.drboylan.com/wolfdoc2.html.

381. See Michael Wolf, *Catchers of Heaven*.

382. For discussion of the more progressive factions in the PI40 group, see Richard Boylan, "Revelations concerning MJ-12," available online at http://www.drboylan.com/mj12org2.html.

383. See Richard Boylan, "Birds of a Feather No Longer: Policy Split Divides 'Aviary' UFO-Secrecy Group," in Boylan and Boylan, *Labored Journey To The Stars*. Available online at: http://www.drboylan.com/aviary2.html.

Chapter 5

US Motivation for Preemptive War against Iraq: Stargate Technology and the 'Return of the Gods'

Introduction

In his 2003 State of the Union address, President George W. Bush declared "the gravest danger facing America and the world is outlaw regimes that seek and possess nuclear, chemical and biological weapons."[384]

In his speech, President Bush eloquently expressed his main motivation for launching a preemptive war against Iraq in order to prevent "a day of horror like none we have ever known." Critics of President Bush's preemptive policy, including the political commentator, Robert Fisk, argue the upcoming US led war against Iraq "isn't about chemical warheads or human rights: it's about oil."[385]

According to another prominent political commentator, Michael Lind, the motivation lies in the preemptive military doctrine championed by neo-conservatives such as Deputy Defense Secretary Paul Wolfowitz, whose policy views were given more prominence after the September 11 attack.[386]

Most, if not all, criticisms of the Bush administration's motivation for going to war focus on a combination of the imperial world views of conservative politicians in power in Washington DC, and corporate interests that drive the political agenda of the Bush administration. This chapter will provide a radically different political analysis of the Bush administration's motivation for going war, and of the explanations offered by his critics.

It will be argued that the focus on either the factors supporting a preemptive war against an Iraq possessing weapons of mass destruction; or on criticisms against US imperialism and corporate interests, are not so much wrong, but simply reflect a limited political paradigm for understanding the motivations behind US foreign policy.

The political paradigm to be used in analyzing the motivations for the preemptive war in Iraq is based on exopolitics.[387] An exopolitical paradigm starts with the premise that there exists an extraterrestrial (ET) presence on Earth about which clandestine government organizations have been withholding knowledge from the general public and elected public officials. Rather than being an unsubstantiated conspiracy theory with little relevance to contemporary policy issues such as a preemptive US war against Iraq, an exopolitical analysis can provide a more comprehensive understanding of what motivates the Bush administration in launching a preemptive attack against Iraq.

Exopolitics as an emerging field of public policy is primarily based on the evidence provided by a range of sources supporting the idea of an ET presence known by clandestine government organizations, who suppress this information from the general public and elected political leaders. The most important evidence comes from former military and government officials who have come forward to give "whistle blower" testimony in a number of non-governmental initiatives to promote disclosure of the ET presence.[388]

Although many disagree over the plausibility of the available evidence and take various positions either for or against the existence of an ET presence and government non-disclosure of this presence, exopolitics is based on the premise that such debate ought not preclude discussion of the implications of such a presence. Therefore, when one examines contemporary international issue such as a US led preemptive war in Iraq, one can explore the viewpoints offered by those using an exopolitical analysis. This allows for a more comprehensive understanding of foreign policy, irrespective of the ongoing debate over the persuasiveness of the available evidence.

An exopolitical analysis is necessary, since those actively involved in a non-disclosure program will use disinformation, intimidation and other strategies to deter witnesses, distort evidence, and deter public attention from the ET presence and how it pertains to a range of contemporary policy issues. Finally, a clandestine campaign of non-disclosure needs to be considered in conducting exopolitical analysis in terms of the likelihood of this influencing and/or compromising available empirical evidence that otherwise would confirm an ET presence.

Therefore, exopolitical analysis has some key differences from more conventional approaches to political analysis, which are based on a traditional social scientific method of a value free, objective analysis of available processes, institutions and actors in the public policy arena.

What follows in this chapter is an exopolitical analysis of a historic ET presence in Iraq that helps explain the motivation for the US led preemptive attack on the regime of Saddam Hussein. In conducting this analysis, I will first examine the available evidence of a historical ET presence in Iraq, and the existence of "Stargate technology" and/or information.

I then analyze the motivations of the Bush administration in launching a US led preemptive war against Iraq, and the role played by Stargate technology and/or information for the war.

What's the Evidence for a Historic ET Presence in Iraq?

The strongest available evidence for a historical ET presence in Iraq comes from cuneiform tablets directly recording the beliefs and activities of the ancient Sumerians whose civilization began almost overnight in 3800 BC. Many of the more than 500,000 cuneiform tablets discovered thus far, describe stories of the Sumerians interacting with their "gods."

Most archeologists initially accepted that these were merely myths and attached little importance to them other than giving insight into the mytho-religious beliefs of the ancient Sumerians. That viewpoint received a major challenge in 1976 when the Sumerian scholar, Zecharia Sitchin, published the first of a series of books on his translations of thousands of Sumerian tablets.[389] Rather than treating the stories of the gods visiting the Earth as myths that had little empirical relevance, Sitchin interpreted the tablets as literal descriptions of events as they occurred at that time:

> All the ancient peoples believed in gods who had descended to Earth from the heavens and who could at will soar heavenwards. But these tales were never given credibility, having been branded by scholars from the very beginning as myths . . . It has taken thirty years of research, of going back to the ancient sources, of accepting them literally, to re-create in my own mind a continuous and plausible scenario of pre-historic events.[390]

Sitchin's translations of Sumerian cuneiform tablets revealed an advanced civilization with many technological achievements across the spectrum of medicine, law, cosmology, economics, politics and social reform. According to one of the world's leading Sumerian Scholars, Samuel Noah Kramer, the Sumerians achieved 39 civilizational "firsts," including: writing (cuneiform), medical science, legal codes, social reforms, bicameral congress, coinage system, cosmology, and cosmogony.[391]

What most intrigued Sitchen was that the Sumerians had precise information on a range of topics that he argues could not have been possible for a civilization at the initial stages of its development without an existing former civilization from which to borrow. According to Sitchin, the Sumerians had detailed knowledge of all the planets in the solar system. They understood the precession of the equinoxes and also had an understanding of complex medical procedures.[392]

Sitchin's claim that the Sumerians were aware of all nine planets in the solar system is remarkable, given that the outermost planets of Uranus and Neptune weren't discovered until the 19th century, and Pluto wasn't discovered until the early part of the 20th century. Even more striking is Sitchin's claims concerning a mysterious tenth planet, Nibiru, that returned to the solar system every 3,600 years.

In the late 1970s two astronomers from the US Naval Observatory, Tom van Flandern and Richard Harrington, began publishing a series of papers supporting the existence of a 10th planet that accounted for the perturbations of the outer planets of the solar system.[393] Hugh McCann, a science writer for the *Detroit News* stated: "If new evidence from the U.S. Naval Observatory of a 10th planet in the solar system is correct, it could prove that the Sumerians . . . were far ahead of modern man in astronomy."[394]

The Infrared Astronomical Satellite (IRAS) discovery in 1983, of a large planet that was close enough to the sun to belong to the solar system, is possible confirmation of the Sumerians' detailed knowledge of all the planets in the solar system.[395]

Concerning the Sumerians' accurate calendar and knowledge of the procession of the Equinoxes, Alan Alford pointed out:

> The uncomfortable question which the scientists have avoided is this: how could the Sumerians, whose civilization only lasted 2,000 years, possibly have observed and recorded a celestial cycle that took 25,920 years to complete? And why did their civilization begin in the middle of a zodiac period? Is this a clue that their astronomy was a legacy of the gods?[396]

As to where the Sumerians could have gained this detailed knowledge of planets in the solar system, the precession of the equinoxes and other puzzling information, Sitchin's translations suggest that the Sumerians provided a clear answer for its ultimate source. They revealed in their tablets that all their knowledge came from a race of extraterrestrial visitors, the "Anunnaki" ("those who from heaven to Earth came") who were not only teachers for the Sumerians, but also played a role in the creation of the human race.[397]

According to Sitchin's translations, the Anunnaki visited the earth approximately 450,000 years ago to establish mining operations for gold needed on their home world after a devastating damage to the atmosphere. According to Lloyd Pye, "the Anunnaki solution was to disperse extremely tiny flakes of gold into their upper atmosphere to patch holes . . . Ironically, modern scientists contend that if we are ever forced to repair our own damaged ozone layer, tiny particulates of gold shot into the upper atmosphere would be the best way to go about it."[398]

Another reason why the Anunnaki may have sought to mine gold for their home world is the consciousness raising properties of gold in its "monatomic state." According to David Hudson, who has patents on the preparation of metals in their monatomic states, monatomic gold was used in the initiation rites of ancient mystery schools and delivered heightened states of consciousness.[399] He believes monatomic gold was the "manna" that sustained the ancient Hebrews in the Sinai desert.

An advanced ET race, understanding the unique properties of gold in its monatomic state as a form of manna for sustaining higher states of consciousness, may well have been engaged in mining operations on worlds with an abundance of gold. Liberally diffused into the atmosphere of their home world—either to repair the atmosphere or to produce manna for all the planet's inhabitants—there may have been a powerful need for gold.

After generations of mining gold around the planet, there was an apparent rebellion among the Anunnaki workers and it was decided that a slave/worker race would be created to continue the mining operations. Humanity was reportedly created from a mixture of the Anunnaki DNA and primates then present on Earth.

Created as a slave worker race, the Anunnaki apparently differed greatly about how to treat the human race. Some preferred to keep humanity in ignorance so as to perform their menial mining operations, but other Anunnaki desired to assist humanity to evolve and develop more sophisticated modes of collective life. The Garden of Eden was a metaphor for competing ET factions who either wanted to keep humanity in its state of ignorance (Jehovah-Enlil faction) or give knowledge to humans (Serpent-Enki faction).

The home world of the Anunnaki, the Nibiru (planet of the crossing), had a long elliptical journey around the sun, and returns to this region of the solar system every 3,600 years.[400] It would be upon the periodic returns of the Nibiru that the factional conflict between the Anunnaki would reach new degrees of intensity. This would be due to both Nibiru's proximity and the gravitational/electromagnetic forces released by its passage through the solar system that brings about tremendous changes both for Earth and Nibiru itself.[401]

When Sitchin's innovative work was first published, it immediately raised great controversy and intense debate between those either for or against his main thesis of a historic ET presence in Sumer that was responsible for starting the remarkable Sumerian civilization. Among those responding favorably to Sitchin's thesis included established popular authors such as Erik Von Daniken, who in 1969, had written the best selling book, *Chariots of the Gods.*

Von Daniken proposed a historic ET presence in different parts of the planet.[402] William Bramley's, *Gods of Eden*, also proved to be popular in his analysis of the historic role of ET races, as has R.A. Boulay's, *Flying Serpents and Dragons: The Story of Mankind's Reptillian Past.*[403]

Less well-known authors/independent archaeologists such as William Henry and Alan Alford have similarly published books supporting Sitchin's thesis.[404] On the other hand, a number of critics objected to Sitchin's translations of key terms, and his literal approach to interpreting Sumerian cuneiform texts.[405]

To support Sitchin's thesis, many authors typically cite biblical texts that make reference to the "gods" that resided on Earth and interacted with humanity. The biblical text most referred to is the apocryphal book of Enoch.[406]

Although the Book of Enoch was excluded in most versions of the Old Testament, it was nevertheless part of ancient Hebrew scholarship and indeed is included in the Ethiopian and Slavic versions of the Old Testament. The Book of Enoch describes a rebel group of angels, the "Nephilim," who numbered 200, settled the Earth and interbred with the human population before being recalled and punished by their superiors, the "Elohim."[407]

[Ch.6] 1 And it came to pass when the children of men had multiplied that in those days were born unto 2 them beautiful and comely daughters. And the angels, the children of the heaven, saw and lusted after them, and said to one another: "Come, let us choose us wives from

among the children of men 3 and beget us children."
And Semjaza, who was their leader, said unto them:
"I fear ye will not 4 indeed agree to do this deed, and I
alone shall have to pay the penalty of a great sin." And
they all answered him and said: "Let us all swear an
oath, and all bind ourselves by mutual imprecations 5
not to abandon this plan but to do this thing." Then
swore they all together and bound themselves 6 by
mutual imprecations upon it. And they were in all two
hundred; who descended in the days of Jared on the
summit of Mount Hermon, and they called it Mount
Hermon, because they had sworn 7 and bound themselves by mutual imprecations upon it.

[Ch.7] 1 And all the others together with them took unto
themselves wives, and each chose for himself one, and
they began to go in unto them and to defile themselves
with them, and they taught them charms 2 and enchant-
ments, and the cutting of roots, and made them
acquainted with plants. And they 3 became pregnant,
and they bare great giants, whose height was three
thousand ells: Who consumed 4 all the acquisitions of
men. And when men could no longer sustain them, the
giants turned against 5 them and devoured mankind.
And they began to sin against birds, and beasts, and
reptiles, and 6 fish, and to devour one another's flesh,
and drink the blood. Then the earth laid accusation
against the lawless ones.[408]

The Book of Enoch provides contextual background for
mysterious verses in the Book of Genesis which describes a
time when the "sons of gods," the Nephilim/Anunnaki, interbred with humanity, and created a race of giants/heroes that
ruled over the rest of humanity. The following passage from the
Book of Genesis, is clearly a summary from the longer account
found in the Book of Enoch: "The Nephilim were on the earth
in those days—and also afterwards—when the sons of God
went to the daughters of men and had children by them. They
were the heroes of old, men of renown."[409]

Supporters of the Sitchin thesis say that this is part of the biblical evidence that an advanced ET race did in fact exist on Earth, had a long interaction with humanity, and even played a role in the creation of the human race.[410]

The greatest support for Sitchin's thesis, according to the evidentiary criteria established in the first chapter, are a number of former participants in clandestine military/intelligence projects involving ET races that played a role in the creation of humanity.

According to Stewart Swerdlow, a gifted psychic who was recruited into the top secret project established at the Montauk Naval/Air force facility, the ET races that established the human race, including the Anunnaki referred by Sitchin, continue to play a powerful role in human affairs.[411]

Another participant in the infamous Montauk experiments, Al Bielak, also described a number of ET races assisting in these clandestine military projects, among whom was a Reptilian race from Orion commonly associated with the Anunnaki.[412] In the most extensive collection of literature available on clandestine government projects involving ET races and technology, Valdamar Valerian details information gained from interviews with whistleblowers and government insiders concerning the historic and contemporary role played by ET Reptilian species in influencing human affairs.[413]

In addition to the growing number of independent archae-ologists, biblical commentators and whistleblowers coming forward to support Sitchin's thesis, a burgeoning number of indi-viduals claim to be in telepathic communication with ET races who reveal information on the historic ET presence in Sumer. The most prominent among these is Barbara Marciniak, whose "channeled works" on the historic ET presence on Earth is a seminal source of information in the New Age community.[414]

Another of these ET "channels" is Jelaila Starr, who is distinguished by her claim to be in touch with beings from Nibiru itself. Starr regularly releases online information from the Anunnaki themselves on her website.[415] She "channels" advice from the Anunnaki elite, the Nibiruan Council, which is designed to assist global humanity in learning of its ET heritage and consciously evolve as a race. She describes how the leaders of the Anunnaki, the brothers Enlil and Enki, whom the

Sumerians later worshipped as gods, decided to resolve the problem:

> Around 250,000 B.C., the astronauts in Africa mutinied. Dissatisfied with mining gold in the hot interior of the earth, they had reached the breaking point and joined together in a revolt.
>
> Enki called Enlil to notify him of the situation. When Enlil arrived at the mining operation, the Anunnaki took him hostage. Enki, although siding with the Anunnaki, asked his men to release Enlil, which they did. Enlil accused Enki of inciting and encouraging the Anunnaki and wanted him brought up on charges before the Council. Both brothers returned to Nibiru to speak before the Council. It was decided that the Anunnaki were more valuable doing the jobs they were trained for than mining gold. Enki believed the solution was to create a worker race to mine the gold . . . . So Enki, being a master geneticist as well as an engineer, along with Ninhursag, retired to the laboratory in Shuruppak to create the workers.[416]

Another popular "channel" is Sheldan Nidle, who claims to be communicating with an ET race from the star system Sirius, and gives extensive information on the historic presence and influence of the Anunnaki in his books and website.[417]

There is great controversy over the extent to which such a disparate collection of evidentiary sources can substantiate the Sitchin thesis of a historic ET presence in Sumer. Of these sources, the whistleblower testimonies, while relatively few, stand out as giving powerful support to Sitchin's thesis.

Despite the controversy generated by such sources, they provide a wealth of information and plausibility that merits closer examination in terms of their public policy implications. Given that exopolitics is based on the premise of an ET presence that is subject to non-disclosure by clandestine government organizations, it is possible to provide an exopolitical perspective on Sitchin's thesis despite the ongoing debate over the consistency and accuracy of the available evidence.

The Historic ET Presence, Stargates and US policy in Iraq

An independent archaeologist who discusses a direct link between the ancient ET presence in Sumer (southern Iraq) and the US motivation for military intervention in Iraq, is William Henry. Henry's main thesis is that there existed in Sumerian times a technological device which he describes as a "Stargate," that the Anunnaki/Nephilim used as an interdimensional and time-space travel device for moving about the galaxy and into higher dimensions.[418] Henry focuses on the following scene described by Sitchin's interpretation of a cuneiform tablet of an Uruk ritual text:

> Depictions have been found that show divine beings flanking a temple entrance and holding up poles to which ring-like objects are attached. The celestial nature of the scene is indicated by the inclusion of the symbols of the Sun and the Moon . . . depicting Enlil and Enki flanking a gateway through which Anu is making a grand entrance.[419]

Rather than a simple temple scene involving the chief Anunnaki of the Sumerians, Anu and his two sons, Enlil and Enki, Henry proposes that the above scene represents a transportation device used by Anu and others from the elite Anunnaki. If so, then such a device is likely to have been located in a Sumerian city such as Uruk, founding city of the Sumerian civilization and the home of Gilgamesh, the famed king of the Epic of Gilgamesh.[420]

Whistleblower testimonies support the existence of "Stargates" as a mode of transportation used by ET races that is part of the exotic technologies currently under development by clandestine organizations in the US and elsewhere.[421] Dr. Richard Boylan, who has a number of "insider" contacts revealed the following about the US government's Stargate technology, which is part of a classified program called "Project Galileo":

> An ex-NSA consultant who has been reliable in the past informs me that government scientists working at

Los Alamos "Nuclear" Laboratory, NM have succeeded
in generating a holographic portal [a "Stargate"]. They
have used this portal to travel across space-time, and
possibly interdimensionally, and have seen into another
world. What they saw there, my informant says crypti-
cally, both frightened and intrigued them. He did not
add any additional details. This research would be a
follow-on to previous secret government successful
research into time travel and teleportation. Los Alamos
physicist Robert Lazar told about the government's
Project Galileo research into time travel, which he
was briefed on when he worked at the S-4 Base south of
Area 51. My NSA contact confirmed that the government has succeeded in time travel, but also considers
it a dangerous technology. Teleportation research conducted at the Lawrence Livermore/Sandia National
Laboratories, CA has had some successful results, as
well. Certain extraterrestrial races have been using
portals of their own devising to visit earth. Now the
U.S. government, ever avaricious to copy ET technology, has created a primitive but working model of
its own.[422]

Dr. Boylan argues that the Stargate technology was the
true reason behind the prosecution of the nuclear scientist,
Dr. Wen Ho Lee, who most likely compromised, in some way,
the clandestine Stargate technology under development:

Dr. Wen Ho Lee, nuclear scientist in the headlines,
worked on that holographic portal project, along with
other scientists. You will recall that Dr. Lee was accused
by the government of copying U.S. "nuclear secrets"
onto a non-secure computer tape. In the previously-lax
security environment of the professorial Los Alamos
Labs, run by the University of California, and accus-
tomed to informal exchange of information among
research colleagues, such "lapses of security" have
been epidemic. If every LANL scientist who took short-
cuts around certain security measures were prosecuted,

Los Alamos would be a ghost town. Why, then, was Wen Ho Lee singled out for such severe and unconstitutional nine months of imprisonment without bail and defamation-by-headlines? What does Dr. Lee know about portal secrets, that the government used the severest measures to silence and discredit him?[423]

A number of individuals claiming to have participated in a clandestine Navy project that has its roots in the Philadelphia experiment and later moved to the Montauk joint Naval/Air Force facility, state that manipulating time and space was the focus of the experiments. According to Al Bielak, the Philadelphia experiment was made possible by the application of ET technology acquired by the US Navy to move objects through time-space and interdimensionally.

This technology, according to Bielak, was both coveted and feared by the US military who were aware of its incredible potential for manipulating the very fabric of time and space, and changing the course of history by manipulating key historic events.[424]

Preston Nichols, who claims to have been a director of the Montauk project, summarized the history of the Philadelphia experiment and the Montauk project as follows:

The origin of the Montauk Project dates back to 1943 when radar invisibility was being researched aboard the USS Eldridge. As the Eldridridge was stationed at the Philadelphia Navy Yard, the events concerning the ship have commonly been referred to as: the "Philadelphia Experiment." The objective of this experiment was to make the ship undetectable to radar and while that was achieved, there was a totally unexpected and drastic side effect.

The ship became invisible to the naked eye and was removed from time and space as we know it! Although this was a remarkable breakthrough in terms of technology, it was a catastrophe to the people involved. Sailors had been transported out of this dimension and returned in a state of complete mental disorientation and horror. Some were even planted into the bulkhead of the ship itself.

Those who survived were discharged as "mentally unfit" or otherwise discredited and the entire affair was covered up. After the war, research continued under the tutelage of Dr. John von Neumann who had directed the technical aspects of the Philadelphia Experiment. His new orders were to find out what made the mind of man tick and why people could not be subject to inter-dimensional phenomena without disaster. A massive human factor study was begun at Brookhaven National Laboratories on Long Island, New York. It was known as the Phoenix Project.[425]

Jamisson Neruda, who claims to be a defector from a clandestine organization embedded within the National Security Agency, states that the most secret and powerful technology currently under development by the NSA concerns the manipulation and control of time-space. Significantly, control of such technology gives the capacity for defense against aggressor ET races; and, by implication, the capacity to conquer ET races:

> Blank Slate Technology [BST] . . . is a form of time travel that enables the re-write of history at what are called intervention points. Intervention points are the causal energy centers that create a major event like the break-up of the Soviet Union or the NASA space program. "BST is the most advanced technology and clearly anyone who is in possession of BST, can defend themselves against any aggressor."[426]

If the above testimonies are an accurate reflection of the advanced travel technology used by various ET races, then it is clear that a "Stargate" or similar ET based technology that facilitates travel through time-space and/or different "dimensions" would be among the most highly prized and valued of technologies. Indeed, whoever was to be in control of such technology, would have the means of conquering and/or protecting a vast number of civilized worlds throughout the galaxy.

Indeed, reports from "super soldiers" such as Michael Relfe, Andy Pero and "Jared" provide evidence of the existence of an elite space military force. This force visits ET worlds and engages in combat with different ET races using Stargate related travel technology that echoes the popular television series and movie, *Stargate*.[427] A particularly vivid experience is recounted in an interview with the "rogue super solider" Jared:

> In one combat situation I was involved in time travel to the future in deep space somewhere with a group of others. One of the persons who shared this experience with me says the year was sometime around 2032. We were sent to a planet called Kalmine somewhere out in the universe.
>
> The species inhabiting this planet were called Zomba's. They are a skeletal type creature about human average height and a strange solid lower jaw that could open far enough to drop down to their chests. Really weird looking. An entire military force was sent here by time shuttle. Thousands of us including female warriors as well. We were in full combat gear, fatigues, helmets, etc. Our weaponry consisted of full armada with tanks, half trucks, the works and all armed to the teeth.
>
> All of these vehicles were very fast even on this rocky terrain due to all being atomic powered. We all carried laser weapons or pulsing weapons and the same with all the vehicles. This planet's terrain was rocky, craggy with no visible structures of any kind. I never saw any trees or vegetation like here on earth either. We were in a low-lying area with these creatures up on higher ground fighting us.
>
> As we would fire our lasers at them and hit them it wouldn't kill them immediately. What it would do is lock onto them and they would give off this blood curdling

scream and bounce and jerk all over the place, so you had to hold your weapon right until it died. It seemed like it would take forever before it died but really was only a matter of seconds but with the air and all it seemed forever.

This planet was oxygenated so we did not have to wear suits or masks or anything for protection. That was the strange thing about it as to why I didn't understand not seeing any vegetation of any kind. As I said we arrived by a time shuttle through a worm hole created and sped through at the speed of infinity so that is why it is possible to go anywhere through the universe in split seconds. The main method of time travel was to literally walk physically through a vortex. We would just jump into the vortex or "wormhole." We called it "Shooting the Vort."

We preferred the vortex over the time shuttle because it was so beautiful and fascinating to sail through, almost identical to what you saw in the movie *Contact*, except it was not contained, we just went through it.[428]

Sitchin missed the significance of the Stargate in his own translations of the above texts and investigations of ET transportation, since he clearly operated in a "conventional paradigm" where transportation occurs through rocket propelled vehicles.[429] Sitchin's focus was on rocket propelled spacecraft in his description of the Anunnaki and their various trips to and from the Earth.

For example, describing the transportation used by the Anunnaki in moving between their earth and space based locations, Sitchin wrote: "The texts reveal that three hundred of them—The "Anunnaki of Heaven," or Igig—were true astronauts who stayed aboard the spacecraft without actually landing on Earth. Orbiting Earth, these spacecraft launched and received the shuttle craft to and from Earth."[430]

It therefore can be concluded that there were two forms of transportation used by the Anunnaki. One was a form of rocket technology familiar to us, which was used by the resident

Anunnaki on Earth. Sitchin described these as the "rank and file Anunnaki" who administered the Earth and humanity according to the dictates of their space based compatriots.[431]

Another transportation technology was a "Stargate" which facilitated travel through time-space and different dimensions. This technology was presumably used only by the elite Anunnaki, who dispensed the tasks of harvesting the Earth's resources to the resident and space based Anunnaki (lesser gods/rebel angels). Interpreting the Babylonian Epic of Creation, one gains an idea of the way tasks were assigned, based on the hierarchy of the Anunnaki, with the "supreme god" Marduk, dispensing tasks to his subordinate Anu, chief of the Anunnaki:

> Assigned to Anu, to heed his instructions, Three hundred in the heavens he stationed as a guard; the ways of Earth to define from the Heaven; And on Earth, Six hundred he made reside. After he all their instructions had ordered, to the Anunnaki of Heaven and of Earth he allotted their assignments.[432]

Thus the Anunnaki operated outposts both on Earth and in Space to maintain their control over the planet. Given the strict hierarchy of authority described by Sitchin in his detailed analysis of the Anunnaki and their interactions with one another and humanity, it is likely that Stargate technology, due to its power and potential to act as a gateway for interdimensional/time travel, would have been strictly monitored and off-limits to the resident Anunnaki and humanity who could only observe its operation.

Due to the nature of Stargates as an advanced form of time-space and interdimensional transportation, there would have been only a limited number of Stargates around the planet depending on the different ET races visiting or residing on the Earth. The Sumerian Stargate would most likely have been located in the most important of the ancient Sumerian cities—the ancient capital of Uruk, home of the ancient kings, which is located in Southern Iraq.

Significantly, after a 12-year lull in excavations, a team of German researchers in 2002 resumed excavations in the buried city of Uruk. Using a magnetometer which is able to detect the presence of man-made objects beneath the soil, and a powerful computer system in Germany, German geophysicists were able to map out the buried structures of the sprawling ancient capital of 5.5 km^2 that was where Sumerian civilization began.[433]

An important event in the Sumerian descriptions of the Anunnaki was the latter's final departure from the planet during a series of cataclysmic events that culminated in the period 1800–1700 BC.[434] Indeed, conventional archeologists support the view that there was a regional cataclysmic event that occurred at that time.[435] If in fact there were two modes of transportation used by the Anunnaki when most of the resident/lesser Anunnaki left by conventional rocket ships, elite Anunnaki most likely left by the Stargate and closed it down.

Predictably, given the advanced technology of the Stargate, it would not have been left unprotected in the interim period between their departure and its reactivation with the prophesied return of the Anunnaki. Different religious/cultural traditions suggest that this departure was a planet wide phenomenon, setting in place the expectation that the "gods" would eventually return.

Prophesied Return of the Gods/Anunnaki

Different religious/cultural traditions, such as Judaism, Christianity, Mayan, Buddhist and others describe an "end times" when there will be a rapid transition throughout the planet to various forms of "divine governance." This "return to divine governance" varies tremendously in terms of the key concepts and beliefs of the different religions and cultures, but essentially means the end of materialistic governance and the beginning of a "golden age" where "divine governance" is made possible through the intervention of God-like beings in human affairs.

For the ancient world of the Sumerians, these God-like beings were the Anunnaki. In the contemporary era, such a phenomenon is described in the guise of a single person, e.g., the

Christ, the Buddha, the Messiah, etc., who brings about divine governance of a region or the planet. Contemporary interest in these prophecies is the recent end of the second millennium in the Gregorian calendar (2000), and the end of the Mayan Calendar scheduled for 2012.

These events have sparked anticipation of a "return of divine governance" and the end of the materialistic belief systems that adherents of religious traditions, or New Age beliefs systems, claim limit the divine potential of individuals.

The notion of a "prophesied return" in the context of the former Anunnaki presence varies in meaning according to three different perspectives. The first perspective is based simply on the idea of the Anunnaki physically returning to resume a prominent role in influencing human affairs and overseeing the use of resources of the planet.[436] In such a scenario, the first wave of Anunnaki would presumably arrive in time to create favorable conditions for the anticipated return of the Anunnaki elite.

This might involve, for example, the lesser Anunnaki first returning and activating the Sumerian Stargate or achieving global influence over key national governments that would be required for the return of the Anunnaki elite. Presumably, this would be heralded as a sacred event that should be celebrated by all humanity.

The authors, Clive Prince and Lyn Picknett, argue persuasively in the book, *The Stargate Conspiracy*, that there has been an identifiable chain of global events involving key religious and political actors preparing humanity for just such a return.[437] Their view is that the whole "end times" phenomenon is the product of a centuries old programming of humans to prepare them for a time when human elites would hand over political power to higher dimensional beings such as the Anunnaki. The Anunnaki would presumably then bring about a return of divine governance by removing recalcitrant political leaders, and appointing their own divinely guided human proxies to govern humanity in accord to a new global religion.

The danger, according to Prince and Picknett, is that such a system of divine governance would essentially limit individual self-expression of religiosity/spirituality and perpetuate a global religion. This would allow humanity to be subtly exploited by ET races.[438]

The second perspective on the "return of the gods/ Anunnaki" is the return of their home world, the planet Nibiru. Indeed, much interest has been generated by a range of books and online web sites devoted to the topic of the return of Nibiru, the home world of the Anunnaki.[439]

Many authors cite a variety of astronomical evidence supporting the idea of a tenth planet that has long been speculated to influence the orbits of Uranus and Neptune ever since it was found that Pluto (discovered in 1930) could not account for these perturbations. As mentioned earlier, in the late 1970s two astronomers from the US Naval Observatory, Tom van Flandern and Richard Harrington began publishing a series of papers supporting the existence of a tenth planet.[440]

The most widely cited reference to support the thesis of a tenth planet that is known but not released to the general public, is a series of press releases by the astronomical team that was searching a part of the sky based on calculations by van Flandern and Harrington suggesting where the tenth planet was located.

In December 1983, the chief astronomer in charge of the Infrared Astronomical Satellite (IRAS) run by the Jet Propulsion Laboratory, Dr. Gerry Neugebauer, announced possible confirmation of such a planet. The *Washington Post* reporter summarizing the announcement wrote: "[a] heavenly body possibly as large as . . . Jupiter and possibly . . . part of this solar system has been found in the direction of the constellation of Orion by an orbiting telescope . . ."[441]

After a total of six major newspapers covered the announcement, there was a retraction of the announcement and public silence by astronomers on the possible existence of a tenth planet. Rumors began to emerge about an active campaign of suppression of information and intimidation by clandestine government organizations.[442]

For example, one of the astronomers at the US Naval Observatory, Dr. Richard Harrington, spoke publicly and wrote articles on the hypothetical planet X. There has been speculation that this directly contributed to his untimely death by "natural causes" in 1992.[443]

A third perspective on what the "prophesied return of the gods/Anunnaki" means can be found in authors who focus on the significance of the upcoming end of the current Mayan 5,200 year cycle. According to John Major Jenkins, the Mayans were aware of the way the solar ecliptic plane comes into alignment with the galactic plane on periodic basis. This makes it possible for more intense cosmic energies to reach the earth from the galactic core.

A corresponding increase or decrease in the level of human consciousness then occurs; parts of the brain either go online or off-line, as these Mayan cycles go through their different phases. According to Jenkins, the year 2012 corresponds to the end of the current Mayan cycle and will lead to a rapid transformation of global consciousness.[444]

Numerous authors refer to this as a New Age of more enlightened global thinking and increased human potential.[445] The "prophesied return of the gods" may therefore signify a rapid growth in human consciousness as dormant parts of the brain come on line when the solar ecliptic aligns with the galactic plane.

In this explanation, humanity itself would develop "god-like" powers which spontaneously become accessible to large numbers of humanity. A number of authors, for example, have been describing the amazing abilities and psychic powers of an increasing number of children worldwide.[446]

In sum, the available information on the "prophesied return of the gods" can be understood to signify an important milestone in the growth of human civilization. The "prophesied return" can be interpreted either literally or metaphorically to mean either a physical return of the "gods"/Anunnaki; the return of a mysterious 10th planet to the solar system; or a rapid growth in the consciousness of humanity as the solar plane comes into alignment with the galactic plane.

Despite the controversy over what precisely such a "prophesied return" signifies, the factors in such a return that most pertain to the preemptive military intervention that occurred in Iraq in March 2003, can be identified and analyzed. The first factor is that an ET transportation device, a Stargate, or some other important ET artifact, may have lain buried in the desert of Southern Iraq which presumably would play a key role in the "prophesied return of the gods." Second, it is possible that there will be a return of a tenth planet that plays a critical role in return of the Anunnaki and/or which significantly impacts on the global environment.

The significance of Iraq, in terms of its location, may play a key role in preparations for whatever contingencies emerge from the appearance of such a planet. Finally, there is the potential for a rapid acceleration of human consciousness as the end of the Mayan Calendar, 2012, approaches. Again, Iraq may play a critical role in such an elevation of human consciousness.

Exopolitical Analysis of US Motivation for Preemptive War in Iraq

Based on available evidence, significant ET artifacts might be located in Iraq, deriving from the historic Anunnaki presence in that country. Any ET technology left behind was likely to have been related to a Stargate and/or other transportation devices that would play a role in a "prophesied return of the Anunnaki."

In addition, many of the cuneiform texts that were stored either in Iraq's National museum or are still awaiting discovery in various underground sites, may have contained important information on "Stargate technology" and/or on the "return of the Anunnaki."

It is likely that clandestine government organizations that strongly influence if not control the Bush administration, were aware of the existence and role of these technologies, and the possible information stored on Sumerian cuneiform texts concerning Stargates and the return of the Anunnaki.

Iraq's former President, Saddam Hussein, most likely had also become aware of such a Stargate's existence or information concerning the return of the Anunnaki, as might be inferred by his architectural projects intent on reviving the grandeur of early Mesopotamian civilizations, and cementing his place as the restorer of Iraq's past glory.[447] In the 1980s Saddam reportedly spent $500 million on restorative projects of Iraq's Babylonian heritage, and even ensured that the center brick on every wall was inscribed with the words: "This was built by Saddam Hussein, son of Nebuchadnezzar, to glorify Iraq."[448]

Significantly, Saddam's permission for a German team of archaeologists to resume excavations in the Sumerian city of Uruk after detailed underground mapping, suggests that this was possibly the location of the Sumerian Stargate, and/or important information concerning the operation of such technology and the prophesied return of the Anunnaki. This knowledge of a buried Stargate or other significant ET artifacts with advanced modes of transportation or knowledge concerning these, was also likely to have been part of the reason why the German, French and Russian governments were publicly opposed to a US-led preemptive war against Iraq.

If in fact both the Hussein regime and the Bush administration believed that a Stargate or Stargate-related information was buried in the sands of Southern Iraq or elsewhere in Iraq, then there was most likely a race to gain access to it and to control it [geopolitical events supporting the existence of such a race will be explored in the next chapter]. William Henry's thesis is that this is indeed the political underpinning of the subsequent military conflict in Iraq.[449]

From the perspective of the Bush administration, control of the Sumerian Stargate, other ET and/or Sumerian cuneiform texts with information on Stargates and the possible return of the Anunnaki, would enable clandestine government organizations to continue their global campaign of non-disclosure of the ET presence.[450] This policy of non-disclosure is clearly implied by the Bush administration's penchant for secrecy and overturning many of the Freedom of Information initiatives from the earlier Clinton administration.[451]

Control of the Stargate, in addition to any other Stargates or related ET artifacts and information that may have been established in the capitals of other ancient civilizations, e.g., the Egyptian, Incan and Aztec, would presumably give clandestine government organizations greater leverage with ET races that are presently interacting with the planet, or are predicted to arrive on the scene in a series of events associated with the "prophesied return of the gods."

At the very least, control of the Sumerian Stargate or knowledge about the operation of Stargate technology would allow clandestine government organizations to dictate the pace of global transformations that ET races promise to introduce to the Earth with their advanced technology, superior knowledge and heightened psychic abilities.

Control of a Stargate or Stargate related information would have allowed Saddam to either activate it and to fulfill prophesy by facilitating the return of an advanced race of ETs, the elite Anunnaki; or pass on Stargate related information to friendly states such as Russia, France and/or Germany.

Saddam likely imagined that in return for his loyalty to the elite Anunnaki, he would have been rewarded with a position of great global authority. Perhaps he even saw himself as some kind of human savior facilitating the return of the gods who would solve all of humanity's problems, and end the rule of clandestine government organizations perpetuating non-disclosure of the ET presence.

Significantly, European governments such as Germany, France and Russia were giving themselves greater leverage in the future control of the Stargate or gaining Stargate related information, by offering diplomatic cover for the Saddam regime as a *quid pro quo* for allowing the resumption of archaeological digging in Uruk and any other clandestine projects in Iraq in which they were involved. These governments and the clandestine organizations associated with them that have access to knowledge of the ET presence, have deep suspicion about the willingness of the US to share information about and control over a Stargate and/or any other ET artifacts discovered in Iraq [again, this will be explored in the next chapter].

Sitchin's thesis of an ancient ET presence in Sumer combined with the notion of a variety of ET transportation devices described by other authors in their research of ancient civilizations, the existence of Stargate technologies revealed by former participants in clandestine government projects, and resumption of archaeological excavations of the first Sumerian capital Uruk in 2002, give support to the idea that a Stargate was buried in the sands of southern Iraq.

The information provided by former participants in Stargate experiments suggest that such technology not only exists, but is at the pinnacle of the exotic arsenals possessed by clandestine organizations associated with different national governments. Whoever controlled such technology, if such testimonies are accurate, literally had a means for controlling life not only on Earth, but also other planets. The existence of Stargate or related technology in Iraq provides important contextual information for understanding the true motivations of the Bush administration in launching the preemptive military attack on Iraq that began on March 20, 2003 and formally ended on May 1, 2003.

Did a Stargate Motivate the US-led Military Intervention in Iraq?

The primary evidentiary support for the above discussion is admittedly thin for conventional public policy experts and may sound better suited to a fictional thriller than serious public debate. From a conventional perspective, a scattered assortment of independent archeological authors, radical exegetical interpretations of biblical texts, the writings of "channels" of ET knowledge, speculative papers from astronomers—hardly constitute a persuasive source of information for understanding the motivations of US foreign policy.

Arguably, more difficult to dismiss are the accounts of former participants of clandestine organizations who claim to have been involved in Stargate related projects in the US. Here too, however, critics may dismiss these testimonies as the work of psychologically disturbed individuals with an axe to grind against various government agencies, or part of a psychological operation (psyop) disinformation campaign by military intelligence services.

Indeed, according to Alexandra Bruce, the testimonies stemming from the Montauk Project are part of a "psyop disinformation" campaign based in the Office of Naval Intelligence to hide the truth about actual events that did occur during the Philadelphia experiments.[452]

The prevailing explanations of a Bush administration as either devoted to eradicating Weapons of Mass Destruction, and/or being driven by oil interests and imperial ambitions will predictably prevail for those unconvinced by the above sources, or who believe the sources are part of a "psyop operation" by US intelligence services.

However, some significant archaeological events did take place both before and soon after the March 20 military intervention in Iraq that lend plausibility to the thesis of Stargate based technology and/or information as the true motivation of the Bush administration or at least key interest groups behind it.

The first archaeological event stems from the behavior of US led military forces once in Iraq, especially after the takeover of the capital, Baghdad. In what was seen as a major error, the US forces did nothing to prevent the sacking and looting of many important Iraqi installations and departments. One of these was the Iraqi National Museum where an estimated 80% of Iraq's ancient artifacts from Sumeria, Babylon and Akkadia were "stolen" from the Museum.

According to one source:

> The museum was the greatest single storehouse of materials from the civilizations of ancient Mesopotamia, including Sumeria, Akkadia, Babylonia, Assyria and Chaldea. It also held artifacts from Persia, Ancient Greece, the Roman Empire and various Arab dynasties.
>
> The museum held the tablets with Hammurabi's Code, perhaps the world's first system of laws, and cuneiform texts that are the oldest known examples of writing—epic poems, mathematical treatises, historical accounts. An entire library of clay tablets had not yet been deciphered or researched, in part because of the US-backed sanctions that restricted travel to Iraq.[453]

What is significant here is the reference to the stolen cuneiform texts that yet awaited translation. It is quite possible that US based clandestine organizations were seeking information that may have either assisted them in finding Stargate technology in Iraq or learning how to use Stargate technology. Reports from Iraqi eyewitnesses, suggested that the "looting" appeared organized and that knowledgeable outside forces were clearly in charge.

Professor McGuire Gibson, one of the world's leading archaeologists claimed: "It looks as if part of the looting was a deliberate planned action . . . They were able to take keys for vaults and were able to take out important Mesopotamian materials put in safes. I have a suspicion it was organized outside the country, in fact I'm pretty sure it was . . .[454]

Again, it needs to be emphasized that many Sumerian cuneiform texts were still awaiting translation and an insufficient number of Sumerian translators are available for the more than 500,000 cuneiform texts thus far discovered. One or more of these untranslated texts may have contained information that was the key to unlocking the secrets behind the use of Stargate technology.

If McGuire is correct, it is possible that a clandestine organization involved in Stargate technology, did in fact lead the looting of the Iraq national museum.

The second archeologically significant event was the radar mapping and start of excavations of the first capital of Sumer, Uruk, by a German archeological team in 2002. Given the prominence of Uruk and its likelihood as the site for a Sumerian Stargate or information on Stargate technology, then the radar mapping and resumption of excavations raised questions over why they were resumed at that time and what was being sought.

Given that political tensions in Iraq had not significantly diminished in 2002, and with the likelihood of it being a site of renewed military conflict with the US, it can be suggested that there were powerful hidden motivations for what on the surface appeared to be a purely scientific dig of an ancient Sumerian capital. With US control of the skies and Saddam's control of the ground, the German archaeological expedition apparently had the permission of both the Saddam regime and US military authorities to do its survey.

The third significant archaeological event was the discovery, announced on April 29, 2003, of the tomb of King Gilgamesh in the ancient Sumerian capital of Uruk, by the same

German archaeological tomb that had begun a sophisticated radar imaging survey of Uruk in 2002.[455]

Gilgamesh was famed for his epic journey to discover the "secrets of immortality" and for meeting a survivor of the "Great Flood" who passed on the secrets of immortality.[456] It would be fair to construe such secrets of immortality as a metaphor for Stargate technology where one could move between different dimensions—literally from the realm of Earth and mortality, to the realm of the gods and immortality.

As a king who was possibly spawned by an Anunnaki-human union, Gilgamesh may well have been aware of Stargate technology and its time-space/interdimensional travel applications. Arguably, the Epic of Gilgamesh was a symbolic story for how humans could activate and use Stargate technology.

The news of the discovery of Gilgamesh's tomb revealed that in the midst of the US-led preemptive war, where military conflict was continuing, the German archaeological team had continued its radar imaging and excavations of Uruk. Presumably, the archaeologists had powerful protection from both the Saddam regime and US military authorities, and were now simply passing on any acquired information through the US military authorities now in charge.

The location and contents of Gilgamesh's tomb would most certainly have been passed on, containing if it did, any secrets concerning "immortality" and possible "Stargate technology."

Conclusion: Implications of the US-Led Preemptive War in Iraq

When all the primary evidence and recent archaeological events are put together, what emerges is a plausible case of a very different motivation for the US led military intervention. Interpretations of the motivations of the Bush administration in launching preemptive war on Iraq in terms of the concerns raised in Bush's 2003 State of the Union address, or the corporate and imperial interests suggested by his critics such as Robert Fisk and Michael Lind, can all be described as part of the surface layer of motivations driving the Bush administration.

At a deeper level, it is likely that there was great anxiety by clandestine government organizations in terms of what would happen if Hussein, with the support of the German and other European governments, gained access to the Sumerian Stargate or other ET technology buried in Uruk, or if the Stargate were to somehow reactivate without clandestine government personnel present to monitor and control the Stargate.

Information concerning either the operation of Stargates or the possible return to Earth of the Anunnaki, would have been of great interest to the US, Russia, European states and to Saddam's regime. President Bush's State of the Union address outlining the need for a preemptive attack on Iraq in most likelihood masked a hidden agenda to gain access to the Stargate and/or other ET technology or information in Uruk and elsewhere in Iraq. Such access would presumably perpetuate clandestine government control over global resources and information at a time of increased ET activity and influence.

Evidence suggests that the motivations for a preemptive war against Iraq had little to do with weapons of mass destruction. **The true motivation was to perpetuate US clandestine government control of information concerning the historic ET presence in Iraq, associated technology and information, and the possible return of the same ET races, the Anunnaki, that sponsored the Sumerian civilization.**

Evidence pointing to the existence of Stargate technology, and the possibility that Iraq possessed artifacts or information on such technology, strengthens the case that the Bush administration simply misled the US and world public over the true motivation for attacking Iraq.

The US argument over the need to respond quickly to the threat of Weapons of Mass Destruction rang hollow when the US did not respond to North Korea's declaration in October 2002, of successfully having a secret nuclear weapons program.[457] Although there are clear strategic differences between Iraq and North Korea meriting a nuanced approach to each case, the radically diverging approaches by the Bush administration to the "weapons of mass destruction" problems in both countries, certainly pointed to something deeper that was motivating the Bush administration for quickly getting into Iraq.

President Bush's State of the Union address even went to the extent of incorporating faked intelligence reports of Iraq purchasing nuclear related material from Niger to strengthen the case for urgent action.[458] Even more disturbing were reports that the Office of Special Plans, a Pentagon group comprising key "Hawks" from the Bush administration, deliberately "spun" intelligence information in a way that justified war against Iraq when most intelligence analysts were simply unconvinced by the available intelligence.

According to U.S. Rep. Ellen Tauscher, (D-Calif) a member of the House Armed Services Committee, "The concern is they [Office of Special Plans] were in the cherry-picking business— cherry-picking half-truths and rumors and only highlighting pieces of information that bolstered the administration's case for war . . ."[459]

Geopolitical events surrounding the US led preemptive war in Iraq suggested that there existed a hidden struggle between competing clandestine government organizations over the control of Iraq's storehouse of ancient ET technology and information. Furthermore, the "prophesied return of the gods" indicated that there was a hidden set of celestial or ET related events that influenced the timing of the intervention into Iraq.

It may well be the case that the country of Iraq in terms of its physical position holds some significance in terms of attaining strategic dominance over the Earth. It may well have been a similar consideration that motivated the Anunnaki choice of the region of Mesopotamia, and Sumer in particular, as the headquarters for its Earth operations. In the next chapter, I will closely examine the geo-political rivalry that has existed between major global powers in attaining access and control to Iraq's treasure chest of ET related artifacts, technology and information.

Notes

384. A full text of his January 28, 2003, State of the Union Address, can be found online at: http://www.whitehouse.gov/news/releases/2003/01/20030128-19.html.

385. Robert Fisk, "This looming war isn't about chemical warheads or human rights: it's about oil," *The Independent* 18 January, 2003: http://www.independent.co.uk/story.jsp?story=370328.
386. See Michael Lind, *Made In Texas: George W. Bush and the Southern Takeover of American Politics* (Basic Books, 2002).
387. For an introduction to exopolitics, see Chapter One.
388. 100 of these officials have already given testimony, with another 300 willing to do so. See Stephen Greer, ed., *Disclosure: Military and Government Witnesses Reveal the Greatest Secrets in Modern History* (Crossing Point Inc. 2001). See also *Executive Summary of the Disclosure Project* (Crozet, VA.: Disclosure Project, April 2001). Available online at: http://www.disclosureproject.com.
389. Zecharia Sitchin, *The Earth Chronicles*, Books 1–6 (New York: Avon Books).
390. Sitchin, *The 12th Planet: Book 1 of the Earth Chronicles* (Avon Books, 1976), p. viii.
391. Samuel Noah Kramer & Hiroshi Tanaka, *History Begins at Sumer: Thirty-Nine "Firsts" in Recorded History*, 3rd ed. (University of Pennsylvania Press, 1989).
392. See his chapter, "The Sudden Civilization," *The 12th Planet*, pages 12–51.
393. For the history of astronomical searches for Planet X, see William Graves Hoyt: *Planet X and Pluto* (The University of Arizona Press 1980), Mark Littman: *Planets Beyond—discovering the outer solar system*, (John Wiley 1988); and Tom van Flandern, *Dark Matter, Missing Planets & New Comets. Paradoxes resolved, origins illuminated* (North Atlantic Books 1993).
394. Hugh McCann, "10th Planet: Pluto's Orbit Says Yes," *Detroit News* (January 16, 1981) 1. Also cited in Jim Marrs, *Rule by Secrecy* (Harper Collins, 2000), 380.
395. For an announcement of the 1983 announcement concerning a mysterious tenth planet, see Thomas O'Toole, "Mystery Heavenly Body Discovered: Possibly as Large as Jupiter," *Washington Post* (December 31, 1983).
396. Alan F. Alford, *Gods of the New Millennium: Scientific Proof of Flesh and Blood Gods* (Eridu Books, 1996) 124.
397. Sitchin, *The 12th Planet*, 52.
398. Lloyd Pye, *Everything You Know Is Wrong* (Madeira Beach, Fl: Adamu Press, 1997) 231–32. Also cited in Marrs, *Rule by Secrecy*, 382.
399. For information on monatomic gold and David Hudson, go to: http://monatomic.earth.com.
400. Sitchin discusses this planet in great detail in *The 12th Planet*.
401. The idea that the Earth periodically experiences massive changes is discussed in books such as Charles Hapgood, *The Path of the Pole*

(Adventures Unlimited Press, 1999); Immanuel Velikovsky, *Earth in Upheaval* (Doubleday, 1955).

402. Erich von Daniken, *Chariots of the Gods* (G.P. Putnam's Sons, 1969).

403. William Bramley, *Gods of Eden* (Avon, 1989); R.A. Boulay, *Flying Serpents and Dragons: The Story of Mankind's Reptilian Past* (Book Tree, 1999).

404. William Henry, *One Foot in Atlantis* (Earthpulse Press, 1998); Alford, *Gods of the New Millennium.*

405. For a detailed critique of Sitchin, see Michael Heiser, "Zecharia Sitchin's Errors: An Overview": http://www.facadenovel.com/sitchinerrors.htm.

406. Ronald Brown, *The Book of Enoch* (Guadalupe Baptist Theological Seminary Press, 2000). An online version of the *Book of Enoch* can be found at: http://wesley.nnu.edu/noncanon/ot/pseudo/enoch.htm.

407. Sitchin describes the Sumerian version of this event in "Mutiny of the Anunnaki," *The 12th Planet*, 312–335.

408. *Book of Enoch*, online version found at: http://wesley.nnu.edu/noncanon/ot/pseudo/enoch.htm.

409. *Holy Bible: New International Version* (Hodder and Stoughton, 1978) *Genesis*, Book 6, verse 4.

410. See Bramley, *Gods of Eden*; Boulay, *Flying Serpents and Dragons* (Book Tree, 1999); and David Icke, *The Biggest Secret*, 2nd Ed. (Bridge of Love Publications, 1999).

411. Stewart Swerdlow, *Blue Blood, True Blood: Conflict & Creation* (Expansions Publishing Co., 2002).

412. For an interview with Al Bielak, see "The Montauk Project and the Philadelphia Experiment," available online at: http://psychicspy.com/montauk1.html.

413. See Val Valerian, *Matrix II: The Abduction and Manipulation of Humans Using Advanced Technology* (Leading Edge Research Group, 1989/90). Online information available at: http://www.trufax.org/catalog/m2.html.

414. See Barbara Marciniak, *Bringers of the Dawn: Teachings from the Pleiadians* (Bear & Co., 1992); and *Earth: Pleiadian Keys to the Living Library* (Bear & Co., 1994).

415. Jelaila Starr, *We Are the Nibiruans: Return of the 12th Planet* (New Leaf Distributing Co., 1999). Website: www.nibiruancouncil.com.

416. Extract from Jelaila Starr, *We Are the Nibiruans: Return of the 12th Planet* (New Leaf Distributing Co Inc, 1999). Available online at http://www.nibiruancouncil.com/html/bookoneexcerpt2.html.

417. Sheldan Nidle, *First Contact* (Blue Lodge Press, 2000). Website: www.paoweb.com.

418. Henry outlines his thesis in his article, "Saddam Hussein, The Stairway to Heaven and the Return of Planet X," which is available on

his website www.williamhenry.net. This is based on his book *Ark of the Christos: The Mythology, Symbolism and Prophecy of the Return of Planet X and the Age of Terror*, both of which are available from his website: www.williamhenry.net.

419. Sitchin, *When Time Began: Book V of the Earth Chronicles* (Avon, 1993) 113–14.

420. In contrast, Henry believes the Stargate was buried in some secret location by the Babylonian king, Nebuchadnezzar, after having been re-taken from Jerusalem. *Saddam Hussein, The Stairway to Heaven and the Return of Planet X*, is available on his website: www.williamhenry.net.

421. For a technical description of time travel/Stargate technology, see Jack Sarfatti, "Zero Point Energy Gravity Physics: Of UFOs, Stargates, time travel and parallel brane worlds," available online at: http://stardrive.org/Jack/scvacuum.pdf.

422. Richard Boylan, "The U.S. Government, Dimensional Portals, and Dr. Wen Ho Lee—The Rest of the Story," available online at: http://drboylan.com/wenhlee2.html.

423. Richard Boylan, "The U.S. Government, Dimensional Portals, and Dr. Wen Ho Lee—The Rest of the Story," available online at: http://drboylan.com/wenhlee2.html.

424. "Interview with Al Bielek," *Connecting Link* (Issue 19, Oct 1993); available online at: http://psychicspy.com/montauk1.html.

425. Excerpt from Preston Nichols & Peter Moon, *Pyramids of Montauk: Explorations in Consciousness* (Sky Books 1995). Available online at: http://psychicspy.com/montauk1.html. See also Preston Nichols & Peter Moon, *The Montauk Project: Experiments in Time* (Sky Books, 1992). For review of the Montauk Project, see John Quinn, "Phoenix Undead: The Montauk Project and Camp Hero Today" (NewsHawk Inc, 1998). Available online at: http://vs03.tvsecure.com/~vs030f1/monew.htm.

426. "Neruda Interviews: Interview 1": http://wingmakers.com/neruda1.html.

427. For two ebooks detailing Michael Relfe's memories of his service, see The Mars Records, published online at: http://www.themarsrecords.com. For an interview of Andy Pero, see "Project Superman," available at: http://www.hostileinvader.com/ProjectSuperman.html. For an interview with Jared, see Eve Lorgen "Secret Project Super Warrior Gone Rogue," *Alienlovebite* (August, 2001). Available online at: http://www.alienlovebite.com/secret_project_super_warrior_gon.htm.

428. See Eve Lorgen, "Secret Project Super Warrior Gone Rogue" *Alienlovebite* (August, 2001). Available online at: http://www.alienlovebite.com/secret_project_super_warrior_gon.htm.

429. Sitchin describes the transportation of the Nefilim/Anunnakin, in his chapter, "The Nefilim: People of the Fiery Rockets," *The 12th Planet*, 128–72. See also Childress' chapter on "Ancient Flight and Aerial Warfare," *Extraterrestrial Archeology*, 147–210.

430. Sitchin, *The 12th Planet*, 327.

431. Sitchin, *The 12th Planet*, 327.

432. Sitchin, *The 12th Planet*, 327.

433. For description of the resumption of archeological digs in Iraq, see Charles Recknagel, "Iraq: Archaeological Expedition Mapping Ancient City Of Uruk," Radio Free Europe, May 3. http://www.rferl.org/nca/features/2002/05/03052002101632.asp.

434. Sitchin describes these events in the third volume of his Earth Chronicles series, *The Wars of Gods and Men* (Avon, 1999).

435. For reference to this regional disaster, see an article by the Chief Archeologist from the University of Chicago, Prof McGuire Gibson, "Nippur—Sacred City of Enlil Supreme God of Sumer and Akkad." First published in *Al-Rafidan*, Vol. XIV (1993) and made available online at http://asmar.uchicago.edu/OI/PROJ/NIP/PUB93/NSC/NSC.html.

436. Such a view is described by a number of "channels" including Sheldan Nidle, *First Contact*; and Jelaila Star, *We are the Niburuans*. Their respective websites are: www.paoweb.net and www.niburuancouncil.net.

437. Lynn Picknett & Clive Prince, *The Stargate Conspiracy: The Truth About Extraterrestrial Life and the Mysteries of Ancient Egypt* (Berkley Books, 1999).

438. Such a scenario is also described by Marshall. Vian Summers, *Allies of Humanity: An Urgent Message About the Extraterrestrial Presence in the World Today* (The Society for the Greater Community Way of Knowledge, 2001).

439. One popular book is Mark Hazlewood, *Blindsided: Planet X Passes in 2003* (Firstpublish LLC, 2001). Hazlewood maintains a website with online excerpts outlining clandestine government suppression of the coming of Planet X: http://www.planetx2003.com/index.html.

440. For the history of astronomical searches for Planet X, see William Graves Hoyt: *Planet X and Pluto* (The University of Arizona Press 1980); Mark Littman: *Planets Beyond—discovering the outer solar system* (John Wiley 1988); and Tom van Flandern, *Dark Matter, Missing Planets & New Comets. Paradoxes resolved, origins illuminated* (North Atlantic Books 1993).

441. Thomas O'Toole, "Mystery Heavenly Body Discovered: Possibly as Large as Jupiter," *Washington Post* (December 31, 1983).

442. For reference to this campaign of intimidation, see Mark Hazlewood, *Blindsided*. See also: http://www.planetx2003.com/index.html.

443. See Hazlewood, *Blindsided: Planet X Passes in 2003.* Website: http://www.planetx2003.com/index.html.
444. Jenkins is author of *Maya Cosmogenesis 2012* (Santa Fe: Bear and Co., 1998); and *Galactic Alignment: The Transformation of Consciousness According to Mayan, Egyptian, and Vedic Traditions* (Inner Traditions International, 2002).
445. Two of the first to identify this upcoming transition were Jose Arguelles and Brian Swimme, *The Mayan Factor: Path Beyond Technology* (Bear and Co., 1987).
446. See Lee Carroll and Jan Tober, *The Indigo Children: The New Kids Have Arrived* (Hay House, 1999); and Drunvalo Melchizidek, *The Ancient Secret of the Flower of Life* (Light Technology Publications, 2000) Vol. 2, 443–54.
447. Henry discusses these projects in *Ark of the Christos.*
448. Quoted in Steve Russell, "'People Will Loot,' Said Rumsfeld, After Pros Snatched Priceless Sumerian Artifacts," *YOWUSA.COM* (June 14, 2003). Available online at: http://www.yowusa.com/Archive/Jun2003/14jun03a/14jun03a.htm.
449. Henry outlines this in his article, "Saddam Hussein, The Stairway to Heaven and the Return of Planet X," which is available on his website: www.williamhenry.net.
450. For more discussion of this history of non-disclosure in the US government, see Chapter Two.
451. See Bill Berkowitz, "Freedom of Information Act on the ropes: *Working for a Change*," Freedom of Information Center, (October 11, 2002). Available online at: http://foi.missouri.edu/federalfoia/foiactonropes.html.
452. Alexandra Bruce, "The Montauk PsyOp," *New World Disorder Magazine*, available online at: http://www.newworlddisorder.ca/issuetwo/articles/bruce.html. See also her forthcoming book, *The Montauk PsyOp: Time Travel, Mind Control & Disinformation.* For more info visit her website at: http://www.chica.bruce.net.
453. See Patrick Martin, "The sacking of Iraq's museums: US wages war against culture and history," *World Socialist Website*, 16 April 2003. Available online at: http://www.wsws.org/articles/2003/apr2003/muse-a16.shtml.
454. Quoted in Steve Russell, "'People Will Loot," Said Rumsfeld, After Pros Snatched Priceless Sumerian Artifacts," *YOWUSA.COM* (June 14, 2003). Available online at: http://www.yowusa.com/Archive/Jun2003/14jun03a/14jun03a.htm.
455. "Lost Tomb of King Gilgamesh Discovered," *BBC News*, April 29, 2003. http://news.bbc.co.uk/1/hi/sci/tech/2982891.stm.
456. For an online account of the Epic of Gilgamesh, go to: http://www.crystalinks.com/sumermythology.html.

457. Andrea Koppel and John King, "U.S.: North Korea admits nuke program," *CNN* (October 16, 2002) Go to: http://www.cnn.com/2002/US/10/16/us.nkorea.

458. Andrew Grice and David Usborne, "The Niger Connection: Tony Blair, Forged Documents and the Case For War," the *Independent* June 5, 2003. Copy available at: http://www.globalpolicy.org/security/issues/iraq/attack/2003/0605niger.htm.

459. Eric Boehlert, "Rumsfeld's personal spy ring," *Information Clearing House* (July 16, 2003) Available online at: http://www.informationclearinghouse.info/article4124.htm.

Chapter 6

America's Triumph & Europe's Angst—The Secret Race to Control Iraq's Extraterrestrial Heritage

After a hastily organized summit meeting in the Azores on March 16, 2003 with his European allies, President George Bush decided to abandon diplomatic efforts for a further UN Security Council Resolution condemning Iraq's lack of progress in fulfilling existing Security Council resolutions concerning any weapons of mass destruction possessed by Iraq.

In a televised address to the Nation on March 17, President Bush gave Iraqi President Saddam Hussein 48 hours to leave Iraq together with his sons to prevent a US led invasion. On March 19, soon after the deadline had expired, President Bush ordered surgical air strikes on Baghdad and the "second gulf war" had formally begun.

In the immediate post-Azores environment of finger pointing over responsibility for the failed diplomatic efforts to maintain global consensus over how to respond to Iraq, Europe and the world watched anxiously for the consequences of the US, British and Australian armed incursion. A prominent critic of President Bush was the Minority Leader of the US Senate, Senator Tom Daschle, who said in a stinging rebuke that he was "saddened that this president failed so miserably at diplomacy that we're now forced to war."[460]

Despite dire predictions of a long and bloody military campaign, resistance by the Iraqi military quickly evaporated when the US led forces reached Baghdad. In a highly symbolic speech aboard the US aircraft carrier *Abraham Lincoln* on May 2, President George Bush declared that large-scale military hostilities in Iraq were over. Contrary to widespread predictions of regional upheaval, the US had apparently succeeded in its preemptive military intervention against the former regime of Saddam Hussein. Although a guerrilla war by remnants of Saddam's regime continues at the time of writing this book, large scale military hostilities appear to be truly over.

It is necessary to analyze the implications of the failed diplomatic efforts to deal with Iraq and the subsequent US-led military incursion from an "exopolitical perspective." This is especially important since, as Chapter Five argued, Iraq holds special significance as a nation that once hosted an advanced race of extraterrestrials whose legacy has not been disclosed to the general public or elected government representatives.

Examining the complex diplomatic maneuvers among major powers concerning the merits of military intervention in Iraq gives important insights into the nature of the alliances between clandestine organizations and their respective perceptions of power as well as the threat related to control over extraterrestrial (ET) assets.

This chapter examines how the need to gain unfettered access to Iraq's ET heritage has played a critical role in influencing US foreign policy in the Persian Gulf region ever since the Carter administration. The chapter analyses how clandestine organizations based in the US, Europe and Soviet Union/Russia have historically maneuvered among themselves to gain strategic advantage in having access to and exploiting ET technology hidden in Iraq.

The chapter argues that the need for a diplomatic solution to the recent international crisis over Iraq resulted from the desire of clandestine groups in Europe, Russia and China to restrict access to these sites by US organizations that have grown rapidly in power and displayed an imperialistic tendency that leads to much anxiety among their European counterparts.

The chapter furthermore claims that the planet is experiencing the use of "exotic weaponry" between clandestine groups struggling among themselves over how to share access and control of ET technology in Iraq, while suppressing the true nature of the conflict to the general public and most elected officials. The chapter also argues that post-war agreement to rebuild Iraq under the new UN Security Council resolution passed on May 22, 2003, marks a new phase in the strategy of clandestine organizations to coordinate their efforts in exploiting Iraq's ET heritage.[461]

Finally, the paper claims that the US triumph in launching a military takeover in Iraq generates *angst* among European clandestine groups concerned over the increased power and imperial pretensions of their US counterparts.

Iraq's Extraterrestrial Heritage and the Clandestine Political Agenda

In 1976, Zecharia Sitchin published the first of his books, *The 12th Planet*, which was based on his translations of ancient Sumerian cuneiform texts.[462] As mentioned in Chapter Five, Sitchin described the technological wonders and knowledge of the ancient civilization of Sumeria, and claimed that the Sumerians were aided by an advanced race of beings called the Anunnaki (Sumerian for 'those who came from Heaven to Earth'). Sitchin's literal interpretation of the Anunnaki as an ET race distinguished his work from earlier translators who viewed the Anunnaki as mythological "gods."

A key component of Sitchin's work relevant to this chapter is his idea of factional war between the Anunnaki that finally contributed to their departing Earth around 1700 BC.[463] Another component is his view that the home world of the Anunnaki is a mysterious "10th planet" of the solar system (Nibiru—planet of the crossing) that periodically returns to the Earth's vicinity every 3,600 years.

As mentioned in Chapter Five, Sitchin's innovative translations when combined with biblical and historical records supporting the existence of ET races in human affairs, made clear the important role played by the Anunnaki in the genesis of humanity. Sitchin's work became very influential and was incorporated and/or supported by the work of other independent archaeologists, historians, "channels" and even a few ex-military whistleblowers.[464]

Nevertheless, Sitchin's translations proved to be very controversial and mainstream archeologists/historians dismissed his work as too speculative in its definitions, premises and conclusions.[465] However, there were very influential clandestine organizations that took Sitchin's work much more seriously.

As mentioned in Chapter Two, from at least 1941, US based clandestine organizations have been engaged in the reverse engineering of downed ET spacecraft, and communicating with different ET races.[466] The most prominent of these organizations was associated with a policy coordinating group comprising senior officials from the Roosevelt/Truman administrations.

President Truman gave executive approval for the creation of this elite policy making body in 1947 in a classified memo wherein he wrote: "Hereafter this matter shall be referred to only as Operation Majestic Twelve."[467] Majestic Twelve was claimed to initially consist of 12 members drawn primarily from the defense and intelligence community and was expanded under the Eisenhower administration.

Over time, clandestine organizations grew rapidly due to the complexity and size of the ET presence, and they remained a public secret with their existence and composition revealed neither to the general public nor to most elected public officials.[468]

The most prominent of the reverse engineering efforts of clandestine organizations have involved a race of ETs commonly described as "Grays" from Zeta Reticulum, similar in appearance to the ETs depicted in Steven Spielberg's famous movie, *Close Encounters of the Third Kind*. The technology possessed by the Grays was far advanced over anything possessed by humanity, and efforts began immediately to learn about and reverse engineer this technology.[469]

As revealed by Col. Corso in his groundbreaking book, *The Day After Roswell*, the Grays possessed propulsion and navigation systems far advanced over any possessed by the US or the USSR.[470] The prevalence of the Grays' ships in the shooting down of ET craft suggested that the US and the USSR were familiar enough with Gray technology in order to begin targeting their craft and creating a planetary defense shield. Certainly, this is what Col. Corso suggested in his work and has been independently confirmed by a number of other prominent military/intelligence whistleblowers.[471]

The content of Sitchin's work describing an ancient ET race would most certainly have aroused the curiosity of clandestine organizations in the US and elsewhere, intent on developing the most advanced technology possible from visiting/resident ET races. The possibility that the Anunnaki described by Sitchin had attained a level of technological sophistication even more advanced than that attained by Grays was something that had to be seriously explored.

Certainly the giant physical bodies possessed by this ancient race of ETs—the Anunnaki—suggested they had reached an evolutionary level in biological terms that was more evolved than the Grays who appeared to be suffering genetic problems. This would have had an impact on the technological advances that could be achieved between these two dissimilar races, especially when it came to the development and application of exotic technology that focused on time/inter-dimensional travel.

Testimonies provided by participants in the Philadelphia/Montauk Projects suggest that important genetic factors influenced the successful use of such technologies. The genetically weak "Grays" would therefore not have been able to develop a whole class of exotic technology that would have been accessible by the more genetically resilient Anunnaki.

If the technological accomplishments of the Anunnaki matched their biological evolution, then the Anunnaki would have technology far surpassing anything currently possessed by any of the clandestine organizations around the planet created to study and reverse engineer ET technology gained from Grays. It would also have been likely that the ETs that assisted Nazi Germany in developing its advanced technology, and "escape" to hidden bases in Antarctica and South America were associated with remnants of Anunnaki hidden on Earth.[472]

The eugenically oriented racial theories that motivated the Nazis would have been compatible with their collaborating with a race of "racially pure" beings, the Anunnaki, who provided an evolutionary model for the biological development of humanity. The technological advances gained through occult communications sponsored by the Thule Society with a racially pure humanoid race hidden in secret underground locations around the planet suggested that the Nazis were collaborating with such an advanced race.

The Nazis believed the "Aryans" were descendants of a race of Nordic blonde haired blue-eyed supermen who had ruled the planet from Thule, ancient capital of this Northern super-race. It can be concluded that the "supermen" the Nazis believed were assisting them and formed the biological model for humanity's evolution, were none other than the Anunnaki that Sitchin had outlined in his work.

Even more perplexing for clandestine organizations aware of Sitchin's work was the idea that the Anunnaki could one day return *en masse* to the Earth and again interact with humanity as they did in the remote past. The idea that the Anunnaki's home world periodically returned to the solar system would most surely have attracted attention in terms of any possible time line and what this meant for humanity. Alternatively, the idea that the Anunnaki could arrive through an exotic transportation device hidden in Iraq such as a "Stargate" (see Chapter Five) would have been another cause for concern.

One way of confirming Sitchin's hypotheses would have been to use advanced communication protocols developed by organizations such as the National Security Agency (NSA) in communicating with different ET races. Dan Sherman described his involvement in Project Preserve Destiny in the 1960s when the NSA began to use psychics for telepathic communications with ET races confirming that Western based clandestine organizations were adopting communication methods similar to those used by the Nazis in the 1930s.[473]

It is likely that Project Preserve Destiny and similar projects in other countries would have been successful in communicating with the Anunnaki.[474] Another means of confirming Sitchin's thesis would have been through "remote viewing programs" that had been secretly sponsored in the early 1970s by a number of US government and military intelligence agencies.[475] It is likely that these and other intelligence gathering efforts confirmed the validity of some if not most of Sitchin's hypotheses.

The confirmation of Sitchin's theses would have had tremendous foreign policy implications. US and European clandestine organizations would undoubtedly have made it a top priority to gain access to these ancient ET sites in southern Iraq to learn as much as possible about the advanced technology used by the Anunnaki, information about their society and their intentions concerning humanity.

Access to these sites would also provide important information about those Anunnaki still resident on Earth and the extent of their collaboration with Nazi forces that possibly still operated in the Antarctic and South America. Furthermore, US and European clandestine organizations would have been interested in learning more about the purported home world of the Anunnaki in case it did indeed return to the vicinity of the solar system in the near future. Finally, the US and Western Europe would have been intent on ensuring that such technology did not fall into the hands of their ideological rivals, the Soviet Union.

The problem for the US and Western Europe, however, was that at the time Sitchin's first book appeared, the Cold War still existed and Iraq was firmly in the Soviet sphere of influence. Although there was strategic cooperation between the US and USSR in dealing with the ET presence ever since the end of the Second World War, the 1945 Yalta Agreement was based on the principle that ET artifacts in various regions of Earth would come under the sphere of influence of the major power that controlled or had an alliance with the host nation.[476]

After a left wing coup in 1958 that deposed the Western-leaning King, Iraq nationalized its oil industries and moved firmly in the Soviet camp. In 1968, the radical socialist Ba'ath Party came to power and increased ties with the Soviet Union developing a socialist system that was secular and dependent on Warsaw Pact countries. The Soviet Union (now Russia) would undoubtedly have known about Sitchin's work and would already have been working to confirm if Sitchin's hypotheses were true through its own secret psychic, remote viewing and other exotic communication projects that it used for intelligence gathering on ET races.

The Soviet Union had a powerful political advantage in gaining access to these ET sites if and when they were found, and exploiting whatever technology and information lay within.

With the unlikelihood that Iraq would cooperate with US/European clandestine organizations in gaining access to these ancient ET sites, these organizations were confronted with a disturbing policy dilemma. If the international status quo remained, then at some point the Soviet Union would locate these ET sites and reverse engineer whatever technology existed; thereby eradicating any technological advantages the West might hold and perhaps gain an advantage in the cutting edge technologies of time/interdimensional travel. Furthermore, if the home world of Anunnaki did return, then the Soviet Union would be best placed to respond to whatever contingencies this created, and dictate how the planet's governments would have to coordinate their activities.

Given the above scenario, it is highly inconceivable that US and European clandestine organizations wouldn't have developed a top secret set of foreign policy goals whose aim was to bring about US/European access to Iraq's buried ET technology. This would have to be achieved without provoking a Cold War confrontation with the Soviet Union who would have been aware of the West's goals and resolutely opposed to US/European access.

All this would have to be achieved without armed conflict between the major powers and without public disclosure of the existence of Iraq's extensive ET heritage and virtual treasure house of ET artifacts and information.

The Secret Agenda to Gain Access to Iraq's ET Technology

Since at least the end of the Second World War, US and European based clandestine organizations have coordinated among themselves a joint policy in gaining access to and using reverse engineering ET technology found around the planet. The most prominent international forum is undoubtedly the Bilderberg group that holds closed meetings on an annual basis.[477] These meetings provide the opportunity for the leading industrialists, politicians, media magnates and military figures from different Western nations to meet and coordinate policies that have global significance ranging from financial and economic policy, to orchestrating political events in order to bring about favorable international conditions for their various agendas.

Less well known is that the Bilderberg group has played a key role in ensuring global non-disclosure of the ET presence, and in discrediting individuals and organizations who are attempting to reveal the true extent of ET intervention in human affairs.[478]

Organizations such as the Bilderberg group and other US/European based clandestine organizations design foreign policy goals that are "secret" insofar as these are not revealed to elected public officials, and revealed only to those officials who are bound by secrecy oaths not to disclose information about the ET presence and clandestine policies to gain access to ET technology. In this way, it has been accurately reported that clandestine organizations have long been able to orchestrate international crises to bring about political conditions that fulfill their foreign policy goals.[479]

The success of the secret foreign policy goals of US/European clandestine organizations in gaining access to Iraq's ET heritage and preparing for a possible return of the Anunnaki, lay in promoting international conditions that would allow US/Europe to gain unfettered access to Iraq without provoking Soviet intervention and a full scale military confrontation during the Cold War.

The way in which this could be done would be to initiate a series of regional crises that would tempt Iraq's staunchly secular socialist regime to take military advantage of these crises. The ultimate result would be Iraq's increasing dependence on Western nations; veering away from its alliance and dependence on the Soviet Union, distracted by its own regional crises.

The solution to the US/European policy dilemma was to sponsor upheaval in Iraq's main rival and regional powerhouse, Iran, that would inevitably force Iraq into a military confrontation with its more powerful neighbor, and thereby create opportunities for greater US and European influence in Iraq.

Traditionally, the US and its allies sponsored Islamic fundamentalism throughout the Middle East region, hoping this would weaken socialism as a viable social political system, and thereby provide for the expansion of US/European influence over territories that might hold extensive ET assets. This had occurred ever since the Suez crisis with the rise of Arab socialism and popular Arab regimes such as that of Egypt's President Jamal Abdul Nasir. According to Lal Khan:

> One of the cornerstones of US foreign policy was to sponsor, organize, arm and foment modern Islamic fundamentalism as a reactionary weapon against the rising tide of mass upsurge and social revolutions. The Jamaat-e-Islami and Ikhwan-ul-Muslimeen [Islamic Fundamentalist Organizations] were singled out for the job mainly due to their viciousness and fanatical neo-fascist character. After the Suez defeat the imperialists gave top priority to this policy. Large sums of money were dished out by the special operations department of the CIA and the Pentagon. They provided assistance in devising the strategy and training of these religious zealots.[480]

Covert sponsorship of Islamic fundamentalism had played an important role in undermining the socialist system established by President Nasir. This proved crucial in the eventual rejection of socialist ideals by his successor, Anwar Sadat, and the eventual movement of Egypt from the Soviet Sphere of Influence into the West. Thus any ET artifacts in Egypt would automatically move from potential Soviet control into the Western camp, in accord with the principles established at the Treaty of Yalta.

Although sponsorship of Islamic fundamentalism had been an important part of covert US foreign policy since the early 1960s, what made the case of Iraq different was that the US would sacrifice an important regional ally in order to destabilize Iraq. The primary focus of this secret agenda for gaining access to Iraq's ET heritage was that the Shah of Iran would be toppled and replaced by a fundamentalist Islamic regime that would create havoc and uncertainty in the Persian Gulf region.

The success of this radical plan rested in a twofold strategy of first withdrawing the traditional support of the US for the Shah of Iran who maintained a tight hold on political power through his powerful security forces; and second, fomenting an Islamic revolution in Iran by allowing the export of revolutionary literature into Iran. The first part of this dual strategy was made possible by the Carter administration, which had begun advocating human rights as an important foreign policy principle for the US in dealing with its global allies, soon after coming into office in January 1977.[481]

Carter's human rights initiative placed pressure on the Shah for political reforms that undermined his tight hold on political power and restrained him from using military force to stay in power. The Shah's inability to pass sufficient reforms to appease the growing Iranian middle class, led to a rapid increase in political dissent.

The second part of this dual strategy was for France to give asylum in October 1978 to an exiled Islamic cleric, Ayatollah Ruhollah Khomeini, who would be given free rein to play a destabilizing role by advocating a radical Islamic State in Iran and undermining attempts to create a liberal secular state by moderate Iranian reformers. France agreed to give asylum to Khomeini after he was expelled from Najaf, Iraq by the Iraqi regime that was under pressure from Iran to silence the outspoken cleric. The role of France in allowing Khomeini to enter France and use it as a base to produce a series of fiery tapes and written pamphlets denouncing the Shah's regime proved critical in sparking Islamic fervor and undermining efforts by moderate political reformers for a secular liberal government under the Shah.[482]

The success of this clandestine two-pronged strategy ultimately led to the collapse of the Shah's regime, and he had to flee from Iran on January 16, 1979. Efforts by moderate Iranian reformers to bring about a modern liberal state were doomed by France's decision to allow Ayatollah Khomeini to return to Iran in this critical period. Three days after the Shah's departure, Ayatollah Khomeini triumphantly flew from France to millions of admiring supporters in Iran to announce the formation of a new government, and formally begin the Iranian revolution.

The Shah of Iran had been sacrificed and liberal Iranian reformers betrayed so a series of regional crises in the

Persian Gulf could be orchestrated by US/European clandestine organizations that would allow them to gain a strategic
foothold in Iraq.

The impact of the Iranian revolution in regional terms was
ominous for the Sunni dominated regimes that surrounded the
Islamic Republic dominated by the Shiites of Iran. Shiites and
Sunnis differ over the legitimate successors to the Prophet
Muhammed, and have historically had difficult relationships
due to the "martyrdom" of key Shiite leaders, such as the
grandsons of the Prophet Muhammad.

For the Sunni dominated Socialist regime of Iraq (Iraqi
President Al-Bakr was forced to resign on July 16, 1979, and
was succeeded by his powerful Vice-President, Saddam
Hussein) the Islamic revolution was a looming threat to the
territorial integrity of Iraq and even the survival of its socialist
regime. Iraq was the most developed society in the Arab world
with high per capita indices in health, education, and public
services.

Iraq's political system was dominated by socialist principles
that made it a very secular and progressive administration in
the region. Iraq, however, had a large Shiite population in
southern Iraq (location of the ancient Sumerian cities in which
lay buried whatever facilities/information left behind by the
ancient Anunnaki).

Iraq Attempts To Take Military Advantage of the Iranian Revolution

The new Islamic Republic of Iran was a dire threat to the
territorial integrity of Iraq since it would undoubtedly influence
the restive Shiite population of Iraq who made up 60% of the
population and resented the Sunni elites (20%) that ruled
Iraq.[483] Furthermore, Iran's Islamic State was an ideological rival
to the Ba'ath socialist system then existing in Iraq.

Saddam Hussein instinctively understood the threat posed
by revolutionary Iran to Iraq, and decided to act while the
Islamic regime was still in its infancy and Iran was preoccupied
by consolidating its regime. More important for Saddam, the

Iranian military had been decimated by the Revolution with its most senior and skilled personnel either escaping the new regime, or being purged by the new Iranian authorities. The mighty Iranian military which only a short time earlier was the most powerful in the region, suddenly was having difficulty finding enough trained pilots and spare parts for its advanced fleets of US supplied aircraft.

The new Iraqi regime under Saddam Hussein decided to strike and launched a devastating attack in September 1980 on its larger and more powerful neighbor, Iran, that resulted in a long eight-year war that quickly ground down into a stalemate. Western states along with wealthy Arab states began to support Saddam's regime with technology, finances and secret armaments.[484] The Soviet Union, preoccupied by its own military difficulties in countering an Islamic revolution in Afghanistan was not able to provide sufficient resources to help Iraq in its war.

The end of the long Iran-Iraq war in 1988 occurred almost simultaneously with a rapidly transforming global political climate. Eastern bloc countries belonging to the Warsaw Pact were beginning to collapse and the mighty Soviet Union was also in the initial stages of its eventual disintegration into 15 independent republics. With the Soviet Union/Russia rapidly losing global influence, Western states gained greater prominence in Iraq. This was especially true for France and Germany, both of which played important roles in directly financing and aiding Iraq in its long war with Iran. Significantly, France had played a direct role in supporting the construction of nuclear facilities in Osirak, Iraq, which were bombed by the Israeli Air force in 1981.[485] Iraq could count on France, Germany and China to fill the strategic vacuum created by the disintegration of the Soviet Union.

Yugoslav, Chinese and German engineering firms provided the technical support for Iraq's construction of a sophisticated network of underground tunnels and bunkers that were used by the Iraqi leadership.[486] Confirming the Yugoslav connection, a *Washington Post* article stated:

> Many of Iraq's military tunnels are believed to have been built by Aeroinzenjering, a Serbian engineering firm

once run by the military of the former Yugoslavia. Hussein maintained a close relationship with Communist leader Tito (Josip Broz), and with Slobodan Milosevic, whose underground tunnels and bunkers bedeviled U.S. and NATO commanders during the 1999 Kosovo air war.[487]

These elaborate tunnel constructions occurred soon after Saddam's elevation to power and would have been motivated both by the threat posed by Iranian missile attack, and Saddam's awareness that Iraq's ancient (ET) heritage, much of which lay buried, was the key to his own grandiose plans for regional dominance.[488] It is significant that he relied primarily on Yugoslav and Chinese engineers, since this would have given him most political flexibility in taking advantage of whatever was found without relying on the Soviet Union or the West.

It is likely that at some point in building these underground constructions throughout Iraq, evidence of Iraq's extraterrestrial civilization was directly encountered. The complex task of studying and eventually reverse engineering these ET assets would have begun. These initial efforts, however, would have been limited by the contingencies of the Iran-Iraq war, the highly advanced nature of these technologies, and Iraq's effort to extract maximum concessions from Soviet/Russian, European and Chinese efforts to study and exploit this technology. It is worth emphasizing that the countries that actively assisted Iraq in its various construction and weapons acquisitions programs were those that were most insistent upon a diplomatic solution to the recent crisis: Russia, France, Germany and China.

US Foreign Policy and the First Gulf War

Despite its tacit support for Iraq in the Iraq-Iran war, the United States (and Britain) had a distinct disadvantage over its European partners/rivals in gaining access to Iraq's ancient ET sites. The Iraq socialist system, its history of human rights abuses, the brutal policies of Saddam that included assassinating his rivals and using chemical weapons on Iraq's Kurdish minorities, Iraq's strong links with the Soviet Union, and strong opposition to the state of Israel, made it difficult for the US to formally improve its relationship with Iraq's regime.[489]

The US Congress, like most institutions comprised of elected government representatives, was simply unaware of the need for US foreign policy to have a cooperative relationship with Saddam's regime in order to exploit the latter's ET assets. Congress would have revolted at any attempt to openly assist what appeared to be a brutal regime run by a despotic ruler. This meant that US based clandestine organizations had to orchestrate international events in a way that would fulfill the secret policy goal of gaining unfettered access to Iraq's ET heritage.

Under the first President Bush, Iraq and Kuwait became engaged in a diplomatic crisis over the overproduction of oil by Kuwait in 1991. Kuwait's overproduction meant that world oil prices were deflated and Iraq's oil production would be insufficient to generate the necessary revenue for Iraq to begin the difficult reconstruction process after its costly war with Iran. This resulted in making Iraq more dependent on Western states and clandestine organizations—a result that Saddam would not have been pleased with, given his undoubted awareness that financial independence would deliver maximum negotiating power with whomever he allowed to exploit the ET resources on his territory.

Even more vexing to the regime of Saddam Hussein, Kuwait was demanding repayment of the war loans it had given to Iraq during the eight year Iraq-Iran war. For Saddam, this was the ultimate affront, given that Iraq had fought a war that directly benefited Kuwait and the other Sunni dominated states in the Persian Gulf. As far as Saddam was concerned, Kuwait should have shown more gratitude for the sacrifice in Iraq's financial and human resources in its debilitating war with Iran. It is unlikely that Kuwait would have taken such a risky policy in dealing with its powerful neighbor had it not been for firm assurances by its main sponsor and historical patron, Britain, that Kuwait would not be abandoned in a conflict with Iraq.

Iraq's longstanding grudge against Britain's sponsorship of Kuwait went back to 1899, when Britain took Kuwait "under its protection."[490] The problem was that Kuwait was then a part of Iraq's Basra district that was ruled by the crumbling Ottoman Empire. When Iraq became independent in 1932, after itself coming under British control after the First World War defeat and collapse of the Ottoman Empire, Basra, Iraq's main seaport, no longer included Kuwait.

Iraqis felt cheated of both the unfettered ocean access and wealth that the territory of Kuwait offered. So odious was this British policy for Iraq's political elites, that ever since its independence, Iraq's leaders have refused to recognize the sovereign statehood of Kuwait, and continued to call for its reintegration into Iraq. In raising its oil production, calling for repayment of its war loans, and its dubious political legitimacy in the eyes of Iraq's political elite, Kuwait was undoubtedly acting in a risky and antagonistic way.

In forcing a change in Kuwait's antagonistic policies, Iraq decided to engage in brinkmanship and massed a large army on its border with Kuwait. At this critical point where Iraq was indicating its intent to possibly invade Kuwait if it did not change its policies, April Glaspie, the US Ambassador to Iraq made what appeared to be a crucial error.

In advising Iraq about the US view concerning the simmering Iraq/Kuwait dispute, she said: "We have no opinion on your Arab-Arab conflicts . . . such as your dispute with Kuwait. Secretary [of State James] Baker has directed me to emphasize the instruction . . . that Kuwait is not associated with America."[491]

Given the history of Iraq's relationship with Kuwait, the risk-taking personal psychology of Saddam Hussein and antagonistic policy of the Kuwaiti leadership, it may well have been predicted that Saddam would interpret this as a green light to invade. Glaspie was appropriately "punished" for her "crucial error."[492]

However, what if this "tragic error" by a senior diplomat was not a mistake? What if Secretary Baker's instruction were intended to provide Saddam with the belief that the US would stand by while he invaded Kuwait and eventually forced a diplomatic solution that would address some of Iraq's historical grievances over Kuwait? Saddam may well have interpreted such a policy as a means by which the US was ingratiating itself with his regime in order to gain access to Iraq's strategic resources, including any ET artifacts that had been discovered.

Saddam may well have viewed this as a *quid pro quo* for allowing the US to gain more influence in Iraq and have access to the hidden/discovered ET technology. Saddam, a risk-taker by nature, may well have been fooled by subtle signals by US policy officials and believed his regime would benefit from launching an attack.

President Bush was a former head of the Central Intelligence Agency and therefore aware and most likely a member of US based clandestine organizations set up to coordinate government policy on the ET presence.[493] Secretary of State Baker, a close friend and former chief of staff for President Bush, would also have been aware of the need for US access into Iraq to monitor and/or control whatever ET technology existed.

Key figures in the Bush administration were most likely aware of any time line that existed in terms of a possible return of the Anunnaki home world. The conflict over Kuwait was an opportunity to lull Saddam into taking the risk of invasion in order to bring about the desired US military intervention that would lead to greater US access to and control over whatever significant ET sites existed in Iraq.

Thus the political crisis that engulfed Iraq and Kuwait and which resulted in Saddam taking the risky policy of military intervention in Kuwait, was orchestrated by US based clandestine organizations that desired unfettered access by the West into Iraq.

Although such a conspiratorial orchestration of international events that led to the first Gulf War in 1991 is undoubtedly controversial, it is consistent with the way in which the ET presence has been systematically suppressed globally. The policy of non-disclosure of the ET presence to the mass media and most elected public officials is made possible by the ability of clandestine organizations to control the mass media by manipulating evidence, intimidating reporters with threats of ridicule or dismissal for investigating UFO reports, and ensuring censorship by editors and media owners.[494]

The same clandestine organizations responsible for this global policy of non-disclosure, has the power to orchestrate international crises and events to bring about favorable policy outcomes.[495] This ability is due to officials in these clandestine organizations being appointed rather than elected, and their policies not being scrutinized in the public arena.

This gives such officials great freedom in formulating and implementing public policy without the supervision and account-ability that elected officials regularly experience. Furthermore, officials in clandestine organizations are appointed without the handicap of short-term election processes that stymie long term planning on the part of elected public officials. In short, orches-trating international events to attain key foreign policy objectives is well within the institutional capabilities and resources of organ-izations led by appointed officials who lack public accountability and supervision.

The possibility that ET technology lay hidden in Iraq, which had a level of sophistication far advanced to whatever had been reverse engineered by recovered ET craft since 1941, would have made unfettered access to Iraq a crucial policy goal for US based clandestine organizations. This would have been accentuated if it were confirmed that the home world of the Anunnaki would soon be returning to the Earth's vicinity of the solar system.

The existence and location of these ancient ET sites, which had likely been discovered by the Iraqis in the 1980s as a result of their extensive underground construction projects, was also possibly known by those states who had long provided techni-cal assistance to Iraq: Russia, France, Germany and China. US based clandestine organizations were therefore at a relative disadvantage to their European partners/rivals in gaining access to this ET technology. US based clandestine organizations orchestrated the first Gulf War in order to provide the US the desired access.

Subsequently, Saddam did go ahead with a war against Kuwait on August 1990, and contrary to the message delivered by Glaspie, he found that the US was resolutely opposed to Iraq's invasion and did not favor any compromise over the territorial integrity of Kuwait. In the protracted diplomatic dialogue over securing Iraq's withdrawal, the first Bush administration ruled out any concessions to Iraq. This meant that Soviet/Russian diplomacy, motivated by awareness that a war would appreciably diminish Russian influence in Iraq and its relative advantage in gaining access to and controlling ET technology, would ultimately fail.

Failure of the Bush administration to support any face-saving compromise ensured that a full-scale war would be fought to "liberate" Kuwait. The US led multinational military intervention that began in January 1991 resulted in the expulsion of Iraq from Kuwait. An important consequence was that the US, for the first time, had a strategic foothold in Iraq with a number of Security Council resolutions giving legitimacy to the continued US presence as long as issues relevant to the Gulf War remained unresolved.

The US Strategic Bind after the First Gulf War

Unfortunately, from the perspective of the first Bush administration, the US was not able to force regime change in Iraq after the end hostilities in the "liberation" of Kuwait. The US sponsorship of a mass uprising by Iraq's Kurdish and Shiite communities did not lead to the fall of Saddam's regime once the rebelling ethnic communities were denied the promised military support from the US led alliance.

Consequently, Saddam's regime was able to reestablish control by brutally suppressing the uprising. This meant US based clandestine organizations were now in a strategic bind in terms of accessing and exploiting the ET technology under the control of Saddam's regime. The US did not have the international authority to forcibly replace Saddam's regime and Saddam undoubtedly felt betrayed by the US. He could be expected to cooperate further with Russian, European and Chinese clandestine organizations in giving access to and exploiting ET technology, and thereby frustrate clandestine US organizations. Clandestine European groups together with their Russian and Chinese partners were in a stronger strategic position to their US partners/rivals in gaining access to and exploiting whatever ET technology existed in Iraq.

Saddam was intent on having his vengeance against the US and Britain by denying all access to them. Given that the US had the most sophisticated reverse engineering program on the planet and was rapidly developing global preponderance as the world's lone superpower, this was a scenario that was deeply disturbing for US officials aware of the possible implications of the ET technology in Iraq to influence the global balance of power. At the same time, European/Russian/Chinese clandestine groups were concerned over the potential for the US to extend its technological superiority and global dominance if it gained access to Iraq's ET technology.

An unexpected obstacle to the plan of US based clandestine organizations to gain access to ET technology in Iraq was the surprise election of President Bill Clinton in 1992. Unlike the first President Bush, Clinton was not privileged to key information concerning the clandestine programs involving ET technology and communications.[496]

As discussed in Chapter Two, since the Kennedy administration, there has been a policy of not disclosing full details of the ET presence and ET technology to sitting Presidents, as this threatened the non-disclosure policy and lack of executive supervision enjoyed by US based clandestine organizations.[497] As a former head of the Central Intelligence Agency, President Bush was aware of information on ETs before he assumed his Presidency.

Indeed, Bush likely played the role of rubber stamping the most significant policies proposed by the clandestine policy coordinating group responsible for ET affairs—MJ-12/PI-40.

Early in his administration, Clinton demonstrated an interest in the ET presence that threatened the non-disclosure policy of clandestine organizations and their political agenda in gaining complete access to Iraq's ET heritage. Clinton's hands-on policy making style was a direct threat to MJ-12/PI-40, the top policy making group for ET affairs. Subsequently, Clinton was denied the information he required if some executive supervision were to occur for ET affairs.[498]

Moreover, key officials in the Bush administration, including Secretary of Defense William Cohen, appeared to be out of the information loop.[499] Predictably, little happened during the Clinton administration for moving ahead with the agenda of gaining unfettered access to Iraq's ET heritage.

The election of the second Bush administration meant that the agenda of clandestine US organizations for gaining access to Iraq's ET heritage could resume. Many former officials from the first Bush and earlier Republican administrations supporting regime change in Iraq were appointed in the new administration. As a result of their association with the Department of Defense, many if not all of these would have been familiar with clandestine activities to reverse engineer ET technology and the true reason motivating regime change in Iraq.

These officials included Secretary of Defense, Donald Rumsfeld; his deputy Paul Wolfowitz; Richard Perle, chairman of the Defense Policy Board, a Pentagon advisory panel; Douglas Feith, Undersecretary of Defense for Policy; and finally, Vice President Richard Cheney, who was Secretary of Defense in the first Bush Administration.[500] The terrorist attacks on September 11, 2001, provided the vehicle for the Bush administration gaining support for eradicating global terrorism wherever it manifested.

Once the Bush administration could make a plausible case that Iraq was a sponsor of global terrorism and that it had concealed weapons of mass destruction that constituted a threat to the US, it could develop the necessary public support for invading Iraq. To achieve this goal, the Office of Special Plans was created in the Pentagon to "invigorate" intelligence assessments of the terrorist threat posed by Iraq. According to intelligence analysts:

> The premise behind the office seemed to be that career analysts inside the intelligence community, and specifically the CIA, were not grasping the hard realities about Iraq and its weapons of mass destruction, and that a fresh set of eyes examining much of the same information could make critical links. [Assistant Secretary] Wolfowitz told the New York Times last year that there is

"a phenomenon in intelligence work that people who are pursuing a certain hypothesis will see certain facts that others won't, and not see other facts that others will."[501]

According to a former CIA counter-terrorism chief, Vince Cannistraro, it's clear "the decision was made within a couple of months of Sept. 11 to get rid of Saddam Hussein. But the administration had to find rationale to do it. So they set up a secretive group through [Douglas] Feith which started producing information on Iraq that was more compatible than the CIA."[502]

The Dangerous Rift between US and European Clandestine Organizations

In the build up to the threatened preemptive war in Iraq, a number of international events had occurred that indicated that clandestine European/Russian/Chinese organizations were at odds with their US partners/rivals. Germany was the first major nation that publicly committed itself to ruling out a preemptive war against Iraq, regardless of progress in the weapons inspection process that began after passage of Security Council Resolution 1441 on November 8, 2002.

Germany's staking out the extreme position made it possible for France, and then Russia, to take up the more moderate position of only calling for military intervention if Iraq failed to comply with Resolution 1441. France and Russia, effectively stymied US efforts in passing a further resolution calling for international military intervention in Iraq to remove any proscribed weapons of mass destruction.

If the diplomatic maneuvering were simply about weapons of mass destruction, then it would be fair to say that the US was acting in a bellicose and imperialist manner in demanding a further UN Security Council Resolution to bring about closure to the weapons inspection process. However, since Western intervention in Iraq has long been secretly motivated by gaining access to Iraq's treasure house of ET technology, the diplomatic behavior of France, Russia, Germany and also China needs to be understood in this context.

Many have viewed the diplomatic opposition by the powerful trio of France, Russia and Germany to a US led preemptive war as being clearly in the interests of the world community united against the horror of an unnecessary war that would devastate the Persian Gulf region, and usher in more acts of terrorism in the Middle East and elsewhere.[503] However, what secretly motivated these nations was the awareness that US access to ET technology in Iraq would constitute a threat due to the growing power of US based clandestine organizations and their secret reverse engineering projects.

US successes in gaining access to and employing reverse engineering ET technology in Iraq would have been a concern for their less well funded and technically proficient partners/rivals in Russia, France, Germany and China. Furthermore, the access enjoyed by the latter in accessing this technology in Iraq, would have given them some insight into the capabilities of this technology and helped balance the technological advantages enjoyed by the US.

More important, European/Russian/Chinese organizations were able to work within whatever constraints imposed by the regime of Saddam Hussein in reaching a preliminary under-standing of the capabilities of this technology. A preemptive war that amounted to a unilateral takeover of Iraq by the US and Britain, was something that European/Russian/Chinese organizations would not support, given the increased opportu-nities to the US in increasing its technological advantages and global dominance.

In short, Europe was in *angst* over the prospect of an already dominant US growing more powerful with acquisition of even more sophisticated ET technology. This would have paralleled the classic story narrated by the Greek historian, Thucydides, who claimed that the growth in Athenian naval power in the 5th century BC led to fear on the part of other Greek city states that allied themselves with Sparta to bring about a long and devastating war that led to the eventual defeat of Athens.[504]

Was the US taking a course that was similar to Ancient Athens, whereby US growth in imperial power would unite other major world states in an opposing alliance that could lead to devastating confrontation?

It is possible that European/Russian/Chinese clandestine organizations had tacitly signaled to their US counterparts that a unilateral takeover of Iraq was not acceptable. The destruction of the Space Shuttle *Columbia* on February 1 certainly was a high profile event that shocked the planet. The timing of the event, however, indicates that it may have been a high profile victim of a clandestine struggle over who would have access and control over Iraq's ET heritage.

In a report to NASA by Larry Park, a Systems Failure Analyst attempting to identify the cause of the *Columbia* disaster, he claims that the disaster was caused by a freak convergence of scalar electromagnetic energy in the mesosphere that struck the Shuttle during its return to Earth.[505] Park's report points to the possible use of "scalar weaponry" in the destruction of *Columbia*. Such weaponry uses an innovative form of electromagnetic energy that, according to a retired US army colonel and scientist Thomas Bearden, was also used in the destruction of the *Challenger* Space Shuttle on January 28, 1986, and other US aviation "accidents" over the last three decades for which these weapons have been developed and used.[506]

According to Bearden, "The *Challenger* was positively killed by the Soviet Union, using the scalar EM weapons through the Woodpecker grid. A host of indicators occurred."[507]

The "Woodpecker grid" according to Bearden, was caused by the activation in July 1976 of powerful Soviet transmitters that beamed a high frequency band of energy around the planet with an enormous power of at least 100 megawatts. "These powerful transmitters were promptly nicknamed 'Woodpeckers' because of the characteristic sound of the chirped signal when received. That is, the received signal made a pecking sound much like a woodpecker's beak hitting a block of wood."[508]

Weather conditions in the mesosphere that Park identified as having caused the *Columbia* tragedy were similar to the weather indicators that Bearden identified as accompanying the destruction of the *Challenger*. The use and possession of scalar weaponry in the arsenals of clandestine organizations around the planet, made it possible and likely that it was used against the *Columbia* to send a powerful political message to the Bush administration over its intended preemptive war against Iraq.

Beginning in mid-February 2003, when the prospective war dominated international diplomacy, an unusual amount of seismic activity had begun to occur around the planet.[509] Although much speculation surrounded the cause and seriousness of these seismic anomalies, it is worth exploring whether the anomalies were caused by advanced weapons technology that was either being tested or extensively used, globally. Existence of advanced weaponry that could produce seismic activity, volcanoes and severe weather conditions was publicly acknowledged by a speech given by former Secretary of Defense, William Cohen, in 1997 at a conference discussing the threat posed by global terrorism: "Others [terrorists] are engaging even in an eco-type of terrorism whereby they can alter the climate, set off earthquakes, volcanoes remotely through the use of electromagnetic waves . . ."[510]

Cohen's speech was not widely reported and indeed has been withdrawn from the public archives of the Department of Defense, thereby suggesting that the development and use of such technology remains highly classified. In a number of books and papers discussing "scalar weapons" capable of the effects described by Cohen, Col. Bearden suggests that such technology has been developed for decades by the former Soviet Union and other states. According to Bearden:

> In January 1960, Khrushchev announced the development of a new, fantastic weapon—one so powerful it could wipe out all life on earth if unrestrainedly used. The New York Times printed part of the story. Khrushchev, of course, was referring to the newly emerging scalar EM weapons. So in early 1960 the Soviets were in at least what we call the engineering development stage for large scalar EM beam weapons, which would be deployed when finished.[511]

He provides extensive evidence that seismic and weather anomalies over the last thirty years have often been caused by these scalar weapons.[512]

If anomalous seismic activity since mid-February, 2003 was caused by scalar weaponry, then it is very likely that a secret military conflict had been occurring between clandestine groups over access and control of ET technology in Iraq. It is likely that European/Russian/Chinese clandestine organizations were active in such a war that was used to restrain US efforts to take sole control of Iraq's ET heritage. The targets of such scalar weapons would have been the numerous underground facilities of each country's respective clandestine organizations around the planet for developing ET technology. The existence of such bases were revealed by Phil Schneider, a former civil engineer employed by military contractors for construction of such bases, in a series of lectures shortly before what appeared to be his murder by a contract killing.[513]

If a secret war between clandestine organizations had occurred both prior to and simultaneously with US military intervention in Iraq, then it was likely that the UN Security Council Resolution reached on May 22, 2003, signaled a "new understanding" had been reached by competing clandestine organizations.

It has been accepted that US intervention could not be reversed and that UN humanitarian assistance and reconstruction would help heal the rift between the major allies. However, there was still intense disagreement over the degree to which power and authority would be shared if the US had formal military assistance from Europe and Russia in containing the upsurge in guerilla violence that emerged after the May 1 cessation of hostilities speech by President Bush.

France's UN envoy, who responded to an appeal by Colin Powell on August 21, 2003 for military assistance in countering guerilla attacks, delivered a revealing statement about the fact that control and power over Iraq's resources continue to be at the core of the dispute between the US and Europe/Russia/China:

> Emerging from a meeting with Secretary General Kofi Annan this morning, Mr. Powell told reporters that "we're looking at, of course, reaffirming our determination to succeed in Iraq. We're looking forward to language that might call on member states to do more." Shortly

afterward, France's deputy ambassador, Michel Duclos, told a Security Council meeting that the economic and political reconstruction of Iraq will not succeed if Washington insists on maintaining sole control of the process. "Sharing the burden and responsibility in a world of equal and sovereign nations also means sharing information and authority," Mr. Duclos said.[514]

Evidence continues to suggest that intense disagreement over the control over Iraq exists and this can easily lead to a violent struggle between clandestine organizations that is kept from the public arena. Given the power of the "exotic" weaponry possessed by clandestine military groups, this means the planet is entering a dangerous period. As long as disagreement exists over the degree to which ET artifacts in Iraq are to be controlled and used by the US, violent opposition by non-US based clandestine groups is likely to occur. This is likely to result in continued instability in Iraq as long as the US refuses to share real power with other major states in the reconstruction of Iraq.

Conclusion: America's Triumph and Europe's *Angst*

The successful military intervention and takeover of Iraq by the US and Britain represent the culmination of a decades long policy of gaining access and control of Iraq's ET artifacts. Originally begun as a cooperative venture between the US and European based clandestine organizations desiring to access and control Iraq's ET assets from the Soviet Union, the shift in geopolitics meant these former allies found themselves on opposing sides of an intense diplomatic struggle over when and how military intervention should occur in Iraq.

Failure of a diplomatic solution to the 2003 crisis over Iraq's purported weapons of mass destruction marked a break between US based clandestine organizations and their former partners, and now rivals in continental Europe who aligned themselves with Russia and China.

Rather than differences between the US and its continental European allies being a temporary diplomatic spat that will disappear as new international issues emerge, it appears that a fundamental change has occurred in the geopolitical alliances and rivalries over the acquisition and control of ET artifacts around the planet. Whatever geopolitical balance was achieved by dividing the planet into "spheres of influence" appears to have been broken with the US action in Iraq, thereby prompting a shift in alliances between clandestine organizations.

Opposition of France, Germany, Russia and China over preemptive military intervention in Iraq has indicated that a major concern of the clandestine organizations of these countries is the growing power of US based clandestine organizations that presumably have the lion's share of access and control of ET technology around the planet. The strategic importance of Iraq in terms of its legacy as a major base of operations for the Anunnaki; the existence of "Stargate technology" in Iraq; the activities of remnant Anunnaki on Earth; and the possible mass return of the Anunnaki and/or their home world; were all sufficient to spark violent conflict between clandestine organizations without public disclosure that such secret military conflict was occurring.

Heightened seismic activities and the destruction of the *Columbia* Space Shuttle were the most visible indicators of the use of powerful exotic weapons such as scalar electromagnetic devices due to concerns over US imperial ambitions in Iraq, and its overstepping tacit international principles that acted as a balance for how ET artifacts were to be accessed and controlled by major states.

In a political climate where the Bush administration appears intent on a foreign policy of preemptive military intervention supported by a small number of loyal allies, there is likelihood of increased global conflict as US based clandestine organizations struggle for best strategic advantage over their European/ Russian/Chinese rivals in accessing and controlling ET artifacts around the planet.

Continental European clandestine organizations find themselves in the unfamiliar positions of having to ally themselves with Russia and China in order to balance the imperial aspirations of US based organizations. If predictions are accurate that the home world of the advanced race of ETs—the Anunnaki described by Sitchin—will soon reappear, this would only heighten concern over the strategic advantages established by US based clandestine organizations and possible conflict with their most determined rivals in Russia and China.[515]

All clandestine organizations are apparently competing for the best strategic position in a race for ET technology and knowledge that may be necessary in a forthcoming ET confrontation/encounter that determines the future of human civilization as we know it. The US led military intervention and takeover of Iraq represents success of a decades-long secret policy of securing US access to Iraq's ET heritage.

The price paid for America's triumph is Europe's *angst* over what the US intends to do with the strategic advantage it enjoys in accessing and controlling Iraq's ET heritage, and the changing balance of power between clandestine organizations over their access and control of ET technology. There appears to no longer be a balance in the ET technologies possessed by clandestine organizations. This spells dangerous times ahead as these organizations try to steer through the challenges of growth in US power, possible return of the Anunnaki, and all the challenges this poses for global humanity.

Notes

460. For a CNN report on Daschle's comments go to: http://www. cnn.com/2003/ALLPOLITICS/03/18/sprj.irq.daschle.gop/index.html. In contrast, Henry Kissinger described the opposition of France and Germany to support a further resolution which would have imposed a formal deadline for Iraq's full compliance with existing Security Council resolutions as the "gravest crisis" in the history of the Atlantic alliance. See Henry Kissinger, "The Atlantic Alliance in its Gravest Crisis," 2003, Tribune Media Services International, 2/9/03: http://www.tmsfeatures.com/tmsfeatures/subcategory.jsp.
461. For a copy of the Resolution, go to: http://www.globalpolicy.org/ security/issues/iraq/document/2003/0522resolution.htm.
462. Zecharia Sitchin, *The 12th Planet: Book 1 of the Earth Chronicles* (Avon Books, 1976).

463. Zecharia Sitchin, *The Wars of Gods and Men: Book III of the Earth Chronicles* (Avon Books, 1996).
464. See Chapter Five for more information on those supporting Sitchin's claims.
465. For criticism of Sitchin's translations, see Michael S. Heiser, "Sitchin's Mesopotamian Rocket Ships: How to Ignore Ancient Mesopotamian Dictionaries," Published online at: http://www.facadenovel.com/sitchinsrockets.htm.
466. For information about the reverse engineering efforts by clandestine organizations within the defense department, see Phillip Corso, *The Day After Roswell* (Pocket Star, 1997). For description of various government agencies involved in these efforts, see Steven M. Greer, *Extraterrestrial Contact: The Evidence and Implications* (Crossing Point Publications, 1999).
467. "President Truman to Secretary of Defense James Forrestal," 24 September 1947; available online at: http://www.majesticdocuments.com/documents/pre1948.html.
468. For documentary evidence dealing with many of these organizations, go to http://www.majesticdocuments.com. For a detailed analysis of these US based organizations, see Richard Boylan, "The Shadow Government: Its Identification and Analysis": http://www.drboylan.com/shadgovt2.html. For an account on how these organizations have grown and become free from executive oversight, see Chapter Two.
469. For details of these reverse engineering efforts, see Philip Corso, *The Day After Roswell*.
470. Corso, *The Day After Roswell*.
471. Corso, *The Day After Roswell*. See also witness testimonies in Greer, ed., *Disclosure*.
472. See Chapter Three for more information on the Nazi-ET connection.
473. Dan Sherman, Above Black. Available online at: http://www.aboveblack.com.
474. A popular psychic "channel" communicating with ET races is Jelaila Starr, *We Are the Nibiruans*. See her website at: http://www.nibiruancouncil.com.
475. For discussion on the intelligence potential of Remote Viewing, see Russell Targ and Harold Puthoff, *Mind-Reach: Scientists Look at Psychic Ability* (London: Jonathan Cape, 1977). For remote viewing of ET races, see Courtney Brown, *Cosmic Explorers*.
476. See Chapter Three for discussion of the global management system set up to deal with ET affairs.
477. For description of the Bilderberg group, see Armen Victorian, "The Bilderberg Group—The Invisible Power House," *Nexus* magazine, 3:1 (Dec '95-Jan '96). Available online at: http://www.nexusmagazine.com/articles/Bilderbergers.html.

478. For discussion of the Bilderberg's focus on the ET question see Richard Boylan, "Bilderberg Council's Internal Struggle over UFO Disclosure," in Boylan and Boylan, *Labored Journey To The Stars*. Available online at: http://www.drboylan.com/bldrbg2.html.
479. See Jim Marrs, *Rule By Secrecy* (Harper Collins, 2000).
480. Lal Khan, "The Menace of Islamic Fundamentalism and the Hypocrisy of Imperialism" 2000. Available online at: http://www.marxist.com/Asia/islamic_fund_ism1100.html.
481. For description of how human rights marked a new phase in US foreign policy, see Michael Salla, *The Hero's Journey Toward a Second American Century* (Praeger Press, 2002) 163–78.
482. For an account of Ayatollah Khomeini's activities in France and their impact on the Shah's regime, see Mohsen M. Milani, *The Making of Iran's Islamic Revolution* (Westview Press, 1988).
483. For an online analysis of the factors driving Iraq's decision to invade Iran, see Federation of American Scientists—Military Analysis Network, "Iran-Iraq War (1980–1988)": http://www.fas.org/man/dod-101/ops/war/iran-iraq.htm.
484. For a description of US support for Iraq during its war, see Bruce W. Jentleson, *With Friends Like These: Reagan, Bush, and Saddam 1982–1990* (W.W. Norton & Company, October 1994). For an online discussion of Western Support, see Kathleen Knox, "Iraq: Relations With The West Haven't Always Been Contentious," Radio Free Europe, March 12, 2003: http://www.rferl.org/nca/features/2003/03/12032003160413.asp.
485. For an account of the actions leading up to the Osirak bombing, see Efraim Karsh and Inari Rautsi, *Saddam Hussein, A Political Biography* (The Free Press, 1993), Pages 126–128. See also, Seymour M. Hersh, *The Sampson Option: Israel's Nuclear Arsenal and American Foreign Policy* (New York: Random House, 1991) 8–13; and Amos Perlmutter, et al., *Two Minutes Over Baghdad* (London: Valentine, Mitchell & Co. Ltd., 1982).
486. Robert Tanner, "Troops begin combing Baghdad tunnels," *Associated Press*, April 09, 2003. Available online at: http://www.militarycity.com/iraq/1756855.html.
487. Dana Priest, "Closing In on Baghdad Will Push War Underground," *Washington Post* (April 5, 2003) A25. Available online at: http://www.washingtonpost.com/wp-dyn/articles/A32294-2003Apr4.html.
488. William Henry describes Saddam's preoccupation with Iraq's ancient (ET) heritage in his book *Ark of the Christos: The Mythology, Symbolism and Prophecy of the Return of Planet X and the Age of Terror*. An article summarizing his thesis is called, "Saddam Hussein, The Stairway to Heaven and the Return of Planet X" and is available online at his website at http://www.williamhenry.net.

489. For an account of Iraq's numerous human rights violations, see Middle East Watch, *Human Rights in Iraq* (Human Rights Watch Books, 1990).

490. For discussion of the historical dimensions of Iraq's claim to Kuwait, see H. Rahman, *The Making of the Gulf War: Origins of Kuwait's Long-Standing Territorial Dispute With Iraq* (Ithaca, 1998).

491. For discussion of circumstances leading to the gulf war see, Hassan A. El-Najjar, *The Gulf War: Overreaction & Excessiveness* (Amazon Press, 2001). For an online transcript of the interview, go to: http://www.whatreallyhappened.com/ARTICLE5/april.html.

492. For description of Glaspie's "punishment," see Andrew I. Killgore, "Special Report: Tales of the Foreign Service: In Defense of April Glaspie," *Washington Report on Middle East Affairs* (August 2002) 49: http://www.wrmea.com/archives/august2002/0208049.html.

493. See Chapter Two for further discussion on the policy coordinating organizations that dealt with ET issues.

494. For further discussion of how the media distorts coverage of the UFO/ET presence, see Terry Hansen, *The Missing Times* (Xlibris Corporation; 2001).

495. See also Jim Marrs, *Rule By Secrecy*; and David Icke, *And The Truth Shall Set You Free*.

496. For evidence that President Clinton was not fully informed of the ET presence and the various US clandestine organizations set up to respond to this presences, see Steven Greer, "Who Are the Controllers?" *CSETI Newsletter*, 3:1 (May 1994): http://www.cseti.org/position/greer/who.htm. See also Presidential UFO Files for more information concerning President Clinton's knowledge of the ET presence: http://www.presidentialufo.8m.com/clinton.htm. See also Chapter Two.

497. See Chapter Two for discussion of the gradual erosion of executive oversight of the clandestine organizations focused on the ET presence and ET technology.

498. For an assessment of President Clinton's policy making style, and comparison with other US presidents, see Thomas Preston, *The President and His Inner Circle: Leadership Style and the Advisory Process in Foreign Policy Making* (Columbia University Press, 2001).

499. Dr. Steven Greer Interview with Art Bell August 30, 2001, available online at: http://www.presidentialufo.8m.com/part5.htm.

500. For discussion of the ascendancy of these neo-conservative thinkers and their views on Iraq, see Steven Weisman, "Pre-emption: Idea With a Lineage Whose Time Has Come," *New York Times* (March 22, 2003): http://www.nytimes.com/2003/03/23/international/worldspecial/23PREE.html.

501. Eric Boehlert, "Rumsfeld's personal spy ring," *Information Clearing House* (July 16, 2003). Available online at: http://www. informationclearinghouse.info/article4124.htm.

502. Eric Boehlert, "Rumsfeld's personal spy ring," *Information Clearing House* (July 16, 2003). Available online at: http://www. informationclearinghouse.info/article4124.htm.

503. For criticism of preemptive war against Iraq, see Richard Falk and David Krieger, "No War Against Iraq," *Waging Peace.org* (August 23, 2002).

504. Thucydides, *History of the Peloponnesian War* (Viking Press, 2003).

505. Marshall Masters, "Failure Analyst Identifies Cause of Columbia Disaster," YOWUSA.com, March 24, 2003: http://www.yowusa.com/ Archive/March2003/scalar1/scalar1.htm.

506. See T.E. Bearden, "Historical Background of Scalar EM Weapons," 1990 paper available online at: http://www.cheniere.org/books/ analysis/history.htm.

507. T.E. Bearden, "Historical Background of Scalar EM Weapons," 1990 paper available online at: http://www.cheniere.org/books/analysis/ history.htm.

508. "Wood Pecker Beams Intersect Over North America," available online at: http://www.cheniere.org/books/ferdelance/s63.htm.

509. For real time and archived seismic records for the US and the world, go to US Geological Survey website at: http://quake.wr.usgs.gov/ recent.

510. Quoted from William S. Cohen, "Q&A at the Conference on Terrorism, Weapons of Mass Destruction, and U.S. Strategy— University of Georgia, Athens," *DoD News Briefing.* Apr. 28, 1997.

511. T.E. Bearden, "Historical Background of Scalar EM Weapons," 1990 paper available online at: http://www.cheniere.org/books/analysis/ history.htm. See also Thomas Bearden, *Fer de Lance: A Briefing on Soviet Scalar Electromagnetic Weapons*, 2nd ed., (Cheniere Press, 2001).

512. T.E. Bearden, "Historical Background of Scalar EM Weapons," 1990 paper available online at: http://www.cheniere.org/books/analysis/ history.htm. In some correspondence, Bearden discusses the possible terrorist uses of scalar weaponry, go to: http://www.cheniere.org/ correspondence/021203.htm. For discussion of the use of scalar weapons in Iraq, see Bill Morgan, "Iraq: World's First Scalar War?" published online at: http://216.247.92.101/pub/bearden/iraq.htm.

513. See Phil Schneider, "MUFON Conference Presentation, May 1995" available online at: http://www.geocities.com/Area51/Shadowlands/ 6583/coverup044.html. See also, "Tim Schwartz, The Mysterious Life and Death of Phil Schneider": http://www.think-aboutit.com/ Underground/mysterious_life_and_death_of_phi.htm.

514. Felicity Barringer, "U.S. Presses U.N. Members to Bear More of Iraq Burden," *New York Times*, August 21, 2003. Available online at: http://nytimes.com/2003/08/22/international/worldspecial/22NATI.html.

515. See Mark Hazlewood, *Blindsided: Planet X Passes in 2003* (Firstpublish LLC, 2001). Hazlewood maintains a website at: http://www.planetx2003.com/index.html. See also Jim McCanney, *Planet-X, Comets and Earth Changes* (jmcanneyscience.com, n.d.). McCanney maintains a website at: http://www.jmccanneyscience.com. See also Nancy Leider, *Zetatalk: Direct Answers from the Zeta Reticuli People* (Granite Publishing, 1999). Leider maintains a website at: http://www.zetatalk.com.

Chapter 7

First Contact: Preparing for Open Interaction with Extraterrestrial Races

Introduction[516]

In the popular *Star Trek* motion picture movie series, First Contact is described as an event featuring the landing of an extraterrestrial (ET) race where a meeting occurs with government officials and news of this is relayed to the public around the planet. Open interaction between members of the general public and the ET race then begins.

In the motion picture series, the Earth makes a transition from a planet emerging from the ruins of devastating war, to becoming a member of a galactic federation of planets that leads to rapid advances in technology that solve many of the world's problems, and open interaction with ET races.

What is instructive in this fictionalized version of Earth's transformation into an interplanetary culture is that there are three parts to the First Contact event: 1. official government representatives meeting with a visiting ET race, 2. a public announcement of this meeting, and 3. open interaction between ET races and the general public.

According to a number of unconfirmed reports, the first part of a First Contact event occurred as early as the 1930s when various ET races began to communicate and even meet with official government representatives in different countries around the world. These reports suggest that meetings took place between Nazi German officials and ET races in 1933, and that President Roosevelt met with ET races as early as 1933.[517] Of these unconfirmed reports the ones that are most supported by whistleblower testimonies are meetings that

occurred between representatives of the Eisenhower administration and different ET races.

The secret meetings, according to these testimonies,
culminated in a Treaty between the US government and an
ET race that was reportedly signed in 1954 by President
Eisenhower himself.[518] One of the reported provisions of the
Treaty was that the ET race concerned would not sign another
treaty with any other national government. Unlike the *Star
Trek* motion picture series, however, the second part of the
First Contact event—public disclosure of a meeting between
government officials and members of an ET race—has not
occurred.

Efforts to promote full public disclosure of the ET presence
and official government involvement with ET races have thus
far proved ineffective.[519] Given the almost 70 years that such
government meetings with ET races have occurred, if whistleblower testimonies are accurate, this would go down in history
as the best kept public secret of all times. There are reports
however, that a partial disclosure campaign has been initiated
through a clandestine acclimation program in which former
public officials from the military and intelligence branches of
government are tacitly given permission to release statements,
give interviews and even write books on the ET presence.

Of these the most noteworthy is a book authored by
Col. Phillip Corso whose strong military credentials gives powerful legitimacy to his claims that he was involved with and even
led a top secret US army effort to reverse engineer ET technology recovered from the 1947 Roswell crash of an ET piloted
craft. The emergence of over one hundred witnesses, who have
given video testimony of their participation in various ET/UFO
related issues, is further evidence that a partial disclosure or
acclimation program is underway.[520] Whistleblower testimonies
have confirmed the existence of such an acclimation program
and its various supporters and opponents in clandestine government organizations in charge of ET affairs.[521]

Absence of full disclosure has delayed open interaction
between ET races and the human population. However, a number of testimonies suggest that there has been rapid growth in
the number of cases of individuals reporting to have had some

sort of interaction with ET races. These interactions range from close sightings of UFOs/ET controlled craft to physical contact with ET races.

The classification system developed by Professor Allen Hynek in 1972 for describing encounters with ET races comprised three types of Close Encounters (CE): CE-1, physical sightings within approximately 500 feet; CE-2, physical evidence such as burns, stalled engines, etc.; and CE-3, physical sighting of an ET in association with a CE-1/CE-2.[522]

Hynek's system has subsequently been extended to include abduction/contact type experiences as a fourth category— CE-4.[523] A fifth category CE-5 has also been added, which involves direct communication with ET races.

According to Dr. Steven Greer, CE-5 cases involve either human or ET initiated communication and interaction which distinguishes it from the first four categories which are all ET initiated.[524] In sum, the growth of human-ET interactions that fall in the CE-3 to CE-5 range confirms whistleblower/witness testimonies that there is an ET initiated program of preparing the human population for open interaction with ET races.

First Contact as an event comprising three parts, has become a long term process that depends on public officials in charge of ET affairs agreeing on a strategy over how, when, or whether this information should be released to the general public. However, rather than First Contact being purely a political process outside the competence of most individuals to directly influence, it is also a social process whereby growing numbers of individuals are having direct interaction with ET races.

This indicates that First Contact involves both top-down political processes, and bottom-up social processes which are essential for its completion and future open interaction between humanity and ET races.

In this chapter, I will review the political and social processes that can lead to the completion of First Contact as a process that has lasted for almost 70 years. I will describe three scenarios that will be most likely to complete First Contact as a political process. I will then analyze First Contact as a social process that focuses on individuals as agents for developing

CE-4 and/or CE-5 interactions with ET races that will inevitably impact on First Contact as a political process.

Indeed, it will be argued that First Contact as a social process involving individual interaction with ET races is a necessary condition for the completion of First Contact as a political process. It will be concluded that First Contact as a social process has the most promising potential for bringing about full disclosure by public officials and thereby completing the First Contact process.

First Contact as a Political Process

The most current phase of First Contact as a political process occurs when responsible officials for ET affairs have encouraged or made possible non-official revelations of an ET presence and official government relations with ET races. These non-official revelations are leaked to the general public in a way that conditions the global population to the possibility of First Contact while simultaneously providing the option of plausible deniability to government officials concerned over the consequences of full public disclosure.

First Contact as a political process is distinguished by the need for those officials in charge of ET affairs to maintain tight control over the release of ET information. Thus there is some degree of tolerance for the release of certain categories of information by former public officials, and intolerance for other categories. For example, recent efforts of President Clinton's former chief of staff, John Podesta, to promote disclosure, indicate tolerance of such public efforts by former officials who presumably have some inside information on the ET presence.[525]

Col. Corso and numerous other former military/intelligence officials are similarly tolerated in their release of information.[526]

Evidence of official intolerance are circumstances surrounding the death of Phil Schneider who went on the public circuit in 1995 with lectures on his participation in the construction of underground military bases and the joint projects with ET races. Schneider was found dead in January 1996. Former whistleblowers testify to the use of the private security agency, Wackenhut, for the intimidation, silencing and even murder of public officials, corporate employees and/or civilian witnesses of ET related projects or activities that are not part of the official acclimation policy.[527]

There are numerous scenarios whereby official disclosure of the ET presence could occur. Rather than examine an extensive list of these scenarios and their nuances, I will concentrate on those three that provide the basic contrasting models by which public disclosure is most likely to occur.

Evidence presented thus far in this book suggests that the debate among officials responsible for ET affairs falls into polarized camps with contrasting views over the extensive political, social and economic ramifications of completing First Contact as a political process. I now explore three contrasting scenarios or models by which First Contact is most likely to be completed as a political process where there is official declaration of an ET presence.

The first scenario involves full disclosure of contact with an ET race having occurred at a certain time, by the US and other governments in announcements to their respective general publics. This would presumably be followed by the open appearance of the announced ET race and full media coverage of the ET presence. In this scenario, the clandestine government organizations responsible for coordinating ET policy at the national and international levels (see Chapters Two and Three) have reached agreement over the best sequencing of events in order to familiarize the general public with the ET presence.

This scenario would presumably be based on widespread cooperation between clandestine government/military organizations and ET races that figure prominently in the public acknowledgement of First Contact. At some point, there would be a more complete disclosure of the historic relations between ET races and various national governments, and an effort to account for the historic non-disclosure policy that kept this out of the public arena for so long.

The above scenario would be the most desirable means of completing the First Contact process, since it involves a high degree of agreement of all parties involved in the process, and a sequencing of events that best prepares the general public for full disclosure. Due to the advanced nature of ET races in terms of their culture, technology and mental abilities, it would be expected that a coordinated effort would be required to prepare the general public with minimal disruptions and anxiety.

It could be expected that resources would be devoted to preparing the general public in terms of the use of movies and other forms of entertainment. The 2002 television miniseries produced by Steven Spielberg, *Taken,* could well be an example of the kind of initiative by clandestine organizations wishing to prepare the general public. In addition, the efforts of former senior public officials such as John Podesta in advocating disclosure of information on ETs/UFOs provides another example of acclimation efforts to bring about completion of the First Contact process.

A second and contrasting way in which First Contact will be completed as a political process is that there will be a mass global intervention of an ET race that becomes known worldwide through widespread media reports that cannot be suppressed or denied by public officials.[528] These mass public sightings and landings would predictably culminate in official recognition of the ET presence, and lead to full disclosure of the historic dimensions of the ET presence and prior governmental relations with ET races.

This scenario would presumably occur without clandestine government organizations responsible for ET affairs having reached agreement to permit such a mass ET intervention, but not being in a position to oppose such intervention. Presumably, an ET race may have reached the conclusion that elite policy makers are unnecessarily endangering the biosphere through a range of clandestine military programs and/or not protecting the global ecosystem in ways that threaten the interests of global humanity.

Covert efforts to militarily prevent such an open ET intervention would most likely have been either attempted and exhausted, or rendered ineffective by preemptive ET military action. Policy makers after such a series of military setbacks, largely unknown to the general public, would have decided that it is counter productive to the interests of the civilian population and the careers of the respective public officials dealing with ET affairs to continue overt military operations against publicly visible ET craft in civilian areas.

Evidence that clandestine US military organizations have actively targeted ET craft in the past and created a global defensive shield to enhance this offensive ability, indicates that covert efforts already have been actively taken to prevent a mass intervention by an ET race.[529]

The mass blackout that affected much of the Northeast of the United States on August 14, 2003, could well be an example of the type of preemptive ET military action that might persuade clandestine organizations to accept the inevitability of mass ET intervention. The cause of the blackout as well as the major blackout in 1965, has been claimed by some to be related to ET activity.[530] The blackout may merely have been the most visible manifestation of a series of preemptive ET actions that affected local military installations otherwise used to prevent a mass ET intervention in the Northeast of the US.

This second scenario is clearly less desirable than the first, since it suggests institutionalized opposition to full disclosure in the form of officials not desiring to move forward in acclimation efforts. Various whistleblowers testify to the opposition of a hard core of individuals termed "the cabal," who are opposed to genuine dialogue and cooperation with ET races.[531]

Presumably, there is division in clandestine organizations over the pace and extent of official disclosure, and ET races may simply decide to bring the matter to a head by deciding to move forward with a mass intervention, forcibly removing those officials and/or destroying any weapons installations being used to prevent a mass intervention. This scenario would obviously be less controlled and predictable and would involve less adequate preparation of the general public for official announcement of the ET presence.

A predictable end result would be a process of public officials having to account for their ET related policies while in office. There may even be special tribunals convened for public/military officials who were most aggressive in their covert operations against ET craft, and/or violations of civilians in clandestine weapons development projects.

The third and least likely scenario is a large-scale military conflict between an ET race and clandestine government organizations that cannot be hidden from the general public. This would take on a characteristic of a "War of the Worlds" in which the presence of ETs is officially disclosed to the general public in terms of an ET race launching an invasion or attempted "takeover." It has been revealed by military-intelligence whistleblowers, that there has been low intensity conflict between the ET race known as Grays/Zetas and clandestine government organizations that sometimes leads to the targeting and shooting down of Gray ET craft.

Michael Wolf, for example, argues that agreements with ET races have often been broken by rogue elements in various clandestine organizations and resulted in unnecessary military confrontation.[532] The development of a global defensive shield using advanced weaponry based on scalar technology and other exotic weapons systems, has given clandestine military organizations a degree of confidence that national governments have some system of defense in case relations with ET races become overtly hostile.

Presumably, the relationship between ET races and clandestine government are quite complex and sometimes degenerate into hostile encounters with the Grays that are kept secret from the general public.

Some insiders claim that an ET invasion scenario could be entirely contrived in order for the military-industrial complex in the US and other countries to gain greater power and resources in their respective countries. Dr. Steven Greer, for example, has stated:

> Since 1992 I have seen this script unveiled to me by at least a dozen well-placed insiders. Of course, initially I laughed, thinking this just too absurd and far-fetched. . . And yet others told me explicitly that things that looked like UFOs but that are built and under the control of deeply secretive "black" projects, were being used to simulate—hoax—ET-appearing events, including some

abductions and cattle mutilations, to sow the early seeds of cultural fear regarding life in outer space. And that at some point after global terrorism, events would unfold that would utilize the now-revealed Alien Reproduction Vehicles (ARVs, or reversed-engineered UFOs made by humans by studying actual ET craft—see the book *Disclosure* by the same author) to hoax an attack on Earth. Like the movie *Independence Day*, an attempt to unite the world through militarism would unfold using ETs as the new cosmic scapegoat (think Jews during the Third Reich).[533]

In the view of Dr. Greer and some whistleblowers/insiders, the whole phenomenon of negative ET races is contrived by clandestine military/intelligence organizations in the US and elsewhere. According to Catherine Fitts, former Deputy Secretary in the Department of Housing and Urban Development, the military industrial complex in the US is eager to legalize its black operations budget that ran for fiscal years 1998, 1999, 2000 at approximately 3.3 trillion dollars (1.1 trillion per year).[534]

A threatened ET invasion would provide sufficient cover to rapidly expand the "official" defense budget that in the 2003 fiscal year was nearly 380 billion dollars, but "unofficially" was closer to 1.5 trillion dollars if Fitts estimates are accurate of the annual amount disappearing into the black budget.[535]

There is also the view that an "invasion" or "takeover" involving the "Grays" could be contrived by an ET race commonly described as Reptilians or Anunnaki, that secretly encourages a military conflict between national governments and the Grays/Zetas. The degree of infiltration by the Reptilian race in US based clandestine organizations (see Chapter Four) makes such a scenario quite possible given evidence of hostility between the Grays and Reptilians.[536] Presumably, the Reptilian/Anunnaki would intervene as humanity's saviors and stage a "false second coming" involving a bio-engineered clone of the historical Jesus using advanced ET technology.[537]

The three scenarios described thus far may occur in the not too distant future and involve political events and policies outside the influence of most individuals. There is however another element to the First Contact process that does focus on individuals. This is the third part of the First Contact process—open interaction between ET races and the general public.

Rather than something that is entirely dependent on public disclosure, such interaction is a social process that can occur independently and even move ahead of the political process. This would happen when large numbers of individuals interact with ET races and begin to openly advocate full disclosure in a way that could result in a political process similar to the 1960s civil rights movement in the US.

From the available evidence of the number of abduction/ contact experiences, it may be concluded that First Contact as a social process has been adopted as a basic strategy by ET races eager to have full disclosure of their presence made known to the general public.

The third part of the First Contact occurs at the individual level whereby an ET race actively makes contact with large numbers of civilians in an effort to prepare them and make them catalysts for official disclosure and transformation of human society. This has a number of important elements that require close examination, since it appears that this has direct influence on full disclosure and the completion of First Contact as a political process.

First Contact as a Social Process

There is extensive public information available on individuals who have experienced direct contact with ET races. The most well known database of information comes from the works of Budd Hopkins, Dr. David Jacobs and Dr. John Mack who, since the early 1980s, have published scholarly articles, books and interviews on the experiences of individuals they describe as "abductees."[538]

These pioneering researchers all used hypnosis for the retrieval of memories which in most cases were buried in the sub/unconscious minds of "abductees." The abductees had no conscious recollection of events other than a vague intuition that something had happened to them, and it probably involved ETs.[539]

Analysis of the information retrieved from these hypnosis sessions instantly provoked controversy over its accuracy and reliability. David Jacobs narrates his own experience in choosing to pursue this research contrary to the advice of those who believed scholarly events needed to focus on the collation and analysis of UFO sightings:

> In 1981, Budd Hopkins published *Missing Time* . . . His book gave UFO researchers the first systematic comparison of abductee experiences and showed that the phenomenon could be studied on a society-wide basis . . . After my meetings with Hopkins, I called [Dr. Allen Hynek] and told him I thought Hopkins was on to something important. Hynek warned me to stay away from the abduction cases because they were eccentric and led us off the main path of sighting analysis. I disagreed and told him that I thought Hopkins' research seemed solid. Hynek reiterated his warning, trying to steer me back to the "correct" course of research. Abduction reports were too bizarre for him; he could not subject them to the kind of scientific analysis that he could use for sightings reports.[540]

Nevertheless, due to the scholarly effort of these pioneers to refine their techniques to eliminate distortion and bias and identify significant patterns and experiences, important information began to emerge.

In the majority of cases, civilians had involuntarily undergone medically related procedures for a genetic program sponsored by the Gray ET race. Justification for these programs provided by the Grays was that they claimed to be suffering genetic deficiencies which threatened their long-term survival. Much information emerged concerning the participation of abducted humans in the creation of a hybrid human-ET race that would presumably provide suitable physical vehicles for the consciousness/souls of the Gray ET race.

The Grays viewed humanity as too primitive because it used only a small proportion of its mental potential, but a mixture of Gray/Human genes could lead to an evolutionary leap that would benefit both races.

According to Dr. David Jacobs, the hybrid programs are clear evidence of a nefarious agenda by ET races that threatens the sovereignty and independence of humanity.[541]

Other researchers, including Dr. Mack, disagree and view the abductions as a phenomenon that is multifaceted in its scope and outcomes. Mack's conclusion is that the human-ET interaction holds many benefits for humanity as evidenced by the heightened consciousness and more socially aware activities of those who have participated in such interactions. Reflecting Mack's approach, Dr. Richard Boylan advocates using less pejorative terms for describing human-ET interactions, such as "contactees" for human participants and "Star Visitors" to describe ET races.[542]

My own conclusion is that the Grays' hybrid program is clearly influencing an evolutionary leap in human consciousness in which a greater proportion of humanity is being born with advanced psychic abilities. A number of authors describe the phenomenon of many psychically gifted youngsters, called "Indigo Children," "Crystal Children," or "Star Children."[543]

These gifted children, in most cases, appear to have no connection to the Grays' hybridization program. If so, then it appears that an evolutionary leap in human evolution is taking place through what the famed biologist, Rupert Sheldrake, describes as an interconnected "morphic resonance" field that is responsible for evolutionary advances in all species.[544] The Grays' hybridization experiments are a likely catalyst for and/or complement to this phenomenon, without necessarily being related to all the instances of psychically gifted individuals.

A small number of researchers argue that many purported ET abductions are in fact conducted by clandestine military organizations desiring to develop advanced mind-control and genetic techniques on the civilian population, and who wish to portray these as ET-related abductions. Reporting on witness testimonies, Dr. Steven Greer claims:

> Those inside the multi-million dollar abduction industry
> have for years told me of suppressed testimony from

abductees who recall human military operatives running the show—essentially controlling the event. Dr. Helmut Lammer and others have documented this hideous abuse of civilians by rogue covert operations. And most important, we have interviewed military and corporate insiders who have described in excruciating detail how they have hoaxed these "alien abductions"—and why.[545]

These MILABs (Military Abductions) may in fact be a clandestine effort to replicate the genetic experiments first pursued by Grays and other ET species, without making the general public aware of who is actually responsible. The experiences of individuals who have participated in projects based in Brookhaven and Montauk, confirm that military clandestine organizations regularly use non-voluntary civilians in their projects and abuse the rights of these civilians.

According to Preston Nichols, "roughly 3/4 or more of all 'alien abductions' are actually being done by government agencies—with no 'alien' involvement at all."[546] Many of the Nazi scientists who were brought into the US under Operation Paperclip were reported to be leading these genetic/mind control experiments for US military/intelligence organizations.

The most infamous of these involved projects MK Ultra and Monarch. "Manchurian candidates" were created that would perform tasks ranging from assassination to "suicide bombings" as a result of the advanced mind control techniques.[547]

Despite evidence of military contrived ET "abductions," most evidence on the abduction phenomenon confirms that large numbers of individuals have had contact with ET races, but hold little conscious recollection of these. The use of hypnosis and other techniques are successful in many cases for bringing these interactions to the active or aware mind state as demonstrated in the pioneering work of Budd Hopkins, David Jacobs, John Mack and others.[548]

Given the sheer number of cases, estimated to be in the millions in the US alone, it is worth exploring how individuals can better prepare for CE-4 and/or CE-5 interactions with ET races and provide positive models for how these experiences can be beneficial.

Human-Extraterrestrial Interaction and Preparing for First Contact

An important preliminary for understanding human-ET interaction in the CE-4 and/or CE-5 range of Hynek's classification system, is discussion of different brain wave frequencies and the partition of the human mind into three parts—conscious, subconscious and unconscious.

These brain wave states operate at different frequencies and trigger different parts of the mind to become dominant.[549] This is significant since, when interaction with ET races occurs, evidence suggests if it is sufficiently intense, it triggers different brain wave frequencies. This accounts for the dream-like quality or "alternative realities" that often figure in reports of encounters with ET races.

Four distinct frequency ranges for the human brain correspond to various mental/emotional activities the brain performs. The Beta brain wave range is 15–40 Hz (cycles per second) and corresponds to the active fully conscious state of mind, e.g., when individuals are actively engaged in their work, having a debate, giving a lecture, etc.

The Alpha brain wave range is 9–14 Hz and occurs when individuals are in a relaxed yet fully conscious state of mind, e.g., listening to music, meditating, taking a walk in a garden, etc. In both beta and alpha brain wave states, individuals are fully conscious and typically have complete memories of activities they perform.

The Theta brain wave range is 5–8 Hz and occurs when individuals are in a deep trance-like meditation, day dreaming, or a having a light sleep. A typical example would be when individuals are driving on a familiar highway and enter into a deeply relaxed state where they simply forget they are driving along different sections of the highway. Individuals are primarily operating from the subconscious part of the mind that is filled with psychic energies that are not readily available to the conscious mind.

Sigmund Freud pioneered the study of this portion of the mind and the role played by repressed psychic energies such as desire, anger, fear, memories, etc., in influencing human behavior.[550] Experiences in this brain wave state typically have a dream-like quality to them and can quickly be forgotten, as in the case of dreams.

The Delta brain wave range is from 1.5–4 Hz, and occurs when in a deep sleep. In this state, the individual is using the unconscious part of the mind where archetypal images are stored. The psychologist who did most work in uncovering archetypal patterns that influence human behavior was Carl Jung.[551]

Jung analyzed the UFO phenomenon and connected it with archetypal patterns embedded in the human unconscious, thereby lending support to the view that UFO experiences occur when Delta brain waves are stimulated.[552] In Delta state, one loses consciousness of what is occurring around them and there is no memory of activities performed.

Although one or more of these brain wave states can occur simultaneously, normally one state is dominant at any time. According to authors/contactees such as Lyssa Royal, ET races typically operate at the Theta and Delta brain wave states as their equivalent of the waking state, only rarely at the alpha, and even less rarely at the beta brain wave states.[553]

In contrast, the dominant brain wave states for humans in the waking state are the higher frequency beta and alpha brain wave states. Indeed, the frenetic pace and stress associated with Western post-industrialized societies typically encourages beta brain wave states.

Testimonies of "abductees/contactees" suggest that ETs have very powerful mental abilities that they typically use to tele-pathically communicate, interact with and even control human subjects. The hypnotic-like mind rapport that abductees/contactees often report when interacting with ETs suggests that the human brain has shifted into the Theta/Delta brain wave ranges. This makes individuals more easily influenced by ET commands because when these brain waves become dominant for humans, there is a shift into the non-waking states associated with the subconscious/unconscious portions of the mind.

The lack of pain abductees report when medical procedures are performed without any anesthesia, suggests the ability of ETs to induce Theta/Delta brain wave states at will.

Evidence suggests that ET races operate at lower brain-wave frequencies that can be both powerful and focused enough to influence even the most resilient of abductees/contactees once a mental link has been established in a CE-4 or CE-5 encounter. Testimonies describe the great difficulty in consciously resisting the hypnotic influence of some ET races that render one receptive to ET commands.

This would account for the dream-like interaction that many witness testimonies provide concerning their ET encounters. Put simply, when interacting with humans, the more powerful and focused mental abilities of the ETs and their low frequency brain wave states appear to shift humans into the brain wave states that are typically not part of one's normal waking consciousness. This makes it difficult for humans to consciously recollect what has occurred.

Not surprisingly, individuals might rationalize an actual ET interaction (either a CE-4 and/or CE-5) as a "daydream" even when tell-tale physical signs (CE-2) might exist. Since there is no conscious recollection of an ET contact to support subconscious/unconscious feelings and physical evidence that contact has occurred, "cognitive dissonance" sets in and dismisses the reality of the interaction. The result is that many individuals may have experienced First Contact!

However, they have no conscious recollection of the contact experience, since their conscious mind goes to sleep or enters a trance-like state; and upon entering normal waking consciousness in the Beta-Alpha brain wave states, the experience is rationalized as a (day)dream and quickly forgotten. This means that any significant messages communicated through the CE-4 and/or CE-5 contact experience are not absorbed by the conscious mind, and simply move into the sub/unconscious parts of the mind for integration.

This helps explain the phenomenon of "missing time" and why hypnosis is regularly used as a means of recalling sub/unconscious memories of what had in fact occurred as a real life event.[554] In an event that illustrates how interaction between an ET race and human might occur, Lyssa Royal recounts the following:

> Janice was sitting at her desk. As the Pleiadian [ET] approached her, the energy field of the ET hit her first.

So even before she looked up, she sensed the energy. Upon sensing that energy, her brain-wave state began to shift. Janice looked up, not because she heard a sound but because she suddenly felt very disoriented as her brain waves shifted very rapidly. The first image Janice saw when she looked up was that of a humanoid (the actual female Pleiadian) dressed in a man's business suit. This was an incongruous vision. We're not talking about a feminine-styled business suit that female executives wear. Instead, this was a straight, boxy business suit that was obviously too big for the female Pleiadian.

This incongruous image was the only way that Janice could make sense of what was coming toward her. Once Janice's ego registered the strangeness of the experience, her consciousness entered what we would call dreamtime—theta consciousness. Her ego was no longer in control. This does not mean that the interaction itself was a dream, no. The interaction itself simply did not adhere to the rules of your *physical* reality, which are organized by the ego. The ego was not the orchestrator of this experience, so the rules changed.[555]

If First Contact is a phenomenon that has occurred for many more individuals than is commonly appreciated (some abduction/contact estimates are in the millions for the US alone), then this adds a new dimension to the whole First Contact process. Rather than First Contact being solely a matter of full government disclosure of the ET presence, First Contact requires a degree of preparation of the human population for an encounter (either a CE-4 or a CE-5) that typically shifts one into an alternative reality framework. Such a "reality shift" makes conscious recall of the ET experience difficult.

Thus, "missing time" or "dreamlike" recollections of actual physical events may in fact signify an actual ET interaction that the conscious mind has rationalized as a dream.

If ET-human interaction occurs far more often than commonly accepted, then official non-disclosure to the general public of First Contact parallels non-recollection of First Contact by large numbers of individuals. If there is some kind of symbiotic relationship between First Contact at the mass public and private individual levels, then it might be predicted that as more individuals become aware of First Contact experiences, this will have an impact on official disclosure of First Contact. In short, the more individuals who consciously prepare themselves to either experience or remember a First Contact event (CE-4 or CE-5), the sooner will official public disclosure of the ET presence occur.

Telepathic communication and physical interaction with ETs involves some degree of mental/emotional rapport that would ordinarily put a human into a trance/dream like state (theta and delta brain waves states) that might make interaction difficult to recall for the conscious mind after the interaction. Consequently, preparation for First Contact inevitably involves some degree of training whereby individuals can consciously operate at lower brain wave frequencies that would occur when interaction (either CE-4 and/or CE-5) with ET races begins.

Official Attempts at Communication with Extraterrestrial Races

According to whistleblower and abduction/contactee testimonies, there are two main forms of communication with ET races. The first is a purely cognitive process, a direct exchange of thoughts—telepathy—which consists either of a voice being distinctly heard inside the head, or holographic visual images appearing again inside the head.

Such communication involves some combination of purely mental energies and stimulation either of the visual cortex and/or the auditory senses without external physical sources causing these sensations. This is the type of communication most often described as occurring with the Gray ET species and appears to be a cognitive process devoid of emotional content. There is widespread agreement among researchers that the Grays do not display emotions, and even lack emotional bodies, thereby making telepathic communication purely a mental exchange of information.

The second form of communication involves direct exchange of information through emotions. An empathic connection is established allowing emotions to be felt, in which a "gestalt-like knowing" occurs. This "gestalt-like knowing" (intuition) is apparently the same way that cetaceans such as whales and dolphins communicate with humans.

According to Joan Ocean, who has researched cetacean communication since the early 1980s, empathic communication works primarily at a cellular level[556] rather than cognitive level, where emotions are exchanged in ways that facilitate deeply transformative experiences similar to mystical states of consciousness.[557]

Those who have communicated with ETs in this empathic manner typically report wave-like feelings emanating from ETs that induce various emotional states that facilitate both a telepathic communication and a gestalt knowing. It appears that the empathic communication uses intuition as the basis for the cellular and cognitive exchange of information. This form of communication is typically associated with ETs that have reached higher evolutionary potentials than the Gray race.

Of the two forms of possible communication with ET races, there is evidence that officially sponsored communication with ET races focuses exclusively on the first form. Confirmation that telepathy is indeed the dominant communication model with ETs comes from the official use of psychics who go through a rigorous training process for telepathic communication with ETs. Dan Sherman served for 12 years in the US Air force and claims to have participated in Project Preserve Destiny, a top secret National Security Agency program in the 1960s that used psychics for telepathic communication with different ET races.

In his book, *Above Black*, Sherman describes the process whereby he was recruited into the program through officials identifying his psychic abilities at a young age.[558] He argues that such potential recruits are "programmed" in ways that make them loyal to authority figures and susceptible to recruitment into the military.

The programming of psychics at a young age appears to have been a part of the infamous MKUltra and Monarch Projects that used mind control programming on children typically from the ages of 10–16. "Mr Coffee," an anonymous psychic recruited into one of these programs, argues that he was sent three letters of acceptance from the West Point Military Academy and Annapolis Naval Academy even though he applied to neither.

He argues that what made him the subject of this very unusual treatment were his advanced psychic abilities and the eagerness of his "handlers" to have him enlist in the military so his abilities could be fully exploited.[559] Dr. Michael Wolf, who claims to have worked in the National Security Agency, claims he pioneered a "mental enhancement" process which "allows utilization of a vastly-increased percentage of the brain, in order for humans to mentally engage the extraterrestrials in full telepathic mental exchange."[560]

The testimony of Sherman and others suggests that clandestine organizations use psychics in their communication with ETs for three main reasons: first, to establish a direct form of communication with ET races whereby the regular exchange of information can take place between senior officials/policy makers and ET races; second, to learn more about ET races that use telepathic and empathic thought/ emotional exchanges as their dominant modes of communication; and third, psychics act as a filter allowing a more tightly managed flow of information between ETs and senior officials/policy makers.

This filtering process guards against senior officials and policy makers being exposed to subtle forms of manipulation by ET races in the communication process, which might compromise the policy making process. According to Jamisson Neruda, some ET races use "suggestive telepathy" that subtly allows ET's to manipulate humans:

> The Grays, and most extraterrestrials for that matter, communicate with humans exclusively through a form of telepathy, which we called suggestive telepathy because to us it seemed that the Grays communicated in a such a way that they were trying to lead a conversation to a particular end. In other words, they always had an agenda, and we were never certain if we were a pawn of their agenda or we arrived at conclusions that were indeed our own.[561]

The use of telepathic communication with ET races suggests that psychics are trained to enter and operate consciously in the theta/delta brain wave states necessary for this form of interaction with ET races.

There are two significant consequence of the filtering process of using psychics for direct communication with ETs. The first is that senior officials and policy makers do not establish direct telepathic communication with ET races, and are thus shielded from CE-5 experiences. Such direct communication would presumably expose these officials to "suggestive telepathy," thereby compromising the policy making process, and possibly leading to "compromised officials" being excluded from the chain of command.

A second consequence is that senior officials do not apparently train themselves to directly communicate with ET races. This means that such officials are not trained to operate in the theta and delta brain wave states in the ordinary waking states, from which they would be able to access higher order personal abilities and knowledge.

Although the purely cognitive telepathic communication process involves accessing higher level mental abilities, it appears that the empathic communication process is what facilitates the highest order of personal abilities through the cellular transmission of emotions and the "gestalt knowing" or intuition that occurs. The conclusion that emerges is that those officials most responsible for deciding the appropriate national policies for responding to the ET presence, are paradoxically kept from developing higher level abilities that might assist them in the policy making process.

President Eisenhower's concern that ET affairs were "not going to be in the best hands" may unfortunately have been institutionalized by the very people most responsible for the policy making process.[562]

Non-official Communication with ET Races

In addition to the "official communication" with ET races that occurs but is not disclosed to the general public, there is non-official communication with ET races. Such non-official communication has occurred from the beginning of human civilization, and involved both the telepathic exchange of information and the empathic communication through the exchange of emotions.

Since antiquity, individuals have claimed to be in direct communication with God, angels, gods, extraterrestrials, etc.[563] One need only look at the founding texts of the Old Testament and the Koran for prominent examples of this powerful communication which profoundly influenced the development of human societies.

Many individuals who claim to have successfully communicated in this way, have historically developed methods for teaching others how to similarly communicate. Many of the ancient "mystery schools" pioneered telepathic/empathic communication as evidenced by individuals and groups such as Madam Blavatsky and the Theosophical Society, Nazi German Occult societies Vrill and Thule, and the more recent phenomenon of "channeling."[564]

Numerous channels claim to be in communication with ET races in terms of CE-5 experiences. Many of these channels provide extensive information on ET races, distinguished by their clarity, coherence and philosophical depth. This makes it difficult to dismiss such communication as contrived, fictitious or part of a government disinformation campaign. It appears that the training that channels use in developing their "lines of communication" with ET races typically involves important lifestyle changes such as meditation, dietary changes, alternative health practices, and establishing harmonious social relationships.

Although there is great variety and intensity in these informal trainings that "channels" undergo, it appears that the common theme is that some rigorous lifestyle changes are necessary for establishing direct communication with ET races. Some ET/UFO researchers such as Dr. Greer and Lyssa Royal facilitate ongoing weeklong workshops in which participants are trained to have CE-5 experiences.[565]

A theme that is common in such trainings and also in the worldwide phenomenon of Crop Circles is the role of "sacred geometry." Sacred geometry is the view, first promoted by the ancient Greeks, that the creation of the universe can be reduced to a core group of geometrical patterns called the "Platonic solids." With the growth in Crop Circles around the planet and the unmistakable role of geometrical patterns in their design, it is worth exploring in some detail how sacred geometry may play a role in stimulating higher consciousness states (theta and delta brain waves) that arise during CE-4 or CE-5 experiences.[566] This will be done without entering into the continuing debate over Crop Circles as physical evidence of CE-2 visitations.

Sacred Geometry and First Contact

Above the entrance to Plato's Academy in ancient Greece was an inscription that read, "Let no one destitute of geometry enter my doors." Plato viewed the contemplation of geometry as the essential requirement for training individuals to discover the deepest philosophical truths. Indeed, Plato was part of a tradition that stretched back to the philosopher Pythagoras and even further back to ancient Egypt and the mysterious builders of the Great Pyramid of Giza.

This ancient "sacred geometry" tradition is exemplified in the current age by prominent authors such as Buckminster Fuller and more generally the Freemasonry movement that believes the most durable and harmonious architectural designs are based on key geometrical patterns and ratios.[567]

The principal geometrical shapes are the five Platonic solids that share a number of characteristics. Each is symmetrical in terms of the number of faces, angles and sides, and they fit perfectly inside a sphere.

The Greeks assigned to each of the Platonic solids what they believed to be the essential elements of the universe: Earth, Water, Fire, Air and Ether/Universe.[568] The five Platonic solids are the Tetrahedron (four triangular faces—fire); Cube (four square faces—earth); Octahedron (eight triangular faces— air); Dodecahedron (twelve pentagonal faces—ether) and Icosahedron (20 triangular faces—water).

It was no accident that the medieval ideal for the ideal human proportions were based on the writings of an architect.

The Roman architect/engineer, Vitruvius Pollio wrote his famous treatise on Architecture in the First century BC.[569] His belief that the human body had ideal proportions that provided the standard for architectural design was widely adopted by medieval artists and architects in Europe. What made Vitruvius' work especially popular was his belief that these ideal proportions were related to a circle and square, the two-dimensional representations of the key Platonic solids—the sphere and cube:

> . . . if a man be placed flat on his back, with his hands and feet extended, and a pair of compasses centered at his navel . . . the fingers and toes of his two hands and feet will touch the circumference of a circle described there from. And just as the human body yields a circular outline, so too a square figure may be found from it. For if we measure the distance from the soles of the feet to the top of the head, and then apply that measure to the outstretched arms, the breadth will be found to be the same as the height . . .[570]

Vitruvius' work especially influenced Leonardo Da Vinci, who was intrigued by how sacred geometry was related to understanding the human body. His famous drawing of Vitruvian Man [See fig. 1] is still used as the standard for drawing human proportions in modern art.

Figure 1—Da Vinci's Vitruvian Man

In the early 1970s, Drunvalo Melchizedek claimed to have been telepathically contacted by the ancient Egyptian teacher, Thoth, and instructed to study and eventually teach sacred geometry and its relationship with life and the elevation of human consciousness.

Melchizedek subsequently developed an elaborate training method based on the sacred geometrical design of "golden mean spiral" that governs the evolution of life flowing through the entire universe. He called his pioneering technique the

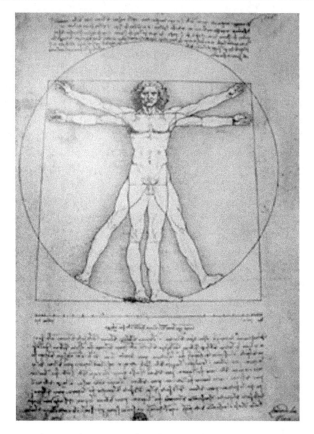

Fig. 1 Da Vinci's Vitruvian Man

"Flower of Life" and it subsequently attracted worldwide attention through his books and videos.[571]

What appealed to many in Melchizedek's work was his ability to analyze innovations in a number of scientific disciplines in terms of sacred geometry and combine this with a deeply rewarding meditative practice. Those who participated in his pioneering workshop programs subsequently produced remarkable innovations in their respective disciplines, suggesting that the exposure to sacred geometry was indeed a catalyst for accessing higher states of consciousness.

His workshop programs have since been extended to include telepathic/empathic communication with cetaceans, suggesting that training in sacred geometry is the key to unlocking these higher order communicative abilities in humans.[572]

In sum, the development of abilities that facilitate communication with ET races (CE-5 experiences) are directly stimulated by geometrical configurations that are found in "sacred geometry." The fact that sacred geometry figures prominently in the Crop Circle phenomenon gives support to views that it is a form of ET inspired communication with humanity. Developing abilities of being fully conscious when experiencing theta/delta brain wave states is therefore aided by awareness and understanding of sacred geometrical structures.

In addition to the role of "sacred geometry" in facilitating higher states of consciousness for individuals, is its role in the important work being conducted on the location of sacred sites around the planet. It is claimed that location of sacred sites, many of which are World Heritage listed, fall along a number of concentric circular arcs that form a multidimensional energy grid around the planet.[573]

This suggests that sacred geometry is also a part of the energy system that sustains sacred sites around the planet; sites which have traditionally facilitated higher states of consciousness. The city of Delphi in ancient Greece, for example, was a sacred site because of its position on this multidimensional grid system and the ability for resident priests/priestesses to spontaneously experience higher states of consciousness.

Sacred geometry therefore appears to be an important means of facilitating the brain wave states associated with higher states of consciousness in which CE-5 experiences occur. Developing an awareness of sacred geometrical patterns that exist in the genesis of life, crop circles, structures like the pyramids, the human body and the earth itself, can therefore be concluded to stimulate the higher dimensional consciousness required for "First Contact."

Completing the First Contact Process

First contact has thus far been described as a process that has yet to be completed due to the absence of an official announcement to the global general public of the ET presence. In the absence of such an announcement, First Contact as a social process gains more prominence since it effectively becomes the only way in which the ET presence can be confirmed and the contact process completed in a way that has social and political significance.

As more individuals learn about and develop the abilities whereby they can establish communication with ET races through CE-5 experiences, this completes the First Contact process for larger segments of human society. Such a social process will inevitably have an impact on the larger political process that will at some time culminate in the First Contact process being completed at the official level.

This suggests that rather than passively waiting for official announcement of the ET presence or desperately struggling for public disclosure, individuals explore consciousness raising techniques and/or lifestyle changes that would make them more receptive to the telepathic/empathic forms of communication used by ETs.

Most important, developing the ability to remain in the waking state while accessing theta/delta brain wave states appears to be critical since this appears to be when First Contact (CE-4 or CE-5 experiences) occurs for individuals.

As a political process, First Contact requires full disclosure of the ET presence, and lies outside the abilities of most individuals to appreciably influence. However as a social process, First Contact requires more individuals making themselves receptive to fully conscious interaction with ET races either through a direct form of telepathic/empathic communication (CE-5) and/or physical interaction (CE-4).

If there is indeed a web of "morphic energy" that is responsible for species diversity and evolution as the biologist, Rupert Sheldrake suggests, then CE-5 experiences can become so common, a policy of non-disclosure of the ET presence will become impossible to maintain.[574]

Official policy of non-disclosure of the ET presence has been in existence for close to seventy years and has created an inertia that has so far proven to be insurmountable for policy makers opposed to non-disclosure. A succession of US Presidents, senior public officials, enlightened policy makers, members of the US Congress, and concerned private citizens, have all attempted and failed to force public disclosure. This has had tremendous political implications for the US and all world nations.

Rather than non-disclosure being a bad policy decision imposed by unenlightened public officials on an ignorant public, non-disclosure is the inevitable policy consequence of an unprepared humanity for the truth of the ET presence. Each individual has the power to change this, and through their private efforts contribute to bringing about an official disclosure of the ET presence.

A New World of profound potential awaits humanity if we are prepared for it!

Notes

516. I would like to especially thank Art Miller for his kindness and hospitality in providing me with living and research facilities while I completed this chapter. Thanks also to Navin Kulshreshtra for helping to arrange for my stay and providing a positive research environment.
517. For references to such meetings, see Branton, *The Omega Files; Secret Nazi UFO Bases Revealed* (Inner Light Publications, 2000). Available online at: think-about-it.com.
518. For discussion of this treaty, see Chapter Two.
519. For a comprehensive discussion of these efforts see Richard Dolan, *UFOs and the National Security State* (Hampton Roads, 2002).
520. See Steven Greer, *Disclosure* (Crossing Point Inc., 2002).
521. See Richard Boylan, "Aviary, Good-Bye; Hello, Acclimation Program," in Boylan and Boylan, *Labored Journey To The Stars.* Available online at: http://www.drboylan.com/aclmatn2.html.
522. Allen Hynek, *The UFO Experience: A Scientific Study* (NTC/ Contemporary Publishing; 1972).
523. See C.D.B. Bryan, *Close Encounters of The Fourth Kind: Alien Abduction, UFOs, and the Conference at M.I.T.* (Alfred Knopf, 1995).
524. Steven Greer is the Director of the CE-5 initiative through the Center for the Study of Extraterrestrial Intelligence (CSETI). Further information available online at: http://www.cseti.org/ce5.htm.
525. Richard Stenger, "Clinton aide slams Pentagon's UFO secrecy," *CNN* (October 22, 2002). Available online at: http://www.cnn.com/2002/ TECH/space/10/22/ufo.records/index.html.

526. See Corso, *The Day After Roswell* (Pocket Books, 1997).
527. See Richard Boylan, "Dialogue with Colonel Steve Wilson," in Boylan and Boylan, *Labored Journey To The Stars*. Available online at: http://www.drboylan.com/colww3a.html.
528. For the historic manipulation of media coverage of ET/UFOs, see Terry Hansen, *Missing Times* (Xlibris Corporation, 2001).
529. See Corso, *The Day After Roswell*. See also Richard Boylan, "Colonel Steve Wilson, USAF (ret.) Reveals UFO-oriented Project Pounce," in Boylan and Boylan, *Labored Journey To The Stars*. Available online at: http://drboylan.com/swilson2.html.
530. Siri Agrell, "UFOs blamed for outage in 1965" *National Post, August 18, 2003*. Available online at: http://www.nationalpost.com/home/story.html?id=728B9A46-EE55-4BBE-AB8B-945F29B31D58.
531. Richard Boylan, "Quotations from Chairman Wolf," in Boylan and Boylan, *Labored Journey To The Stars*. Available online at: http://www.drboylan.com/wolfqut2.html.
532. Richard Boylan, "Quotations from Chairman Wolf," in Boylan and Boylan, *Labored Journey To The Stars*. Available online at: http://www.drboylan.com/wolfqut2.html.
533. Steven Greer, Cosmic Deception: Let the Citizen Beward (Disclosure Project, 2002). Available online at: http://www.disclosureproject.org.
534. Catherine Austin Fitts, "The $64 Question: What's Up With the Black Budget?—The Real Deal," *Scoop: UQ Wire* (23 September, 2002). Available online at: http://www.scoop.co.nz/mason/stories/HL0209/S00126.htm.
535. For an investigative report on the 1.1 trillion that annually goes missing from DOD and other government agency budgets, see Kelly Patricia O'Meara, "Wasted Riches" *Insight Magazine* (Sept. 28, 2001). Available online at: http://www.insightmag.com/main.cfm/include/detail/storyid/108588.html.
536. Courtney Brown discusses such conflict in his discussion of the "Reptilian Agenda" in *Cosmic Explorers* (Signet Book, 2000) pages 297–320.
537. See Stewart Swerdlow, *Montauk: The Alien Connection* (Sky Books, 1998). For online discussion of this scenario, see Michael Salla, "Preserving Human Sovereignty and Independence In Responding to Extraterrestrial Intervention," (Exopolitics.org 5/5/2003). Available at: http://exopolitics.org/Exo-Comment-6.htm.
538. See Budd Hopkins, *Missing Times* (Ballantine Books, 1990); Jacobs, *Secret Life: Firsthand Accounts of UFO Abductions* (Touchstone Books, 1993); John Mack, *Abduction: Human Encounters with Aliens* (New York: Ballantine Books, 1994); and Mack, *Passport to the Cosmos: Human Transformation and Alien Encounters* (Three Rivers Press, 2000).

539. For detailed discussion of the use of hypnosis in abduction cases, see Budd Hopkins, "Hypnosis and the Investigation of UFO Abduction," *UFOs & Abductions: Challenging the Borders of Knowledge*, ed., David Jacobs (University of Kansas Press, 2000) pages 215–40.

540. David Jacobs, *The Threat* (Simon and Shuster, 1998) pages 17–18.

541. Jacobs, *The Threat*.

542. Richard Boylan and Lee Boylan, *Close Extraterrestrial Encounters: Positive Experiences With Mysterious Visitors* (Wildflower Press, 1994); and Richard Boylan & Lee Boylan, *Labored Journey To The Stars* (2003): www.drboylan.com. See Lee Carroll and Jan Tober, *The Indigo Children: The New Kids Have Arrived* (Hay House, 1999); Doreen Virtue, *The Crystal Children: A Guide to the Newest Generation of Psychic and Sensitive Children* (Hay House, 2003). See also Paula Peterson's interview of Richard Boylan, "Star Kids: Our Future Hope," (February, 2003) Available online at: http://www. drboylan.com/strkidsfuture.html.

543. Rupert Sheldrake, *A New Science of Life* (Inner Traditions Intl., 1995).

544. Steven Greer, "Decoy, Distract and Trash," (Disclosure Project, 2002). Available online at: http://www.disclosureproject.org/ddt.htm.

545. Quoted in John Quinn, "Phoenix Undead: The Montauk Project and Camp Hero Today," (NewsHawk Inc, 1998). Available online at: http://vs03.tvsecure.com/~vs030f1/monew.htm.

546. See Ron Patton, "Project Monarch: Nazi Mind," *The Conspiracy Reader: From the Deaths of JFK and John Lennon to Government-Sponsored Alien Cover-Ups*, eds., Al Hidell & Joan D'Arc (Citadel Press, 1999) 197–213. Available online at: http://www.aches-mc. org/monarch.html.

547. See Hopkins, *Missing Times*; Jacobs, *Secret Life*; and Mack, *Abduction*.

548. For a discussion of brainwaves and the different mental/emotional activities associated with these, see Anna Wise, *The High-Performance Mind: Mastering Brainwaves for Insight, Healing, and Creativity* (J.P. Tarcher, 1997); and Elmer Green and Alyce Green, *Beyond Biofeedback* (Delacorte Press, 1977).

549. See Sigmund Freud, *Introductory Lectures on Psychoanalysis* (Liveright, 1989).

550. Carl Jung, *The Archetypes and The Collective Unconscious—Collected Works of C.G. Jung Vol. 9 Part 1* (Princeton University Press, 1989).

551. Carl Jung, *Flying Saucers: A Modern Myth of Things Seen in the Skies* (Princeton University Press, 1979).

552. See Lyssa Royal, *Preparing for Contact*.

553. See Hopkins, *Missing Times*.

554. Lyssa Royal and Keith Priest, *Preparing for Contact: Metamorphosis of Consciousness* (Royal Priest Research Press, 1993) p. 83.
555. For discussion of how emotions are transmitted through cellular communication, see Candace Pert, *Molecules of Emotions: The Science Behind Mind-Body Medicine* (Simon and Schuster, 1999).
556. Joan Ocean, *Dolphin Connection: Interdimensional Ways of Living* (Spiral Dolphin Connection, 1989). Ms. Ocean has a website at: www.joanocean.com.
557. Dan Sherman, *Above Black: Project Preserve Destiny Insider Account of Alien Contact & Government Cover-Up* (One Team Publications, 1997). See also website: http://www.aboveblack.com.
558. John Quinn, "Phoenix Undead: The Montauk Project and Camp Hero Today," (NewsHawk Inc, 1998). Available online at: http://vs03. tvsecure.com/~vs030f1/monew.htm.
559. Richard Boylan, "Quotations from Chairman Wolf," in Boylan and Boylan, *Labored Journey To The Stars.* Available online at: http://www.drboylan.com/wolfqut2.html.
560. Neruda Interview, #1: www.wingmakers.com.
561. See "Testimony of a Brigadier General Steven Lovekin," *Disclosure,* ed. Greer, p. 235.
562. See Zecharia Sitchin, *Divine Encounters: A Guide to Visions, Angels and Other Emissaries* (Avon Books, 1996).
563. An excellent overview of occult societies is Lyn Picknett and Clive Prince, *The Stargate Conspiracy* (Berkley Books, 2001).
564. For online information on Dr. Greer's workshops, see website of the Center for the Study of Extraterrestrial Intelligence, http://www. cseti.org. For online information on Lyssa Royal's seminars/ workshops see: http://www.lyssaroyal.com.
565. For discussion of crop circles and the geometrical patterns found, see Werner Anderhub and Hans Roth, *Crop Circles: Exploring the Designs & Mysteries* (Lark Books, 2002); Freddy Silva, *Secrets in the Fields: The Science and Mysticism of Crop Circles* (Hampton Roads, 2002); and Nick Kollerstrom & Busty Tayler, *Crop Circles: The Hidden Form* (Wessex Books, 2002).
566. See Buckminster Fuller, *Synergetics* (MacMillan Publishing Co., 1982).
567. For discussion of how each element corresponds to a Platonic solid, see Plato's "Timeaus," *Timaeus and Critias,* ed. H.D. Lee (Viking Press, 1972).
568. Vitruvius, *The Ten Books on Architecture,* tran. Morris Hickey Morgan (New York: Dover Publications, Inc., 1960).
569. Vitruvius, The Ten Books on Architecture, Book III. p. i.2.
570. His two books are *The Ancient Secret of the Flower of Life,* Vols. 1–2 (Light Technology Publications, 1999/2002). Melchizedek has a website for his training technique: http://www.floweroflife.org.

571. The training schedule for Melchizedek's workshops can be found online at: http://www.floweroflife.org.

572. For discussion of the world grid and sacred geometry, see David Hatcher Childress, *Anti-Gravity and the World Grid* (Adventures Unlimited Press, 1987).

573. *A New Science of Life.*

574. Rupert Sheldrake, *A New Science of Life.*

About the Author

Dr. Michael E. Salla has held academic appointments in the School of International Service, American University, Washington DC (1996–2001), and the Department of Political Science, Australian National University, Canberra, Australia (1994–96). He taught as an adjunct faculty member at George Washington University, Washington DC, in 2002. He is currently researching methods of Transformational Peace as a Researcher in Residence in the Center for Global Peace (2001–2004) and directing the Center's Peace Ambassador Program which uses transformational peace techniques for individual self-empowerment.

Dr. Salla has a PhD. in Government from the University of Queensland, Australia, and an MA in Philosophy from the University of Melbourne, Australia. He is the author of *The Hero's Journey Toward a Second American Century* (Greenwood Press, 2002) and co-editor/author of three other books. He has authored more than seventy articles, chapters, and book reviews on peace, ethnic conflict and conflict resolution and conducted research and fieldwork in the ethnic conflicts in East Timor, Kosovo, Macedonia, and Sri Lanka.

Index

IF YOU LIKED THIS BOOK, YOU WON'T WANT TO MISS OTHER TITLES BY DANDELION BOOKS

Available Now And Always Through
www.dandelionbooks.net And Affiliated Websites!!

TOLL-FREE ORDERS—1-800-861-7899 (U.S. & CANADA)

Non-Fiction

Stranger than Fiction: An Independent Investigation Of The True Culprits Behind 9-11, by Albert D. Pastore, Ph.D... Twelve months of careful study, painstaking research, detailed analysis, source verification and logical deduction went into the writing of this book. In addition to the stories are approximately 300 detailed footnotes Pastore: "Only by sifting through huge amounts of news data on a daily basis was I able to catch many of these rare 'diamonds in the rough' and organize them into a coherent pattern and logical argument." (ISBN 1-893302-47-4)

Ahead Of The Parade: A Who's Who Of Treason and High Crimes— Exclusive Details Of Fraud And Corruption Of The Monopoly Press, The Banks, The Bench And The Bar, And The Secret Political Police, by Sherman H. Skolnick... One of America's foremost investigative reporters, speaks out on some of America's current crises. Included in this block-buster book are the following articles: Big City Newspapers & the Mob, The Sucker Traps, Dirty Tricks of Finance and Brokerage, The Secret History of Airplane Sabotage, Wal-Mart and the Red Chinese Secret Police, The Chandra Levy Affair, The Japanese Mafia in the United States, The Secrets of Timothy McVeigh, and much more. (ISBN 1-893302-32-6)

Another Day In The Empire: Life in Neoconservative America, by Kurt Nimmo... A collection of articles by one of Counterpunch's most popular columnists. Included in this collection are: The Son of COINTELPRO; Clueless at the State Department; Bush Senior: Hating Saddam, Selling Him Weapons; Corporate Media: Selling Dubya's Oil War; Iraq and the Vision of the Velociraptors: The Bleeding Edge of Islam; Condoleezza Rice at the Waldorf Astoria; Predators, Snipers and the Posse Comitatus Act, and many others. (ISBN 1-893302-75-X)

Palestine & The Middle East: Passion, Power & Politics, by Jaffer Ali... The Palestinian struggle is actually a human one that transcends Palestine... There is no longer a place for Zionism in the 20th century... Democracy in the Middle East is not safe for US interests as long as there is an atmosphere of hostility... Suicide bombings are acts of desperation and mean that a people have been pushed to the brink... failure to understand why they happen will make certain they will continue. Jaffer Ali is a Palestinian-American business man who has been writing on politics and business for over 25 years. (ISBN 1-893302-45-8)

America, Awake! We Must Take Back Our Country, by Norman D. Livergood... This book is intended as a wake-up call for Americans, as Paul Revere awakened the Lexington patriots to the British attack on April 18, 1775, and as Thomas Paine's *Common Sense* roused apathetic American colonists to recognize and struggle against British oppression. Our current situation is similar to that which American patriots faced in the 1770s: a country ruled by 'foreign' and 'domestic' plutocratic powers and a divided citizenry uncertain of their vital interests. (ISBN 1-893302-27-X)

"Evil Fire Made to Burn"—A True Account of the World's Greatest Cover-Up, by Gary... In the spirited Indiana Jones tradition, Gary Vey, editor of an internet underground website, viewzone.com, finds himself transported from a sleepy New England suburb to a waking nightmare in the barren Alaskan tundra, the unpredictable vortices of Yemen and ultimately the wilderness of the Australian Outback. Eden accidentally stumbles into what turns out to be the most startling revelation of his life. Besieged by his newly-discovered destiny as prophesied translator of ancient texts, he learns he holds the key for unlocking secrets that have the power to change the course of history. From that point on, Eden becomes one of the most wanted—and haunted—persons on the planet. (ISBN 1-893302-41-5)

The Perennial Tradition: Overview Of The Secret Heritage, The Single Stream Of Initiatory Teaching Flowing Through All The Great Schools Of Mysticism, by Norman D. Livergood... Like America, Awake, this book is another wake-up call. "It was written to assist readers to awaken to the Higher Spiritual World." In addition to providing a history of the Western tradition of the Perennial Tradition, Livergood also describes the process that serious students use to actually *realize*—bring to manifestation—their Higher Consciousness. "Unless we become aware of this higher state, we face the prospect of a basically useless physical existence and a future life—following physical death—of unpleasant, perhaps anguished reformation of our essence." (ISBN 1-893302-48-2)

The Awakening of An American: How America Broke My Heart, by Meria Heller, with a Foreword by Catherine Austin Fitts... A collection of choice interviews from Meria Heller's world-famous www.meria.net rapidly growing radio network that reaches millions of people daily. Dr. Arun Gandhi, Greg Palast, Vincent Bugliosi, Mark Elsis, William Rivers Pitt, Mark Rechtenwald, Nancy Oden & Bob Fertik, Howard Winant, Linda Starr, Dave Chandler, Bev Conover, John Nichols, Robert McChesney, Norman Solomon, Stan Goff and Mark Crispin Miller. (ISBN 1-893302-39-3)

America's Nightmare: The Presidency of George Bush II, by John Stanton & Wayne Madsen... Media & Language, War & Weapons, Internal Affairs and a variety of other issues pointing out the US "crisis without precedent" that was wrought by the US Presidential election of 2000 followed by 9/11. "Stanton & Madsen will challenge many of the things you've been told by CNN and Fox news. This book is dangerous." (ISBN 1-893302-29-6)

America's Autopsy Report, by John Kaminski... The false fabric of history is unraveling beneath an avalanche of pathological lies to justify endless war and Orwellian new laws that revoke the rights of Americans. While TV and newspapers glorify the dangerous ideas of perverted billionaires, the Internet has pulsated with outrage and provided a new and real forum for freedom among concerned people all over the world who are opposed to the mass murder and criminal exploitation of the defenseless victims of multinational corporate totalitarianism. John Kaminski's passionate essays give voice to those hopes and fears of humane people that are ignored by the big business shysters who rule the major media. (ISBN 1-893302-42-3)

Seeds Of Fire: China And The Story Behind The Attack On America, by Gordon Thomas... The inside story about China that no one can afford to ignore. Using his unsurpassed contacts in Israel, Washington, London and Europe, Gordon Thomas, internationally acclaimed best-selling author and investigative reporter for over a quarter-century, reveals information about China's intentions to use the current crisis to launch itself as a super-power and become America's new major enemy... *"This has been kept out of the news agenda because it does not suit certain business interests to have that truth emerge... Every patriotic American should buy and read this book... it is simply revelatory."* (Ray Flynn, Former U.S. Ambassador to the Vatican) (ISBN 1-893302-54-7)

Shaking The Foundations: Coming Of Age In The Postmodern Era, by John H. Brand, D.Min., J.D.... Scientific discoveries in the Twentieth Century require the restructuring of our understanding the nature of Nature and of human beings. In simple language the author explains how significant implications of quantum mechanics, astronomy, biology and brain physiology form the foundation for new perspectives to comprehend the meaning of our lives. (ISBN 1-893302-25-3)

Rebuilding The Foundations: Forging A New And Just America, by John H. Brand, D.Min., J.D.... Should we expect a learned scholar to warn us about our dangerous reptilian brains that are the real cause of today's evils? Although Brand is not without hope for rescuing America, he warns us to act fast—and now. Evil men intent on imposing their political, economic, and religious self-serving goals on America are not far from achieving their goal of mastery. (ISBN 1-893302-33-4)

Democracy Under Siege: The Jesuits' Attempt To Destroy the Popular Government Of The United States; The True Story of Abraham Lincoln's Death; Banned For Over 100 Years, This Information Now Revealed For The First Time! by C.T. Wilcox... U.S. President Lincoln was the triumphant embodiment of the New Concept of Popular Government. Was John Wilkes Booth a Jesuit patsy, hired to do the dirty work for the Roman Catholic church—whose plan, a well-kept secret until now—was to overthrow the American Government? (ISBN 1-893302-31-8)

The Last Atlantis Book You'll Ever Have To Read! by Gene D. Matlock... More than 25,000 books, plus countless other articles have been written about a fabled confederation of city-states known as Atlantis. If it really did exist, where was it located? Does anyone have valid evidence of its existence—artifacts and other remnants? According to historian, archaeologist, educator and linguist Gene D. Matlock, both questions can easily be answered. (ISBN 1-893302-20-2)

The Last Days Of Israel, by Barry Chamish... With the Middle East crisis ongoing, *The Last Days of Israel* takes on even greater significance as an important book of our age. Barry Chamish, investigative reporter who has the true story about Yitzak Rabin's assassination, tells it like it is. (ISBN 1-893302-16-4)

The Courage To Be Who I Am, by Mary-Margareht Rose... This book is rich with teachings and anecdotes delivered with humor and humanness, by a woman who followed her heart and learned to listen to her inner voice; in the process, transforming every obstacle into an opportunity to test her courage to manifest her true identity. (ISBN 1-893302-13-X)

The Making Of A Master: Tracking Your Self-Worth, by Jeanette O'Donnal... A simple tracking method for self-improvement that takes the mystery out of defining your goals, making a road map and tracking your progress. A book rich with nuggets of wisdom couched in anecdotes and instructive dialogues. (ISBN 1-893302-36-9)

The Clear and Simple Way: The Angel Lessons, by Judith Parsons... a book about heart, with heart. Parsons, known throughout the world for her spiritual workshops and seminars, shows us how to transform our lives into infinite "presents"—"gifts" and moment-by-moment experiences—of peace, joy and self-fulfillment. (ISBN 1-893302-43-1)

Cancer Doctor: The Biography Josef Issels, M.D., Who Brought Hope To The World With His Revolutionary Cancer Treatment, by Gordon Thomas... Dr. Josef Issels treated more than 12,000 cancer patients who had been written off as "incurable" by other doctors. He claimed no miracle cures, but the success record of his revolutionary "whole person treatment" was extraordinary... the story of his struggle against the medical establishment which put Dr. Issels in prison, charged with fraud and manslaughter. (ISBN 1-893302-18-0)

Fiction

Ticket to Paradise, by Yvonne Ridley... Judith Tempest, a British reporter, is searching for the Truth. But when it starts to spill out in her brilliant front page reportage of Middle East suicide bombing in retaliation for Israeli tanks mowing down innocent Palestinian women and children, both 'Tempest' and 'Truth' start to spell 'Trouble'—with a capital 'T', joke her friends and colleagues. A non-stop mystery thriller that tears along at a reckless pace of passion, betrayal, adventure and espionage. (ISBN 1-893302-77-6)

The Alley of Wishes, by Laurel Johnson... Despite the ravages of WWI on Paris and on the young American farm boy, Beck Sanow, and despite the abusive relationship that the chanteuse Cerise endures, the two share a bond that is unbreakable by time, war, loss of memory, loss of life and loss of youth. Beck and Cerise are both good people beset by constant tragedy. Yet it is tragedy that brings them together, and it is unconditional love that keeps them together. (ISBN 1-893302-46-6)

Freedom: Letting Go Of Anxiety And Fear Of The Unknown, by Jim Britt... Jeremy Carter, a fireman from Missouri who is in New York City for the day, decides to take a tour of the Trade Center, only to watch in shock, the attack on its twin towers from a block away. Afterward as he gazes at the pit of rubble and talks with many of the survivors, Jeremy starts to explore the inner depths of his soul, to ask questions he'd never asked before. This dialogue helps him learn who he is and what it takes to overcome the fear, anger, grief and anxiety this kind of tragedy brings. (ISBN 1-893302-74-1)

The Prince Must Die, by Gower Leconfield... breaks all taboos for mystery thrillers. After the "powers that be" suppressed the manuscripts of three major British writers, Dandelion Books breaks through with a thriller involving a plot to assassinate Prince Charles. *The Prince Must Die* brings to life a Britain of today that is on the edge with race riots, neo-Nazis, hard right backlash and neo-punk nihilists. Riveting entertainment... you won't be able to put it down. (ISBN 1-893302-72-5)

Waaaay Out There! Diggertown, Oklahoma, by Tuklo Nashoba... Adventures of constable Clint Mankiller and his deputy, Chad GhostWolf; Jim Bob and Bubba Johnson, Grandfather GhostWolf, Cassie Snodgrass, Doc Jones, Judge Jenkins and the rest of the Diggertown, Oklahoma bunch in the first of a series of Big Foot-Sasquatch tall tales peppered with lots of good belly laughs and just as much fun. (ISBN 1-893302-44-X)

Synchronicity Gates: An Anthology Of Stories And Poetry About People Transformed In Extraordinary Reality Beyond Experience, by Stephen

Vernarelli... An inventive compilation of short stories that take the reader beyond mere science, fiction, or fantasy. Vernarelli introduces the reader to a new perception of reality; he imagines the best and makes it real. (ISBN 1-893302-38-5)

Daniela, by Stephen Weeks... A gripping epic novel of sexual obsession and betrayal as Nazi Prague falls. The harboring of deadly secrets and triumph of an enduring love against the hardest of times. Nikolei is a Polish/Ukrainian Jew who finds himself fighting among the Germans then turning against them to save Prague in 1945. Nikolei manages to hide himself among the Germans with a woman working as a prostitute. (ISBN 1-893302-37-7)

Unfinished Business, by Elizabeth Lucas Taylor... Lindsay Mayer knows something is amiss when her husband, Griffin, a college professor, starts spending too much time at his office and out-of-town. Shortly after the ugly truth surfaces, Griffin disappears altogether. Lindsay is shattered. Life without Griffin is life without life... One of the sexiest books you'll ever read! (ISBN 1-893302-68-7)

The Woman With Qualities, by Sarah Daniels... South Florida isn't exactly the Promised Land that forty-nine-year-old newly widowed Keri Anders had in mind when she transplanted herself here from the northeast... A tough action-packed novel that is far more than a love story. (ISBN 1-893302-11-3)

Weapon In Heaven, by David Bulley... Eddy Licklighter is in a fight with God for his very own soul. You can't mess around half-assed when fighting with God. You've got to go at it whole-hearted. Eddy loses his wife and baby girl in a fire. Bulley's protagonist is a contemporary version of the Old Testament character of Job. Licklighter wants nothing from God except His presence so he can kill him off. The humor, warmth, pathos and ultimate redemption of Licklighter will make you hold your sides with laughter at the same time you shed common tears for his "God-awful" dilemma. (ISBN 1-893302-28-8)

Adventure Capital, by John Rushing... South Florida adventure, crime and violence in a fiction story based on a true life experience. A book you will not want to put down until you reach the last page. (ISBN 1-893302-08-3)

A Mother's Journey: To Release Sorrow And Reap Joy, by Sharon Kay... A poignant account of Norah Ann Mason's life journey as a wife, mother and single parent. This book will have a powerful impact on anyone, female or male, who has experienced parental abuse, family separations, financial struggles and a desperate need to find the magic in life that others talk about that just doesn't seem to be there for them. (ISBN 1-893302-52-0)

Return To Masada, by Robert G. Makin... In a gripping account of the famous Battle of Masada, Robert G. Makin skillfully recaptures the blood and gore as well as the spiritual essence of this historic struggle for freedom and independence. (ISBN 1-893302-10-5)

Time Out Of Mind, by Solara Vayanian... Atlantis had become a snake pit of intrigue teeming with factious groups vying for power and control. An unforgettable drama that tells of the breakdown of the priesthood, the hidden scientific experiments in genetic engineering which produced "things"—part human and part animal—and other atrocities; the infiltration by the dark lords of Orion; and the implantation of the human body with a device to fuel the Orion wars. (ISBN 1-893302-21-0)

The Thirteenth Disciple: The Life Of Mary Magdalene, by Gordon Thomas... The closest of Jesus' followers, the name of Mary Magdalene conjures images of a woman both passionate and devoted, both sinner and saint. The first full-length biography for 13 centuries. (ISBN 1-893302-17-2)

ALL DANDELION BOOKS ARE AVAILABLE THROUGH WWW.DANDELIONBOOKS.NET... ALWAYS.

CPSIA information can be obtained
at www.ICGtesting.com
Printed in the USA
BVHW040430170719
553471BV00031B/846/P

9 780996 708999